ॐ

Visveshwaraya Namaha!

Sri Shiva Lila

ॐ

Ganeshaya Namaha!

"Salutations to Lord Ganesha!
Who removes and overcomes all obstacles,
And grants success in every endeavour."

Ganashtakam

ॐ

Mrityunjayaya Namaha!

Sri Shiva Lila

The play of the Divine in the form of Lord Shiva

As found in the

Sri Shiva Mahapurana

and

Sreemad Bhagavata Purana

Lives of saints as given in the

Periya Puranam

by

Sekkizhar

Narrated by

Vanamali

Aryan Books International
New Delhi

Sri Shiva Lila

ISBN-10: 81-7305-221-2
ISBN-13: 978-81-7305-221-7

First Published: 2002

Reprinted in **2016** by:

Aryan Books International
Pooja Apartments, 4B, Ansari Road, New Delhi-110 002 (India)
Tel.: 23287589, 23255799; Fax: 91-11-23270385
E-mail: aryanbooks@gmail.com
www.aryanbooks.com

Computer Typeset and Printed in India at
ABI Prints & Publishing Co., New Delhi

ॐ

Mrityunjayaya Namaha!

DEDICATION

"The recompense that a son makes to the mother that bore him, is to make people exclaim. What austerities did this man's mother perform to beget such a son!"

Thirukkural by Thiruvalluvar

To
my beloved son
Janardan
with all my blessings

ॐ

Gagatpitre Namaha!

In youth, the venomous snakes of sound and sight,
Of taste and touch and smell,
Fastened on my vitals and slew my discrimination.
Alas! My heart bereft of the thought of Shiva,
Swelled in arrogance and pride!
Therefore O Shiva
O Mahadeva! O Shambho!
Forgive me, I pray, my transgressions.

Now in my old age, my senses have lost the power of proper judgment and action.
My body is weak and senile from afflictions,
But even now, my mind instead of meditating on Shiva,
Runs after vain desire and hollow discussions.
Therefore O Shiva! O Mahadeva! O Shambho!
Forgive me I prey, my transgressions.

I bow to Him who bestows on the sages direct knowledge of ultimate Truth.
I bow to the teacher of the three worlds,
Dakshinamurthi, the Lord Himself,
Who dispels the misery of birth and death

Adi Shankaracharya

ॐ

Shivaya Namaha!

PREFACE

by

His Holiness Sri Dayandaji Maharaj — Rishikesh

The Veda presents the cause of the entire *jagat* as Mayin, wielder of *maya*, who does not come under the spell of *maya*, The Mayin is Maheswara — the Lord of all. He is not only the intelligent cause of the *jagat* but He is also in the form of the *jagat*. Space, Time and everything in space and time, are His manifestations and therefore not separate from Him. He is therefore both the father and the mother of the universe. Every form is His form and you can invoke Him in any given form. If you look at this Maheswara from the point of view of any manifest force or law, He becomes a *devata*. If you give a name in Sanskrit to this *devata*, the name will be descriptive of the form. Thus the name Vishnu means that the Lord is all-pervasive. The word Brahma means the one who is big without a limit. The word Rudra means the cause of tears as the giver of the fruits of actions and also one who is the remover of all tears. In any of the names and forms of worship, you can invoke the Maheswara as the one who is the cause of manifestation, sustenance and dissolution.

In the *Shiva Purana* the whole *lila* of Maheswara is presented in a style that offers the readers a scope to explore and discover. One gets to know what it takes to be almighty. An insight of every virtue in its infinite measure is unavoidable as one goes through any Purana. The author, Vanamali, presents the Lord as one who is invoked as Shiva as depicted in the *Shiva Purana*. The author's devotion to the Lord imbues her pen with facility of expression and helps the reader discover the glories of the Lord and leads to devotion. The author is a recipient of the Lord's blessings and by converting these blessings in the form of presenting the glories of the Lord, she becomes once again the recipient of the Lord's blessings in abundance.

ॐ *Namashivaya!*

Dayananda Ashrama
Rishikesh,
5th May 2001

Swami Dayananda

ॐ

Giripriyaya Namaha!

CONTENTS

PART – II

ॐ *Namashivaya*

ॐ

Panchavaktraya Namaha!

ACKNOWLEDGEMENTS

Our grateful thanks go to Nan Koheler and Joseph Baxter, U.S.A. It was only due to their kindness and help that we have been able to get photos of the original paintings of Sri Harish Chandra Johari and his disciples, Pieter Weltevrede and Patrick Prather.

ॐ

Panchavaktraya Namaha!

INTRODUCTION

ॐ *"Trayambakam yajamahe sugandhim pushtivardhanam,*

Urvarukamiva bandanath, Mrityor mukshiya-mamritath."

"I worship the fragrant, three-eyed one in order to give me perfect health and release me from the coils of mortality as effortlessly as a ripe gourd falling from its stalk and grant me immortality."

Yajur Veda

Puranic literature springs from a deep need in the heart of the human being for fulfilment. It plumbs the depths of our psyche, which cradles in it, an unconscious and indescribable longing for the Supreme, and comes out with the most fantastic images and conceptions, which have baffled the mind of modern man. Those who have been brainwashed by modern scientific preconceptions, whose imaginations have been stifled by strict adherence to a truth which only the senses can see, may find it difficult to read the *Puranas* and to understand their deep insight into human nature. But those, whose intellects have not been stunted by these constricting notions, will delight in the absolute freedom of expression and the amazing flights of imagination to which the human mind can soar. What must be remembered is, that the forms of the gods are not mere flights of fancy but they are meant to reveal the many facets of Truth, which are not perceivable to the five senses. These five senses are limited at best and deceitful at worst, for their main aim is to conceal a Truth, which is incomprehensible to them. The modern world-view knows only of heat and motion, energy bursting out in the Big Bang, some fifteen thousand million years back and expanding into a system of galaxies which are running down from a state of maximum heat and concentration, to a state of cold stillness and disintegration, during the course of a vast period of time. Life and consciousness, as we know them, are claimed to be secondary phenomena, which will pass away into the cold ambiguity of death in this meaningless dance of the elements. Consciousness has no special significance in this view of the cosmos. The scientific outlook is quite sceptical about ultimate values. There is no purpose, no plan in the universe and intelligence itself is only a by-product of matter, condemned to perish in the course of time. For one who is convinced of this view, the *Puranas* will only be a source of amusement. Which modern mind can believe in oceans of milk and five-headed gods!

The *Puranic* view of creation unlike the modern scientific view has its basis in the will of the Supreme Being. The ancient sages or *rishis* of India knew that matter is only a derivative of consciousness and contains within it, in seed form, the fundamental knowledge of its own inner spiritual potency, just as the whole of the mighty banyan tree is contained in its tiny mustard-like seed. There is an invisible field of energy prior to, and underlying the whole of this visible field. This field is unmanifest and not within the grasp of our five senses. The entire field of visible objects is only a projection of this. The *rishis* were well aware of this. Lord Krishna calls this field, *avyaktha* or the Unmanifest from which all this manifestation has sprung. Beyond even this field is the vast field called *chidakasha* or the field of consciousness, which is potent with the power to create. This field is also called *Shakti* or the creative aspect of the Divine. It is the feminine principle that is capable of all action and creation and hence it is known as the Divine Mother. The universe and all this phenomenon of life cannot really be called a creation, but a projection of the Divine Consciousness that appears inert but which is actually pulsating with life. The creation is not a making of something out of nothing, by someone, but it is a projection of that which has eternally existed. Science may have discovered many physical and chemical laws that govern the universe but it is yet to discover those transcendental laws that are fundamental to it. These spiritual laws are eternal and inherent in Nature.

Based on a cyclical conception of Time, *Puranic* history has a much wider scope than the modern, limited concept of human history. Modern history, being linear, has no idea of where and when the line started and where it might end. What was there, before the beginning and what will come after the end? These are questions that the modern historian cannot answer. Only the unthinking mind will be satisfied with such a concept of history. The *Puranas*, however, give us cosmic history. An intelligent reading of them would enlarge our vision and give us a totally new concept of the history of the universe. We will be made to feel that the history of the human being is not as simple or as short as modern historians would have us believe. H.G. Wells who was one of those writers who was most *Puranic* in his thinking, says, "Amongst the ancient people, the Indian philosopher alone seems to have some perception of the vast ages through which existence seems to have passed."

The modern concept of history may have something meaningful to say about the recent past of the Homo sapiens but it can throw no light on our distant past, our future and our significance in cosmic history. The *Puranas* on the other hand give the right interpretation of the human being as being made up of consciousness, evolving towards higher levels of perfection and having an existence along with other intelligent and conscious beings. It raises the history of man, from a meaningless episode in the infinity of Time to a meaningful progress from man to God! The *Puranas* are based on the intuitions, inspirations and revelations of the enlightened sages of ancient India and thus have more value, culturally and spiritually than copperplate inscriptions and stone tablets. Modern history has no spiritual value. *Puranic* history on the other hand is based on the intangible verities of life which will lead us to the best and highest spiritual core within us. The Hindu deities like Shiva, Vishnu and Shakti, never had a location on earthly space and time except in images. But they are spiritual verities — the manifestations of the Supreme Being. Material objects are mere shadows compared to these.

"In whatsoever way a man approaches Me, so shall I approach him," is what Lord Krishna says in the Sreemad Bhagavad Gita. God is willing and capable of moulding Himself into whatever form His devotee imagines Him to be. Here there is no question of whether something or someone has taken place in a particular form, at a particular place, in a particular spot of time Faith transcends the bonds of time and space and the Infinite Being is capable of moulding Himself into infinite forms to delight the hearts of His devotees. To limit Him into one form and one mould is to set boundaries to His infinity and His omnipotence. Just as the great rivers and mountains and oceans of this country are an expression of the natural forces, working from within the earth, so also our *Puranas* are the expressions of the Indian mind which saw in the most trivial incident, an expression of the immense variety of the Supreme. The *Puranas* seek to give a meaningful interpretation of the omniscience and omnipotence of the Supreme Being who is a loving, spiritual reality, who can be communed with, prayed to and visualised in various forms of spiritual glory. Thus the *Puranas* provide valuable glimpses of eternal truths that transcend the scope of modern history.

The forms of the various gods are really condensed books of spiritual wisdom. The seers or sages of the *Puranas* who saw these forms were really scientists of a high order whose investigations were not limited by their preconceptions. To consider their findings as childish nonsense, fit for the ignorant is the same as considering algebraic symbols to be the scribbling of a lunatic! No literature in the world has succeeded in making the formless God into a tangible reality, with such vivid and realistic descriptions as the *Puranas* have done.

Modern physics has blasted the theory of matter being static and inert. The atom was discovered to be not a solid block but a nucleus of empty space around which whirled energy particles. Even these particles were found to be not things, but interconnections between other things. Quantum physics thus reveals a basic oneness of the universe. We cannot decompose the world into independently existing small units. The more we penetrate into matter the more we realise that it is made up of a complicated web of relations between the various parts of a unified whole. This network of relations is intrinsically dynamic and not static. It is always in a state of motion. This is very similar to the Indian concept of matter, which states that matter has to be understood as having dynamic equilibrium. The seers understood this perfectly and tried to bring it forcibly into the minds of the lay people by their vivid descriptions of the gods and their interaction with the world. Very often these ideas would be given graphic form as in the case of the dancing Shiva which depicts the dance of creation and destruction which goes on all the time.

The *Vedas* speak of the Supreme, as Brahman, who is the Absolute in its Unmanifest, formless aspect. The *Puranas* however bring this Absolute down, from its indescribable, glory, to the din and clamour of this earthly existence, by giving it a million forms and names. The rightness or wrongness of such an experiment is not the question here, but whether it has any utilitarian value. The mind of the human being is incapable of visualising the formless and the unmanifest. It is not used to think in abstractions. Some path, some way, however strange, has to be made to cut out a path to this Infinite, Formless, Absolute. The ancient *rishis* of the *Puranas* found such a way in the creation of the gods. The Divine in its multifarious forms has become a living reality in the minds of the Hindus by the depiction of the gods as given by the sages. Who is to say with absolute certainty what is real and what unreal? The Einsteinian theory of relativity has blasted the Copernican theory that matter alone is real. Einstein declared that everything in the world is relative and nothing is absolute. The sages of the *Upanishads* said the same thing in a different way. They said that the Absolute alone is real and everything else is relative. The mind has a thousand mansions and each one has a reality of its own. In every state of consciousness like waking, dreaming and deep sleep, our experience of reality is totally different. The biologist sees a completely different view of reality when he examines a leaf under a microscope. The *rishis* of the *Puranas* in their heightened states of awareness discovered many, many gods and their forms. Their names are all *mantras*, or special sounds, which give a clue to their forms. Each one of them is only a pointer to the Supreme Reality. Each one of these forms and names has a particular part to play in the spiritual evolution of humankind. Each *Purana* speaks of the *Bhagavan*, the Supreme Person. But each *Purana* calls Him by a different name. This is because the *Bhagavan* is not an individual but an archetype, which is capable of taking on any form by which He or She is invoked. An anthropomorphic veneer is put on Him or Her for we can only think of the highest and most idealistic concept, which the human mind can conceive. In this way, the seer saw to it that no fixed form was given to that Absolute, for

He/She is formless. The great sage Vyasa wrote all the eighteen *Puranas* but in each of them he extolled that particular deity alone, as being the Supreme. In the *Bhagavata Purana*, Krishna is the supreme incarnate. In the *Devi Purana*, the goddess is the Supreme incarnate. In the *Shiva Purana*, it is Shiva, who is the Supreme. Thus the mind was made to realise that the Supreme, being formless, is capable of taking any form and any of these forms, can take us to that ultimate Truth. Hence the great efficacy of *Puranic* literature. It allows the mind of man to take the quantum leap from the form to the formless. It does this, by rocking our usual human conceptions and rocketing us to the unknown by means of a vast array of symbols and strange descriptions. Like the Buddhist koans which defy our usual concepts and activate us to think in a different fashion, so also the forms of the gods defy the norms of common thought and instigate us to leap into the unknown and discover the reality underlying this amazing array of mind-boggling descriptions. The total effect creates a tremendous impact of divine consciousness on the mind.

The ancients saw that just as the sun, moon and planets weave an intricate pattern in the sky, so also they weave the same intricate patterns in the tissues of our bodies and the fabrics of our mind. Hence they discovered the science of astrology to show how the planets rule our physical and psychic bodies. So also within us, are all the gods and it is because of their existence that the slightest movements of our bodies and reflexes are carried out. These gods can heal both body and soul. All philosophy and art, and even all scientific knowledge have to be based on a knowledge of these gods, who form the energy particles of the spiritual field which was known to the ancient seers. They had knowledge of past and future because of their intimate connection with these gods and therefore they knew the secret of moulding human life into a living, spiritual present. The modern scientific mind has forgotten this path and is unable to commune any more with these pulsating gods of the universe and this is the cause of our deep-rooted unrest and anxiety, despite all the comforts which science has provided us. Modern science has provided us a wonderfully fashioned and comfortable chair but the floor on which the chair rests, is shaky so how can we relax comfortably on it? Consciousness alone is the foundation of all existence and the gods are the spiritual essences of which it is made up. It is only by discovering these gods within ourselves that we will be able to see this fabric of the universe as a divine tapestry, on which is woven the milky way of life.

ॐ *Namashivaya!*

Panchakshari Stotram.

Nagendraharaya Trilochanaya, bhasmangaragaya Maheswaraya,
Nityaya Shuddhaya digambaraya,
Tasmai nakaraya, Namashivaya!

Mandakini salila chandanacharchitaya, nandiswara pramathanatha Maheswaraya,
Mandarapushpa bahupushpa supuchitaya,
Tasmai makaraya Namashivaya!

Shivaya Gauri vadanabja bala-suryaya dakshadwaranashakaya,
SriNeelakantaya vrishadwajaya,
Tasmai shikaraya namasivaya!

Vasishtakumbhodbhava Gautamarya, munindra devarchita shekharaya,
Chandrarka vaishwanara lochanaya,
Tasmai vakaraya Namashivaya!

Yajnaswaroopaya jatadharaya, pinakahastaya sanatanaya,
Divyaya devaya digambaraya,
Tasmai yakaraya Namashivaya!

Panchaksharamidam punyam ya padeth Shiva sannidhau,
Shivalokamavapnothi Shivena saha modate.

ॐ

Sri Gurave Namaha!

Invocation to the Supreme Guru.

Guru Brahma, Guru Vishnu, Guru Devo Maheswara!
Guru Sakshatha Param Brahma,
Tasmai Sri Guruva Namaha!

The Guru is none other than
Brahma, Vishnu and Shiva!
The Guru is verily the Parabrahman itself.
To that divine Guru do I make my prostrations!

ॐ

Gurave sarva lokanam,
Bhishaje bhavaroginam,
Nidhaye sarvavidhyanam,
Dakshinamurthaye Namaha!

I bow to Lord Dakshinamurthy, the preceptor of the whole universe, Who removes the ills of mortal existence and confers all supreme wisdom.

Dakshinamurthy stotram by Adi Shankara

ॐ

Giripriyaya Namaha!

PART – I

"Karana charana kritam vaak kaayajam karmajam va.
Shravana nayanajam va manasam vaparardham,
Vihitamavihitam va sarvametath kshamasva,
Jaya Jaya karunabdhe Sri Mahadeva Shambo!"

Hail to Thee O! Mahadeva! Thou art the ocean of compassion!
Pray forgive me for whatever wrong actions I might have done either knowingly or unknowingly,
Through the organs of my action and perception or through the mind.

ॐ

Mahadevaya Namaha!

CHAPTER I

THE GREAT GOD

"Behold Him,
With a rolled palmyra leaf stuck into His ear lobe,
The rider on the bull,
The wearer of the pure white moon on His locks,
Smeared with hot ashes from the cremation ground,
The stealer of my heart...."

Saint Sambandar

In the bewildering galaxy of gods of the Hindu pantheon, Lord Shiva stands out as one of the oldest and one of the best loved. He is as old as the Indian culture, perhaps even older. At the time of the cosmic dawn, before the creation of man, he appeared as the divine archer, pointing with his arrow to the unrevealed Absolute. The world is his hunting ground. The universe resounds with his presence. He is both sound and echo. He is intangible vibration as well as infinitesimal substance. He is the rustling of the withered leaves and the glossy green of the newborn grass. He is the ferryman who ferries us from life to death, but he is also the liberator from death to immortality. He has innumerable faces. His forms are eleven as described in the *Vedas*. The sky and the season vibrate with his intensity and power. He grips, supports, releases and liberates. He is both the disease and the destroyer of the disease. He is food, the giver of food and the eating itself. His divine majesty and power are depicted through symbolic and at the same time highly realistic descriptions of an awe-inspiring figure, at once far and distant and cold, shut up in his remote Himalayan fastness, as well as close and kind and loving, a living, throbbing symbol of the divine.

He was worshipped by the wild tribes which roamed across the subcontinent before the dawn of history, as the divine Shaman. They contacted him by the use of certain narcotics and by various different types of esoteric rituals. Next we see him on the terracotta seals of the Indus civilisation. There he is shown as Pasupati, the Lord of beasts, surrounded by the wild ones of the jungle. He is also shown as the *yogi* sitting in various meditative postures. The *rishis* of the *Vedas* looked up at the Himalayas and saw in them his hair, they found his breath in the air, and all creation and destruction in his dance — the *Thandava Nritta.* The *Rig-veda,* the oldest religious text known to humankind, refers to him as Rudra, the wild one, who dwelt in fearful places like crossroads and shot arrows of disease. Sacrifices were constantly offered to appease him. This was the time when religion was dominated by female deities. Soon the cult of Shiva fused with that of the great mother-goddess, Shakti who later came to be known as Durga, Uma, Parvati and so on. Male and female are but complementary halves of the whole truth and some images portray Shiva as Ardhanareeswara, in which one part is male and the other female.

He is also mentioned as the enigmatic first emanation from the Brahman as *Iswara.* Thus he is the Great Lord, Maheswara, and the Great God, Mahadeva. He is one of the Immortals, Unborn and Deathless. The *Shiva Purana* equates him with the Supreme Brahman of the *Vedas.*

He is also the endearing personal god, Shambunatha and the innocent Bhola with a naive nature. On the other hand he is Dakshinamurti, the Supreme teacher who gave the teaching of the *Vedas,* the *sastras* and the *tantras* to the *rishis.* He is also the master of every art, the supreme dancer, Nataraja, the supreme musician, composer of the *Sama Veda.* Though normally pictured in his fierce aspect, yet he can take the form of Sundaramurti, the handsome one and entice anyone. To the wicked, he is Bhairava or Rudra of fierce aspect. Depending on the needs of the devotees he is capable of taking on many forms.

His forms, attributes, decorations, weapons, attendants and activities are given in great detail so that he becomes a living reality. As Rudra, he is full of wrath and destruction but as Shiva, he is filled with all auspiciousness. He has two natures — one wild and fierce, the other calm and peaceful. Of all the deities, he is the one who is most easily propitiated. Moreover in compassion there is none to compare with him. He is the friend of the unfortunates, the blind, and the lame, the goblins and the ghouls. Those who are despised by others, find a place in his entourage. Demons, vampires, ghosts and goblins who are feared by all, are his close attendants. Snakes, which normally people dread, and run away from in horror, wind themselves lovingly round his neck. His companions are the ghosts and the goblins, the deformed and the ugly. He is averse to none. He does not belong exclusively to the gods or the sages. His greatest devotees are Kubera, king of *yakshas*, Ravana, king of the *rakshasas* and Shukra the *guru* of the *asuras*. Wizards, sorcerers, witches and magicians also worship him. Every spirit, malefic or compassionate, seeks Shiva's grace. His attendants are the *ganas* who are a wild bunch of hooligans and social misfits. They are ugly, deformed and misshapen. They take intoxicating liquors and drugs like *bhang*. They are a totally lawless set of beings that only Shiva can control. Instead of curbing their eccentricities, Shiva joins in their wild revelries and sings and dances with gusto to the accompaniment of their cacophonous music. But he also keeps them in check. Because of him, they are forced to desist from doing too much damage in the world. He is the Supreme *Yogi*, uncaring of material wants, ever immersed in the immensity of his divine bliss. Death stands in dread of him and the word inauspicious does not exist in his dictionary. Bedecked with skulls and bones, Shiva wanders in cremation grounds, dancing to the light of funeral pyres, smearing his body with the ashes of the dead. Dangerous forests infested with cannibals and wild beasts as well as the icy, inaccessible peaks of the Himalayas are his favourite haunts. In the forests he is adored by the wild tribes as Kirata, the hunter. Shiva means the auspicious one, yet everything about him seems inauspicious. He dwells in dark and gloomy caves and jungles, dances in cemeteries lit by the fire of burning pyres, rattling skulls and drums. He smears himself with ash from these pyres, drinks poison and smokes narcotics and enjoys the company of ghosts, ghouls and goblins. The unorthodox and the casteless, who stood outside the traditional fold, saw in him, the non-conformist who sought for ultimate truth, beyond ritual, beyond society, beyond matter. He was the first *tantrik* as well as the first *siddha*. These casteless ones sought his blessings before dabbling in their magic rites, their sorcery and their alchemy.

The Brahmins or the orthodox priest caste thus found it difficult to accept this wild and fearsome god. Like the priest-king Daksha, they held him in contempt. They refused to offer him any portion of their *yajnas* or sacrifices given to the other gods. The story of the Daksha *yaga* shows how by the sheer power of his truth, which is the truth of all creation, Shiva came to be accepted as the great god. He transcends the duality of good and evil, right and wrong, auspicious and inauspicious. The *Sanatana Dharma* or the ancient code of the Hindus, forces the human mind, time and time again, to accept the fact that the divine is all that exists, both clean and unclean, both pure and impure, both auspicious and inauspicious. The same code, which gave us the caste system, also gave us the image of Shiva, the non-conformist, who challenged all social codes and sought a truth, which lay beyond all apparent dualities. There is nothing or nobody that can be said to be beyond the pale of society. The divine accepts every creature, however ugly or malformed. All the rites and rituals that are employed by the human being, groping his way to godhead, have to be accepted by the divine, for that also comes from him alone. Shiva is a symbol of this all-inclusive catholicism of the Hindu view of the deity and thus the Brahmins were forced to accept him into the fold of their conservative beliefs. By the time the *Upanishads* were written, Shiva had become a most important deity. He, who was considered to be inauspicious and impure, eventually, came to be known as Shiva, the auspicious one. He became the inspiration for theatre, dance and drama and was a favourite figure for painters and sculptors.

In the Hindu trinity, Brahma is the creator, Vishnu the sustainer and Shiva, the destroyer. The divine trinity thus ensures the cycle of existence. The Shaiva Siddhanta School of philosophy however does not accept Shiva as being just one of the Trimurtis or one of the trinity. To them, he is the Supreme Brahman to whom both Brahma and Vishnu offer obeisance. He is called *Pati* or Master with the five important functions of godhead, which are, creation, maintenance, destruction, veiling and grace. The human soul is called *pasu*, or creature, which is tied with the *pasa*, or rope of bondage. This bondage consists of three types of impurities. The first is *avidya* or primordial ignorance. Next comes the bondage accruing from our actions, which is known as *karma-mala.* Last is *maya-mala* or the impurity caused by attachment to the world of *maya.* To get rid of the last two impurities, four types of approaches are prescribed. The first is the way of the servant or *dasa marga.* This consists of performing the external acts of worship, like gathering flowers for worship, cleaning the vessels used in worship, sweeping the temple and so on. This leads to *salokya.* The devotee will be taken to the abode of Shiva at the time of death, where he or she will reside forever. The second way consists in intimate service to God, in the way of conducting of rituals, intimate communion with him, speaking about him and writing about him and so on. This is called the *satputra marga* or the path of the good son. This leads the devotee to *samipya* or close proximity to God. The third way is called *sakhya-marga* or the path of friendship and includes internal worship like meditation and communion, which leads to *sarupya.* In this the devotee attains the form of the deity at the time of death. The last is *jnana marga*, or the path of wisdom by following which the devotee attains *sayujya*, or union with God.

As said before, these disciplines can remove only the first two impurities caused by action and attachment to the world — *karma-mala* and *maya-mala.* The bondage of ignorance or *avidya* can only be removed by the grace of God. Thus Shiva is known as Pasupati or the Lord of all human creatures who are bound by these impurities. Shiva accepts all those who are despised and rejected by others. He destroys the negativity in all and purifies them. He is thus the regenerator and reformer. He destroys pomposity by his simplicity and prudery by his defiance of orthodoxy. He is the destroyer of the ego, which is what traps the human being in the ocean of life and death. He can also destroy sorrow, pain and misery. Though he seems a fearsome figure, he is the one who can remove all the fearful influences that threaten our life. Like the lotus, even though rising from the slime of the pond, is the symbol of purity, so Shiva is the symbol of purity even though dabbling in impurity.

His physical body, clothes and ornaments are also unique. He is white as camphor and wears his hair in matted locks, coiled in the shape of a shell. He has a blue neck because he drank the deadly poison that stuck in his throat. He has three eyes. The third eye on his forehead denotes him to be the lord of *yoga.* This inner eye distinguishes truth from illusion and conquers lust. He is Chandrachuda for he wears the crescent moon as an adornment for his hair. Like the waxing and waning of the moon, he is in tune with the rise and fall of the cosmic rhythm. He is Krittivasa or one who wears animal hides. His upper body is covered with the skin of the black antelope, the elephant hide covers his loins and the tiger skin is his seat. His androgynous nature is often shown by his wearing the male *kundala* in his right ear and the female *tatanka* in the left. He wears a garland of skulls and carries a skull in his hand as his begging bowl and often drinks out of it in order to show the frailty of mortal life. He also bedecks himself with *rudraksha* beads. His vehicle is the bull Nandi, which represents restrained power. In his right hand he holds the antelope representing all the creatures that are under his protection. Verminous mongrel dogs scorned by all, run after him, in his wanderings. Snakes slither up and down his body. His weapons are the trident, the three prongs of which represent the trinity. He also carries a staff and a noose — the *pasa* that binds all creatures to mortality. His two bows are known as Pinaka and Ajagava. He is the source of the primeval sound, *Aum* and carries the drum, *damaru* while dancing. The boom of the drum represents the vibrations of cosmic energy. He is the master of music and plays on the *Rudra-veena* or lute, designed for him by Ravana. He also carries a bell on his person. He is prepared to make the most enormous sacrifices for the protection of the world. Though depicted in the trinity, as the destroyer, yet he is the one who protected the world by swallowing the dreaded poison that the serpent evicted. He is the one, who cut the fall of the divine Ganga and thus saved the earth from being drowned in the deluge of her waters. There is no end to his mercy and his kindness. He is prepared to sacrifice himself for the sake of the world.

Modern physics pictures matter, not as passive and inert but as continuously dancing and vibrating. The physicists speak of the continuous dance of sub-atomic particles, which goes on all the time. They have actually used the words, "dance of creation" and "energy dance." When we look at a sculpture of the dancing Shiva, the Nataraja, this description of the physicists, comes forcibly to the mind. The

Nataraja is the personification of this cosmic dance. Modern photographic techniques have been able to project the particle tracks emanating from the dancing image of Shiva. This image is a concrete symbol of the great principle that the seers tried to portray; that life is a rhythmic interplay of birth and death, creation and destruction. The scientists have shown this in their bubble chambers. Shiva's cosmic dance depicts the mad gyrations of energy particles. His *damaru* or drum beats to the rhythm of the cosmic vibrations and his energy or Shakti, is the divine mother, the goddess, Durga or Parvati, the enchantress who creates and nourishes and gives suck to all beings, human and sub-human. All are infants of this divine mother.

The Greeks who came to India around 300 BC saw in Shiva a reflection of their own god Dionysius. He was the rebel who opposed their classical divinities and sought salvation in esoteric rituals. By the time of the Christian era, the cult of Shiva had captured the minds of all and had spread from Kashmir in the north, to Kanyakumari at the very tip of the Indian subcontinent. Now we will look into *Puranic* literature and see how the concept of Shiva is dealt with.

ॐ *Namashivaya*

"O head of mine, Bow down to the Head (of the universe) Who wears a crown of heads on his Head. Who receives alms in a skull, O head of mine! Bow down to him!"

Saint Appar

"O Destroyer! By that supremely peaceful form of yours Which is auspicious and blissful and destroys sin, Give us the knowledge Supreme"

Sri Rudri. Yajur Veda

ॐ

Maheshwaraya Namaha!

CHAPTER II

THE CREATION

Salutations to the Supreme Person, the boundless Being, who wields His triune power for the purpose of creation, preservation and dissolution, the indwelling Spirit within all beings and the unseen director of everything.

Sri Shuka in the Sreemad Bhagavatham

It was *Mahapralaya* — the night of Brahma where nothing existed. There was neither night nor day, no light or darkness, neither joy nor sorrow. All animate and inanimate creation had merged into that infinite essence. There was neither sun nor moon nor planets. The whole firmament was one complete void, pulsating with life.

That alone existed! **That** which the *Vedas* call Brahman — the One without a second. **That**, One, alone existed — the one Existence, the one Consciousness, the one Bliss — *Satchidananda.* It is incomprehensible by the mind. It has neither beginning nor end. It has no second. It has no decrease or development. It is immeasurable, changeless, formless and without attributes. It is the all-pervasive and sole cause of the changing universe, filled with forms. **That** alone existed and **That** alone exists. **That** is the only Reality, all else is *mythya* or unreal. In the course of Its own sport or *lila*, It emanated out of Itself, an auspicious form of Its own, endowed with all power, qualities and knowledge. This was the form of *Iswara.* It is the form of pure *sattva* undiluted by *rajas* and *tamas.* It is the form of harmony alone, with no activity or inertia. It is a form that can go everywhere and take on all forms. It sees all, and is the cause of all and It sanctifies everything.

In the *Puranas*, creation is cyclic in nature. A vast period of *shrishti* or creation is followed by another vast period of *pralaya* or dissolution. There is no absolute beginning for creation and thus, no absolute end.

Time is therefore not linear as in modern thought but cyclic. Brahma is the creative aspect of the Supreme Being. It is he who conducts the work of creation. Shiva is known as the destructive aspect of that same consciousness and Vishnu, the harmoniser or the one who keeps the balance and sustains the creation. A cycle of the creative activity of Brahma is only one day of Brahma and an equally long cycle, constitutes his night. The immensity of Brahma's lifespan can be imagined only if we convert it into human years. One human year of three hundred and sixty days corresponds to just one day of the gods. So three hundred and sixty human years is only one year for the gods. Twelve thousand such celestial years make one *chaturyuga* or the four *yugas* into which cyclic time is divided. One thousand such *chaturyugas* constitute one day of Brahma and an equal number make his night! Each cycle of creation has its own Brahma, whose total lifespan is one hundred such years. The immensity of the period of time involved, in human calculations, cannot be imagined. It will come to three hundred and eleven and forty billion human years. The human mind can scarcely imagine the period of Brahma's life. A cycle of creation is only one day of Brahma and of dissolution, his one night. The inherent tendencies generated by the *jivas* in one cycle remain latent during his night and return to that *avyaktha* from which they have come and sprout into existence at the commencement of his day.

In every cycle of creation it is Time which commences the act of creation. The first principle to be manifested is the Lord's power, as Time. In itself, time is without any modification. It is insubstantial and without beginning or end. It gets its expression at the beginning of creation when it causes the stirring of the three *gunas* or modes of Prakriti or Nature. These *gunas* are called *sattva*, *rajas* and *tamas*. Time is the basis of the sport of the Supreme for His creative manifestations. It is without beginning and without end. A period of evolution is followed by a period of involution, called *pralaya*, in which all things remain, in a latent state. At the end of one cosmic cycle, the Lord's power of illusion, *maya* withdraws all things into itself. At the commencement of a new cycle of evolution, the Lord's power as Time starts a new process by which all things come into existence once again. During *pralaya*, the universe is in a state of latency and after *pralaya* it is in a state of manifestation. This is all a play of the Supreme Lord.

The dissolution of the universe takes three forms, based on Time, substance and the attributes of Prakriti. The first is called *nitya-pralaya*, which is the daily dissolution based only on Time, which all of us experience every day when we go to sleep. Each night is a *pralaya* for each individual soul. When he or she sleeps, there is no world and no individuality. Both are in a latent state, submerged into consciousness. The moment the person awakes, the world appears and individuality asserts itself. The second type of dissolution is called *naimittika-pralaya*, or *mahapralaya*, which is the night of Brahma, when the creator, Brahma, goes to sleep. This happens after one day of Brahma, which lasts, for a thousand *chaturyugas*. In the night of Brahma, the creator, Brahma sleeps for another thousand *chaturyugas* and the whole universe up to Satyaloka or the world of Brahma goes into a state of involution. After this cosmic night is over, the Lord's power as Time, begins to operate and creation and evolution go on as described at the beginning of this chapter.

The third type of dissolution is called *prakritika-pralaya*, when all the categories and attributes of Prakriti go into total dissolution into their ultimate cause, Prakriti, which itself reverts into the *Iswara* and then into the Brahman. This will last for aeons. All things will remain in a latent state. When creation begins once again, all things come out in a reverse order. By the fiat of the Absolute, as mentioned earlier, the first to appear is the Lord's power as Time. It stirs the *gunas* of Prakriti at the beginning of each creative cycle. Out of the cosmic womb of Prakriti comes the cosmic *ahamkara*, or cosmic ego, which splits into *sattva*, *rajas*, and *tamas*, the three *gunas* or attributes of Prakriti. The third aspect is the appearance of the *tanmatras*, or the subtle energy of the elements, which are capable of evolving into the *bhutas* or gross elements. The fourth aspect of creation is the projection of the ten *indriyas* — the five organs of knowledge and the five organs of action. The fifth is the formation of the mind and the presiding deities of the organs, all from the *guna* of *sattva*. The sixth is the creation of *avidya* or ignorance, which clouds and distorts the minds of living beings.

In His sportive manifestation, the *Iswara* assumes the limitation of *rajas* and creates, in the form of the Creator, Brahma. From then on it is Brahma who creates all things. In the seventh aspect of creation Brahma brings into existence the six types of unmoving beings. These are plants that bear fruit without flowering, vegetation that is destroyed when the fruits are destroyed, creepers that spread on supports, the grass family including bamboo, creepers that stand without support and trees with flowers and fruit. They are all characterised by these features. They look insentient but they have internal reactions. They have infinite varieties and they draw their nourishment from the roots upwards.

The eighth creation is that of beasts. *Tamas* is predominant in them so that they cannot think of the morrow and are interested only in food and other physical needs. Their sense of smell is acute. They are without reasoning capacity. There are twenty-eight categories of such species moving on the earth and twenty-eight categories flying in the sky. The ninth creation is that of the human species. Humans are dominated by the *guna* of *rajas* and are compelled to act through desire. Next comes the creation of the gods or super-human beings, which are eight in number. Brahma brings out these four types of creation at the commencement of every cosmic cycle of creation. The universe existed, as it is now even before each *pralaya* and will continue to exist, as it is now, after each *pralaya.* During *pralaya* it is in a latent state and after *pralaya* it is in a manifested state. That is the only difference.

The Supreme Purusha is known as Sadashiva according to the *Shiva Purana.* He is the *Iswara* or supreme embodiment of the godhead and is of pure *sattvic* form. Together with His Shakti or the feminine principle within Himself, He decided to create a third one, in order to enjoy the bliss of His own Being. In the nectarine essence of the ocean of His mind, where thoughts were the waves, where *sattva* was a precious gem, where *rajas* was the coral and *tamas* the crocodile, there appeared the most charming of all persons, who appeared to be a veritable ocean of immeasurable majesty. He had the lustre of a blue sapphire; His glorious eyes were like the newly opened petals of a lotus and were filled with love. He wore silk garments that were golden in colour. He had infinite patience and infinite love.

In a golden, mellifluous voice He asked, "What is my name and my task?" The *Iswara* answered, "As you are all-pervasive and all expansive, you will be known as Vishnu. You will have many other names as well.

By the performance of *tapasya* you will acquire all knowledge."

Then Vishnu performed severe penance for a thousand celestial years and from his body water currents of various types began to flow. The twenty-four *tattvas* or principles also emanated from him. The Supreme Brahman, in the form of divine waters, pervaded the entire void. Vishnu reclined on the body of the celestial serpent and went to sleep on these cosmic waters. Hence he got the name "Narayana," or the one who reclines on water. Except for that primordial Being, there was nothing else.

Lord Narayana lay on his serpent bed, all alone, absorbed in blissful self-awareness. It was the cosmic slumber in which all creation remained in a subtle state. After a period of a thousand *chaturyugas*, his power as Time, stimulated his suspended powers and he opened his brilliant eyes. The whole universe was within him, lying in cosmic dissolution. As his inner gaze turned to these latencies within himself, they burst out of his navel in the most wondrous form of a lotus. It had the brilliance of a million suns and it illumined the expansive wastes of the cosmic waters like the rising sun illumining the quarters. The All-pervading Being entered the lotus and immediately there appeared the form of Brahma who thus came to be known as the lotus-born and the self-born and is the embodiment of the *Vedas*. As Brahma turned his head in all the four directions, he sprouted four faces and when he looked up, he got his fifth face. His complexion was red. He looked around and saw himself seated on the lotus surrounded by the cosmic waters. He knew not who he was, nor where. The lotus stalk waved to and fro in the midst of the gigantic waves, lashed by the winds of dissolution.

Alone and helpless, he became afraid. "Who am I and where have I come from?"

Thinking thus, he climbed down the stalk for a hundred divine years and could not find its beginning. Despondent, he climbed up again and heard a celestial voice telling him to perform *tapasya*. Thus for another hundred divine years he performed severe penance and then in his purified mind, the truth of the Lord as the Indwelling Spirit, dawned on him. He had been unable to find this truth in his search in the outside world for this truth can only be seen within. He saw him, the Lord

Narayana, lying on *Adishesha*, his serpent-bed. The serpent's thousand jewelled hoods cast their glow over the cosmic waters, dispelling the darkness. He saw the incredibly beautiful form of the Lord that included within itself the whole universe. His clothes were like the evening clouds covering the mountains. His floral wreaths were made of all the various flowers of the world. He saw him, whose smile removes the sorrows of the world and all his wondrous accoutrements. Simultaneously Brahma saw the lotus coming out of the Lord's navel with himself sitting in it, amidst the turbulent cosmic waters. Seeing that wondrous form of brilliant hue, Brahma was suffused with delight and asked him, "Who are you? Who am I? Pray enlighten me."

Lord Narayana covered him with his brilliance and said, "Welcome to you, O grandsire. Do not be afraid. I shall confer on you all that you desire."

Then Brahma, provoked by the quality of *rajas* was filled with pride and said, "Who are you to confer anything on me. I am the Self-born, the eternal, all-pervasive Brahma, the grandfather of the whole of creation."

Lord Vishnu said, "I know you, as the Creator. For this purpose you have been born from the lotus, sprung from my navel. But you are not to be blamed for not knowing me. You have fallen a prey to my illusion and have forgotten your source. Know me to be the Supreme Brahman and the only Truth."

Spurred by the Lord's power of *rajas*, a terrible anger rose in Brahma's mind and he fought a wordy duel with Vishnu. At that moment Sadashiva appeared in the form of a huge column of fire before them, having neither beginning nor end. Both Vishnu and Brahma were bewildered at the sight of this enormous column of fire and they decided to find its source. Taking on the form of a boar, Vishnu, the soul of the universe, sped to the nether-worlds in order to find out the beginning of that wondrous column. Brahma took the form of a swan and flew up to the top of the column, trying to gauge its summit. For many aeons, Vishnu, in the form of the boar, penetrated to the bowels of the universe and thus got the name of "Svetavaraha" or the white boar. At last, exhausted he came up. Brahma too soared up in the form of a swan for many aeons and failed to see the top of the column. He decided to return and admit his defeat to Vishnu. Suddenly he noticed the beautiful *keora* flower, which is famous in the worship of the gods, drifting down. Although it had been on its downward course for many years, it had lost neither its fragrance nor its lustre. He asked the flower where it was coming from and the flower answered that it was coming from somewhere in the middle of that primordial column and that it had been travelling for vast ages. Then Brahma thought of a perfect way of convincing Vishnu that he had indeed seen the top of that mysterious Being. He asked the flower to accompany him and to swear that it had met him at the top. The flower agreed and he returned triumphantly. Vishnu took his word for granted, especially since he had a witness to prove the fact. But suddenly out of the column, the mighty voice of the mysterious Lord pronounced these words, "Thou O Vishnu! will in future be considered as equal to Me. Thou shall be worshipped as the Supreme Himself."

Then out of that fire there appeared the fearful form of *Kala Bhairava* who was commanded by Sadashiva to chastise the deceitful Brahma. *Bhairava* pounced on him and caught hold of his fifth head and threatened to cut it off. Then that compassionate and deeply forgiving soul, Vishnu, begged the Lord to forgive Brahma. Sadashiva relented and told the repentant Brahma, "O Brahma, in order to assume the role of Supreme Lord, you resorted to deceit. In future you shall not be honoured by any one and you will not have any temples." Thus it is, that to this day, Brahma, the Creator has no temples or devotees.

Then turning to the *keora* flower, Sadashiva said, "Due to the fact that you have been an accomplice to this deceit, you will no longer be used in my worship."

The flower begged for forgiveness, "If I'm not to be included in thy worship, O Lord, the very purpose of my existence will be lost. Pray forgive me." Then Sadashiva relented and said that though his words could not be withdrawn, the flower could continue to be used in the decorations of temples. And so it is, to this day.

This column of fire was in the shape of a *linga*. The word *linga* actually means a sign or a characteristic. Brahman, the cosmic spirit has no *linga* or characteristic. But since the mind needs something concrete to hold on to, Shiva is depicted in the form of the *linga*. Shiva's *linga* is the divine phallus, the source of the seed of the cosmos, containing within it the entire universe of living and non-living beings. All life is created from it and returns to it. The *yoni* or sign of the female, forms the base of the *linga* and together they represent the union of man and woman, Shiva and Shakti, the cosmic spirit combined with the cosmic Prakriti or nature through which the whole of creation comes into being. Usually there is a pot of water suspended above the *linga* in order to cool it since its origin is from the fiery *linga* which stretched to infinity and whose nature none could fathom.

The day on which Sadashiva thus manifested himself as a column of fire was the day on which the constellation *ardhra* was in ascendance, in the month of *Margashirsha*, November/December. Those who worship Shiva on that day will be blessed. The place where that great Being manifested himself as the column of fire was on the hill of Arunachala and hence a most holy centre of worship sprang up there in course of time.

To those two — Brahma and Vishnu, who had been humbled — Sadashiva explained, "I am the Supreme Brahman. My form is both manifest and unmanifest. I am both Brahman and *Iswara.* My form as *Iswara* can be known through all the forms of the various deities and my form as Brahman can be known through this formless *linga.* Shiva can be worshipped through his formless aspect as the *linga*, as well as his aspect with form. All other gods including both of you will have aspects with form."

When Shiva takes on a form, he has five faces corresponding to his fivefold powers of creation, maintenance, annihilation, concealment and liberation. The syllable "A" , comes from the northern face, the syllable "U" from the western, the syllable "M" from the southern and the *bindu* or dot from the eastern face. The *nada* or sound comes from the middle face. All these five unite to form the mystic sound of *AUM.* From these five sounds is born the five-syllabled *mantra*, *Na-ma-shi-va-ya. AUM* indicates all knowledge. The entire set of *mantras* and all the four *Vedas* have sprung from that. Different things are achieved by different *mantras* but *Omkara* alone achieves everything. By the repetition of this root *mantra*, both enjoyment and salvation can be attained.

At that time, *AUM*, the sound of eternity, which is the form of the Lord, as *nada*, or sound filled the air and all the quarters. It filled the hearts of Brahma and Vishnu with indescribable bliss. The sound manifested in a luminous form before the clear gaze of Vishnu, who was pure and free from all negative thoughts. The first syllable "A" blazed like the sun to the right of the column and then the sound "U" appeared in the middle and finally the sound "M", glittering like the lunar sphere, appeared to the left. Vishnu then meditated on the universal Being, enveloped by that sound and wished to examine the column of fire once again. Into his calm mind, the Truth was revealed. The column of fire was the Supreme Brahman. *Nada* is one of His forms. The creator or Brahma is expressed by the sound "A", the enchanter or Vishnu, by the sound "U" and the Rudra or Shiva by the sound "M".

Both Brahma and Vishnu eulogised the Great Supreme. "Obeisance to Thee, of the bodiless form. Obeisance to Thee, of the formless lustre. Obeisance to Thee the Lord of everything. Obeisance to Thee as the perfect sound, *AUM.*" Thus they praised their preceptor and prayed that he would take on a form that could be worshipped. The voice said that he would incarnate himself through the body of the Creator, Brahma and would be known as Rudra. Shiva and Rudra would be the same principle. The voice also declared that Brahma should engage himself in the work of creation and Vishnu, of protection. Rudra would be the cause of dissolution. Vishnu would be the bestower of salvation on all. In order to please Brahma and Vishnu, Sadashiva, took the form of Dakshinamoorthi, the preceptor of the world. He faced south or *dakshina* while Brahma and Vishnu faced north. He placed His lotus hands on their heads and slowly taught them the great *mantra* and the Supreme Knowledge.

The Iswara's Shakti or power manifested in three forms. As Saraswati, the goddess of speech she became the consort of Brahma, as Lakshmi, the goddess of wealth, she was to become the wife of Narayana or Vishnu and as Kaali, she would stay with Rudra.

The voice continued, "Know Me to be the Supreme Brahman, the eternal, the endless, the perfect and the unsullied. Vishnu has *tamas* within but *sattva* outside. He will be the protector and sustainer of all the worlds. Brahma who creates, will have *rajas* both within and without and Shiva who causes dissolution, will have *sattva* within but *tamas* outside. This is the position of the *gunas* in the three deities. O Vishnu! Spread your glories far and wide by taking up various incarnations. Remember that there is no difference between you and Shiva. He who worships you, worships Shiva and vice versa."

Both Brahma and Vishnu once more eulogised the form that now disappeared from view. Brahma looked around to find that he was alone once more. He was puzzled as to how he should proceed with the work of creation. So he meditated once again on Vishnu who appeared before him in all his glory. When Brahma told him of his predicament, Lord Vishnu blessed Brahma and told him that the knowledge of creation would come automatically to him. He would be able to create all things without any external aid, for everything was contained in seed form within the lotus, on which he was sitting.

Brahma now created the seven sages: Marichi from his eyes, Brighu from his heart, Angiras from his head, and Pulaha, Vasishta, Kratu, and Daksha from his vital breaths. Narada was created from his lap and Kardama from his shadow. *Dharma* came from his right breast. From his back came *adharma* or unrighteousness, which is the seat of death, the terror of the worlds. From his heart came desire, from the eyebrows, anger. From his lower lip came greed and from his mouth, speech. From his urinary system came all the oceans and from the anus, the spirit of evil. From his mind were born the four boy sages known as Sanaka, Sanandana, Sanatana and Sanatkumara. He begged them to proceed with the task of creation. But these pure souls were ever established in *atmic* consciousness and refused to obey their father. At this disobedience on the part of his offspring Brahma frowned with rage and out of that frown there appeared a boy with a red complexion. He cried out, "O father, give me names and places of positions." Because he cried as soon as he appeared, Brahma called him Rudra, which means "Don't cry". This is the story as given in the Bhagavatha *Purana.* Brahma gave him eleven names and forms along with appropriate consorts and told him to create. Unfortunately Rudra's creations were as fierce looking as himself so Brahma told him to stop creating. He told him to do *tapasya* and thus Rudra did *tapasya* and came to be known as Shiva, or the auspicious one.

Since the work of creation was not progressing at all, Brahma prayed to the divine to help him. At that time his body became divided into two halves, one of which was a man, called Swayambhu Manu and then other a woman, called Shatarupa. They became husband and wife and from that time onwards, creation proceeded by way of sexual relationships.

ॐ Namashivaya

"O Resident of the mountains! We sing this hymn to you to propitiate you. Be pleased to make our world prosperous, Our minds peaceful and our bodies free from disease."

Sri Rudri. Yajur Veda

"Let the blue-necked one make us happy. He who rises in crimson splendour in full view of the cowherds, the water maidens and the creatures of the world."

Sri Rudri. Yajur Veda

"O Thousand-eyed One! O Many quivered One! May you be pleased to unstring your bow, flatten the tips of your arrows and become peaceful and well disposed towards us."

Sri Rudri. Yajur Veda

"Let the weapons of your bow liberate us from pain and your quiver be directed against our enemies."

Sri Rudri. Yajur Veda

ॐ

Shambave Namaha!

CHAPTER III

SANDHYA

"He in whom this universe, prior to its projection,
Was potentially present like a tree in a seed,
And by whom it came into existence by the magic of His own will,
Or like a great *yogi* creating out of His own power,
To that Dakshinamurti, the Supreme Being,
Who came in the form of a benign *Guru*,
I offer my profound salutation".

Dakshinamoorti Stotram

The *Shiva Purana* says that after having created the seven sages, Brahma reflected within his mind and from his mind there arose the fascinating form of a woman. She was called Sandhya since she appeared at that time when day meets night. She was the perfection of womanly beauty and on seeing her, the minds of Brahma as well as all the other sages became extremely agitated. When Brahma felt the pangs of the emotion called love, another handsome being appeared out of his thoughts. He had a golden complexion, a fine nose, wonderful, sensuous lips and fine eyes, with titillating eyebrows. On seeing Brahma, this person bowed before him and asked Brahma to give him a name and some occupation.

Brahma's mind was already agitated by the pangs of love and he spoke thus, "You will be known as Manmatha since even at your birth you have started to torment all our minds with thoughts of love. You will also be known as Kama since you will be able to take on any form you wish. Your power will be greater than the powers of all the gods put together. With this form of yours as well as the five flower arrows that you have been born with, you will be able to enamour and captivate the minds of men and women and thus ensure that creation will continue. No living being, not even the gods, will be able to defy you. Even I, as well as all the sages, who are assembled here, have come under your sway. The minds of all living beings will be an easy target for your flower arrows. Invisibly you will be able to enter the hearts of all people, thrilling them and making them lose their reasoning capacity. You will be able to arouse ecstasy in everyone."

Kama's five arrows are: the ability to delight, to appeal, to delude, to wither and to kill. Even sages are unable to resist these five arrows. When he was given all these powers, Kama decided to try them out immediately in the presence of Brahma and the sages. He fitted his arrow on his bow and immediately a beautiful, fragrant breeze started to blow, churning the minds of all those present and as his arrows sped from his bow, those present, started gazing at Sandhya and wishing to possess her. Kama did not stop until everyone had completely lost his or her power of reasoning. Sandhya was also a victim. She started giving shy glances at all of them in turn and looking provocatively at them. Kama was delighted at the success of his first venture. Brahma however had enough sense to realise that he was behaving badly and mentally thought of the Lord and begged him to help him control his emotions. Lord Shiva appeared and chastised him for harbouring sensual feelings for his own daughter.

(The same story is told in another way in the *Bhagavad Purana.* Brahma created Saraswati, the goddess of speech and then fell in love with her. His sons reprimanded him for his incestuous feelings. He forsook his body and took another body and then married Saraswati.)

Brahma felt ashamed of his emotions. He directed his anger against Kama who was the perpetrator of all the misdeeds. "Since you are the cause of all our shame, O Kama, one day you will direct your arrows at the great Lord Shiva and then, you will be severely punished for your crime!"

Hearing this Kama became quite despondent, "Why O grandfather, have you cursed me like this? I have done nothing wrong. I have only carried out your orders. You, yourself said, that all of you, including Vishnu and Shiva would become targets for my arrows. I merely wanted to test the efficacy of your words."

Brahma was pacified by this and said, "Your mistake was to have made me fall in love with Sandhya who is my own daughter. However don't be afraid. Even though Shiva will curse you, you will be reborn soon after."

Saying this, Brahma vanished from view. The patriarch, Daksha, who was one of those born from Brahma now presented his daughter Rati to Kama and asked him to accept her as his wife. On seeing the beautiful daughter of Daksha, Kama was pierced with his own arrows and happily agreed to marry her. She was indeed a fitting wife for him. She was capable of charming the whole world and was expert in all the varieties of love-making.

After watching all these proceedings, Sandhya felt sad and bereft. She felt most ashamed at her own behaviour, for the feelings of lust that had churned her mind. She decided that she could no longer bear to remain in the body which had cast a spell on her own father as well as the Lords of the quarters. She went to the Himalayas and started to do *tapasya.* Brahma sent the sage Vasishta to instruct her. The sage took on the body of a young *brahmachari* and taught Sandhya the method of worshipping Shiva, the three-eyed God.

"O dear Lady," he said, "worship Lord Shiva, the Lord of all the *devas*, with this *mantra*, '*Aum Namashivaya*'. Perform all rites in silence and fast at the end of each period of worship." Having advised her thus, the sage left.

After performing severe penance, Shiva appeared before Sandhya and blessed her. He told her to cast off her body in the sacrificial fire of the sage, Medatithi after which she would be reborn as Medatithi's daughter. The man, on whom she fixed her mind at the time of death, would be the person she would marry in her next life. Having blessed her thus, the Lord disappeared from view. Sandhya went to the hermitage of the sage, Medatithi as instructed by Shiva and just before she entered the fire, she thought of the young *brahmachari* who had instructed her in the worship of Shiva and wished that she would have him as her husband in her next life. Her body became the sacrificial offering. As it was totally purified by contact with fire, it was taken up to the heavens where it was divided into two portions. The upper half of her body became *pratah-sandhya* or dawn, which is the time, which is especially propitious for the gods. The lower half became *shyama-sandhya* or dusk, which is especially pleasing to the manes. At the end of the sacrifice, the sage Medatithi found a baby lying in the heart of the fire. He lifted her up tenderly and cared for her as his own child. Fire had cleansed Sandhya of all her sins and she shone like molten gold. The sage gave her the name, Arundhati. She grew up in the hermitage and when she came of age, her father gave her in marriage to the sage, Vasishta. He was the young *brahmachari* on whom she had concentrated her mind at the time of entering the fire. Arundhati became famous for her chastity and purity, and is still to be seen shining in the sky as an evening star — at the time known as *sandhya* or twilight.

ॐ *Namashivaya*

"O Lord! Eternal like a mountain! On the very day you enslaved me, did you not appropriate, My soul, my body and my belongings! Today if anything untoward happens to me, Be it good or be it bad, Have I any mastery over this?"

Saint Manikkavachakar.

"Prostrations to the golden-armed commander of cosmic forces, the Lord of the four quarters. Prostrations to the source of all the green-leafed trees of Nature, the Lord of all creatures. Prostrations to the golden-hued one, the self-effulgent, the Lord of all paths."

Sri Rudri. Yajur Veda

"Prostrations to the one seated on the bull, the giver of food, destroyer of sins. Prostrations to the ever-green one, the wearer of the sacred thread, The chief among the healthy and strong. Prostrations to the Lord of the universe, The shield against the phenomenal world."

Sri Rudri. Yajur Veda

ॐ

Ambikanathaya Namaha!

CHAPTER IV

DURGA

"If one could but be privileged to see
The arched eyebrows, the rosy red lips,
The budding smile, the wet matted locks,
The milk-white sacred ash on the body of coral hue,
And the sweet lifted foot,
Even human birth on this earth would be desirable."

Saint Thirunavukkarasar

Brahma was very unhappy over his chastisement by Lord Shiva. He went to meet Daksha and his other sons and consulted them about what should be done. The reason why Shiva had reprimanded him was because he had harboured sexual feelings for his own daughter, Sandhya. Shiva's lack of feelings originated from the fact that he was a *yogi*, who had no knowledge of women or passion. In order to make him suffer the pangs of love, Brahma decided to get the help of Kama and his wife Rati and make Shiva fall in love.

"Unless that primordial being Shiva indulges in sexual sport, creation will continue to be mediocre. In the case of Shiva, who is extremely detached, only Kama's power can prevail." Thus saying, Brahma requested Kama to go and try his wiles on Lord Shiva. He also created Vasanta or spring to be Kama's permanent companion and thus aid him in his exploits. "O Kama, for the benefit of the world, please go and try to enchant Shiva. Wherever Shiva goes, you should follow him and shoot your arrows at him so that he will be inclined to take a wife. Over mountains or lakes, through forests or peaks, follow him wherever he goes and charm him. You alone have the power to do this. He is averse to women and is in full control of himself."

Hearing these words of the Creator, Kama accompanied by his attendants, Vasanta and the gentle *malaya* breeze, left for the harsh mountains, caves and dales over which Shiva roamed. Along the icy fastness of the Himalayan regions Kama stepped and wherever he went, the season changed. No longer did the cold winds blow. Instead the gentle *malaya* breeze, fragrant with the perfume of a thousand flowers swept the region. All the trees bloomed simultaneously. Spring burst into bloom with all its profusion of flowers but Shiva was not beguiled. He was immersed in *atmic* bliss. Arrow after arrow sped from Kama's sugar-cane bow. Both he and Rati tried all their tricks. All living beings fell a victim to their charms, but not Shiva. He alone was unaffected. In fact, he did not even notice what was happening. Kama's ego was subdued and he returned dejectedly back to Brahma.

"O Brahma! Listen to me. Though I tried my best to enchant Shiva, he remained unaffected. In complete control of his senses, he continued to remain in a state of *samadhi* despite all my efforts to shake him out of it. Wherever Shiva went Rati and I followed him closely and darted arrow after arrow at him but neither he nor his *ganas* were moved by them. Whenever he came out of *samadhi*, I placed many pairs of birds and animals before him, all engaged in mating games. He remained unmoved. Never did my arrow find a vulnerable point in him. Vasanta who accompanied me also did his best. He covered the mountain slopes with fragrant flowers and the lakes with lotuses. Seeing all this abundance of nature, even the sages fell a prey to passion. Need I then speak about the state of ordinary mortals! But there was no wavering to be seen in the demeanour of Lord Shiva. He did not even evince anger at me. What could I do but return. I assure you that there is no one in the whole world who is capable of arousing lust in him. If you want him to marry, you will have to produce someone who is capable of arousing his love." So saying Kama returned to his abode followed by his wife, Rati and his troop of helpers.

Brahma was quite dejected at this news and did not know what to do. Brahma's nature was *rajasic*, active and energetic, while Shiva's was *tamasic*, passive and contemplative. In between stood Vishnu, the cosmic saviour, totally *sattvic*, always interested in maintaining the cosmic order. He preserved the cosmic balance between the aggressiveness of the

Creator, Brahma and the regressiveness of the destroyer, Rudra. Thus Brahma, Vishnu and Shiva stand for *shrishti*, *sthiti* and *samhara*, creation, preservation and destruction. Brahma realised that if Shiva became totally dispassionate about the world, the cosmic balance would be destroyed since a certain amount of tension is always necessary to keep up the work of creation. Suddenly he thought of calling on Lord Vishnu, who was the primary cause of Brahma's own creation. The moment he thought of him, Vishnu, the lotus-eyed one, four-armed and blue in colour appeared before him and smilingly asked him what he wanted. Brahma repeated his tale of woe and told Vishnu how he had sent Kama to enchant Shiva and failed miserably.

Vishnu smiled to hear this tale and said, "O Brahma! How is it that this delusion has befallen you? Don't you know that Shiva is the *Mahayogi*, free from all illusion, ever immersed in the bliss of the Self. How could you ever think of making him fall a prey to Kama's wiles? O Brahma if you really want Shiva to marry, then you will have to pray to Shiva himself. You know his Shakti is a part of him. Shakti is his feminine counter-part and is known as Shivaa. If that goddess takes on a human birth, she will definitely become his wife, for she is a part of him. Command your son, Daksha to do penance and propitiate that goddess and induce her to take birth as his daughter and ask Daksha to give her to Shiva in marriage. Remember, at that time when all three of us came out of that formless Brahman, it was declared that Lakshmi would be my feminine counterpart, Saraswati, yours and Sati, Shiva's. Sadashiva incarnated himself as Rudra and came out of your brows. He is now residing in Kailasa awaiting the advent of Shivaa in the form of Sati, daughter of Daksha. Therefore make all preparations for her advent." Thus saying, Lord Vishnu blessed Brahma and vanished from view.

As soon as Vishnu left, Brahma began to meditate on Shivaa or Durga, the feminine counterpart of Shiva. The goddess is *vidya* and *avidya*, both knowledge and ignorance. She is nothing but the Supreme Brahman. Pleased with his penance, the goddess Durga appeared before Brahma. She was as dark as night, with four divine arms, one of which carried the blue lotus and the other a sword. The third was raised in the *mudra* of blessing. Her eyes were dark and lustrous and gleamed like the pearls, which adorned her dishevelled tresses. The mystic third eye on her forehead was closed. She was as beautiful as the autumn moon. The crescent moon bedecked her broad forehead. She was seated on a magnificent lion that gazed at her lovingly with its tawny eyes.

On seeing this wondrous apparition, the divine Shakti, Brahma folded his palms and eulogised her; "Obeisance to Thee O Goddess! You are the eternal energy of Brahman who has manifested herself in many forms. In the form of Lakshmi you have found a place beside Vishnu; in the form of the Earth, you hold everything within yourself. You are both action and non-action; you are the cause of both creation and destruction. You are that primary energy of both movable and immovable objects and you are capable of enchanting everyone. Though unmanifest, you are capable of taking on infinite manifestations. You are eternal Time which holds the worlds in thrall."

Hearing this hymn of Brahma's, the goddess was pleased and asked him what he wanted from her. Brahma replied, "O goddess, the great God Shiva, who has manifested himself as Rudra through my forehead is now residing in Kailasa. He performs penance all alone and refuses to take a wife. You are his eternal *shakti.* He is the Lord of *yoga* and cannot be tempted by any woman. But as you know, the path of *yoga* or restraint has to be balanced by the path of *bhoga* or enjoyment. You alone in the entire world are capable of exciting Lord Shiva, as you enchanted Vishnu in your form as Lakshmi. O mother of the universe, I pray you to be born as Daksha's daughter and bewitch the Lord who is totally detached from worldly life. At the moment Daksha is performing penance with his mind directed to you. Be pleased to grant his wish that you should be born as his daughter, Sati." The goddess agreed to his request and after blessing him, she vanished from view.

She appeared before Daksha, who was practising penance on the seashore as told by Brahma. Her beauty charmed Daksha and bowing low, he sang a hymn of praise to her. She was pleased by his devotion and asked him to choose a boon. Daksha said, "O mother of the universe! As you know Rudra has incarnated himself as Shiva but so far he has not taken a wife. You alone are capable of enacting this role, so kindly deign to be born as my daughter and become Shiva's wife. This is the boon that I crave for."

Hearing these words, the goddess said, "O Daksha! You have spoken rightly. I'm the only fitting mate for Shiva. I am his beloved in every manifestation, so I shall incarnate myself as your daughter. Return to your abode and remain in prayer. Your wish will soon be fulfilled. But there is one condition O Daksha! If at any time in the future, you show disrespect to me or to Shiva, I shall withdraw into myself and cast off my body." Thus saying the goddess disappeared from Daksha's view.

ॐ Namashivaya

"Prostrations to the robber chief, armed with quiver and arrows. Prostrations to the deceiving, elusive chief of marauders. Prostrations to the wandering, ever evasive chief of forest thieves!"

Sri Rudri. Yajur Veda

"Prostrations to the chief of thieves, ever alert in defence and eager to strike. Prostrations to the chief of dacoits, who moves about in the night, carrying swords. Prostrations to the red-capped resident of the mountains, who steals our belongings."

Sri Rudri. Yajur Veda

"Prostrations to you who are both seated and reclining. Prostrations to you who are both sleeping and awake. Prostrations to you who are in the static and the dynamic. Prostrations to you who are in both the chiefs and the assemblies."

Sri Rudri. Yajur Veda

ॐ

Pinakine Namaha!

CHAPTER V

SATI

"Young doe of deer is she, or tender bud of a divine flower.
Or the early stage of fragrant honey,
Or the beautiful tendril of the young coral beneath the waves of the sea.
Or the early streaks of the rays of the moon.
Or the miniature bow on which Cupid practised".

Sekkizhar in Periyapuranam

Daksha now retired to his own hermitage and Brahma requested him to get married and thus get progeny in order to increase the population of the world which was sadly under-populated in those times. He married two ladies called Asikni and Virini. By his second wife he begot many sons who were sent by him towards the west with instructions to create. They reached the famous lake known as Narayana *saras.* When they touched the waters of that holy lake, their intellects changed and they decided to perform austerities at that beautiful spot. Hearing of this resolve of the sons of Daksha, the sage Narada went to that place and advised them to give up their desire for children and concentrate on the Lord and thus enlighten themselves. The intelligent sons of Daksha realised the truth of his words and gave up their attempt and wandered about as *yogi*s, in their search for truth. Hearing of the fate of his sons, Daksha, undaunted, begot another thousand sons by his other wife. When they came of age they also went to the lake called, Narayana. As soon as they touched the holy waters of the lake, their minds changed. Once again Narada went to them and advised them to search for God rather than for wives and they also went the way of their brothers and roamed about as *yogi*s.

Daksha was grief-stricken at the loss of all his wonderful sons.

Hearing of the dastardly trick which Narada had played on him, he cursed Narada and said, "Since you are the one who has made my sons into homeless vagabonds, roaming about in search of God, you, O Narada, will never have a proper home for yourself. If you stay longer than a few hours at any one place your head will burst. You will be condemned to be a cosmic wanderer, never resting for long at any place, always on the move."

Narada was not a whit put out by this curse. He thanked Daksha for his kindness in having cursed him thus. The curse ensured that he could always roam about the world singing the praises of Lord Vishnu on his lute. This was just what he liked to do. One finds that the devotees of Lord Vishnu are always peaceful of disposition and never given to violent outbursts of temper even if they are abused.

Having lost all his sons, Daksha decided that he would try his hand at begetting daughters who were not likely to wander off like sons. He then begot sixty daughters. As soon as they came of age he got them married. Ten were married off to Dharma, the lord of Righteousness, thirteen to the sage Kasyapa and twenty-seven to the moon, Chandra. The rest were married off to various people and the progeny of these daughters slowly started to fill the world. It was at this time that Daksha had his quarrel with his son-in-law, the moon. It appears that Daksha made a habit of quarrelling with all his sons-in-law, as we shall see. Chandra, the moon-god had married twenty-seven of Daksha's daughters. These are the twenty-seven lunar asterisms, but Chandra showed a marked preference for Rohini, the fairest amongst them. The others complained to their father and Daksha cursed Chandra that his beautiful body would wane and wither. As the curse took effect, the moon became weaker and weaker. He was terrified and went to Vishnu who advised him to go to the supreme physician, Vaidyanatha, or Shiva. He was the custodian of the sacred herb, Soma, because of which he is also known as Somnatha. Shiva cured Chandra, but each time he returned to his own abode, the dreaded malady struck again. At last Chandra begged Shiva to cure him completely. Shiva agreed to do so and gave him a place in his own tresses. The crescent moon, *chandrakala*, adorns the locks of Shiva and thus Shiva got the name, Chandrashekara. Daksha could not forgive Shiva for having saved one whom he had cursed.

It was now that Daksha remembered the promise made to him by the goddess Durga that she would be born as his daughter. Therefore he and his wife prayed to the goddess and she appeared and told them to do certain purificatory rites and she would soon take birth in the womb of Virini, Daksha's wife. True to her word, the goddess Shivaa, also known as Durga, Kaali etc., was born to Daksha. At the time of her birth there was a gentle shower of rain and flowers from the sky. She showed her divine form to her parents and they eulogised her with many hymns. She then became a baby once more and started to cry, as all new-born babes would do. She was called Sati. As a child her favourite pastime was to sit in one place and draw portraits of Shiva, whom she had never seen in this birth. All her songs were of Shiva or Rudra.

One day, Brahma accompanied by the sage Narada went to Daksha's abode and told Sati that her desires would be fulfilled and she would secure Lord Shiva as her husband. She approached her mother and informed her that she was going on a year's penance in order to secure Shiva as her husband.

She then started to do severe penance in order to propitiate Shiva. Every month she worshipped Shiva in various ways, undergoing rigorous tortures of her body until one full year had passed. At the end of the year she concluded her worship and sat and concentrated on the three-eyed Lord, the all-merciful. Even the sages came to see Sati for she had reached an exalted state which even they had failed to reach after many years of *tapasya.* The sages approached Lord Vishnu and begged him to intercede with Shiva on Sati's behalf. Accompanied by Brahma and Vishnu, they went to Kailasa and praised Shiva. He was delighted and asked them to name their desire and he would fulfil it. They jointly begged him to accept a wife, just as Vishnu had accepted Lakshmi and Brahma, Saraswati.

Hearing this Shiva spoke, "*O Devas*! Only a person of imperfect knowledge will desire marriage. It is a great bondage. I am a *yogi*, ever delighting in the bliss of the Self. I'm always engaged in *tapasya* and totally detached from the world. What interest would I have in marriage? Moreover I'm the friend of ghosts and goblins. I visit the burning ghats and crematoriums. My body is covered with the ashes of cremated bodies. Serpents and reptiles are my ornaments. Which woman would want to marry me!"

Again the gods begged him to reconsider their request for it was imperative for the good of the world that he should have a consort. Hearing their words, Shiva smiled and said, "All right. I can never refuse the requests of my devotees so I shall take a wife, but remember she will have to be a very special type of woman. When I am a *yogi*, she will have to be a *yogini*, and when I desire her she will have to be a wife. When I go into *samadhi*, she should not approach me for she will be burnt into ashes in the fire of my austerity. If she refuses to believe in what I say, I will abandon her. Consider all these factors O Brahma, and then tell me if such a woman can be found amongst your creation!"

Brahma was delighted at these words and said, "Indeed O Lord, such a woman has been born, as the daughter of Daksha. She is known as Sati and is a fitting mate for you. At present she is performing rigorous penance in order to secure you as her husband. She is the same mother Goddess, who has taken on the form of Lakshmi and Saraswati." Vishnu also spoke highly of Sati's qualities and urged Shiva to grant their request as well as Sati's wish. Shiva agreed.

On the eighth day of the bright half of the month of *Asvini*, Sati observed her final fast, which concluded her one-year worship of Shiva. She was sitting in the forest engrossed in meditation on his form when Shiva appeared before her. He showed her his incomparable form with five faces, three eyes and crescent moon adorning his locks. He was holding the trident and drum. His face was brilliant and Sati could hardly gaze at him. She lowered her eyes shyly and knelt at his feet.

Although he knew her desire, he asked her to choose a boon for he wanted to hear her express her wish boldly to him without any reserve. But she was very shy and would not speak. Again he urged her to openly express her desire. At last she whispered, "O Lord, why do you play with me? You know my desire. Let me have the bridegroom of my choice."

Hardly had she finished when he replied, "You shall indeed be my wife O Sati!" Delighted to hear these words she could not speak a word but could only smile sweetly at him. Looking at her fascinating form, even the stern, ascetic heart of Shiva melted with the emotion of love and he gazed tenderly at her. At last Sati spoke, "O Lord, be pleased to approach my father and ask him for my hand in the accepted mode of conduct." Shiva agreed and she bowed to him and returned to her parents' palace with great joy. Her friends informed Virini that Shiva had granted Sati, the boon for which she had been doing *tapasya.* Both Daksha and Virini were very happy to hear this. They were wondering how to proceed in this matter when Brahma appeared before them accompanied by his consort, Saraswati. Shiva had requested him to go to Daksha and formally ask for his daughter's hand in marriage, for that was her wish. Brahma said, "O Daksha! That which we have all desired has now come to pass. He who could not be tempted by Kama's arrows has now fallen a prey to your daughter, Sati. The great Lord has now abandoned meditation on the Self and is now thinking only of Sati. Therefore allow me to go and let Shiva know that you have given your consent."

Daksha readily gave his consent and Brahma went and reported the matter to Shiva who was waiting in a fever of impatience about the outcome of his proposal. Shiva was delighted to get the news. When a devotee gives all her heart to him, the Lord in turn becomes equally impatient to give his love to her. Without further debate, Shiva collected his fearsome-looking attendants and told Brahma and the sages to accompany him.

On a Sunday, in the bright half of the month of *Chaitra*, Shiva accompanied by Brahma, Vishnu and all the sages as well as his own *ganas*, proceeded to the kingdom of Daksha. The bridegroom was clad in the hide of an elephant and tiger. He had matted locks with the crescent moon peeping from them and serpents adorning his neck.

Daksha and his wife welcomed the party with great delight. Daksha requested Brahma to conduct the marriage rites. Brahma complied with the request and gave Sati to Shiva. It was a union of Shiva and Shakti, the ideal couple. Shiva firmly grasped her trembling hand in his and lead her three times round the sacred fire as was customary. The rest of the ceremonies was concluded and Shiva left the place, seated on the bull, Nandi, with Sati placed on his lap, in front of him. All the gods accompanied the bridal party to a certain distance. Then Shiva and Sati, escorted by his *ganas*, proceeded to the Himalayan ranges, which was his abode.

ॐ *Namashivaya*

"Prostrations to you who are in the forms of carpenters and chariot-makers. Prostrations to you who are in the forms of hunters and fishermen. Prostrations to you who are in the forms of hounds and their keepers."

Sri Rudri. Yajur Veda

"Prostrations to the resident of the mountains, who is present in all beings. Prostrations to the one with the bow which rains heavily through the clouds. Prostrations to the short one, who is beautiful. Prostrations to the ancient one, who transcends time, space and matter. Prostrations to the venerable old one, who expands through prayers."

Sri Rudri. Yajur Veda

"Unattached, unattached, unattached am I (to the body, mind and intellect)
I alone and changeless exist in the form of consciousness and bliss.

I am ever pure and free, without change of form and nature.
I am ever full...I alone exist, changeless.

I am eternal and without boundaries,
Immutable and unshakeable.
I alone exist,
Changeless in the form of consciousness and bliss"

Dasisoka by Adi Shankaracharya

ॐ

Shashishekaraya Namaha!

CHAPTER VI

SATI AND SHIVA

"Be attached to Him, who is without attachment.
Hold on to that attachment.
Then only will you be able to leave other attachments."

Saint Thirvalluvar

Sati was the perfect mate for Shiva. She had no interest in anything except in following him and pleasing him, but this did not mean that she had no mind of her own. On the contrary, though she was Sati, she was also Durga and Kaali and when she made up her mind nothing could deter her, as we shall see. But for the moment she cared not for the loss of the luxuries of palace life where she was waited upon, hand and foot. All she wanted was to roam about wildly in the wake of her strange husband, across the desolate Himalayan ranges and peaks, inhabited by wild animals, followed by his hoard of goblins, the *ganas*. At first he hardly glanced at her but she cared not for his apparent lack of interest and continued to follow him.

One day he suddenly asked her, "Why do you follow me?"
She answered, "Because I'm your wife."
"Why did you marry me?" he queried.
"Because I'm incomplete without you," she replied.
"I have nothing to offer you,"
"But I ask for nothing but you," she countered.
"I have no parentage or lineage or possessions. These strange creatures alone are my kith and kin."
"I want nothing but you. Those whom you consider your own, are also my own," was her reply

Her tenacity and love at last won him over completely and he ordered his *ganas* to leave them in peace and that he would call them when he needed them. Then the Lord took Sati in his arms and sported with her as any man with a newly-wed wife. He never left her side even for a moment and even if he did, he would return suddenly and close her eyes from behind, so that she would tremble and cling to him for support. He would suddenly become invisible and then catch her and make her shriek with fright and then appear before her so that she would again rush into his arms in apparent terror. Sometimes he would gather flowers for her hair and adorn her with garlands. Sometimes when she looked into a deep pool in order to admire her face, he would come behind her and gaze into the water. She was the dark monsoon cloud from behind which the full moon was peeping, for Sati was the colour of ebony and Shiva, fair as the moon. Then he would gather lotuses from the lake and decorate her dark body with flowers. Very often he would help to dress her after her bath and anoint her with sandalwood perfume and apply musk on her breasts.

When winter set in, Shiva thought of Kama and Kama arrived accompanied by Vasanta. With the arrival of spring, trees and creepers bloomed and blossomed in the Himalayan glades in accord with the inclination of the Lord. Lakes were covered with full-blown lotuses while the gentle *malaya* breeze drenched the air with perfume. Spices like cloves and cardamom added to the fragrance, making the bees dizzy with delight. The nights were bright with the moon, in a sky devoid of clouds. In this enticing atmosphere, Lord Shiva consorted with Sati for many years. Just as ropes bind an elephant, he seemed to be bound by the loveliness of her face and her charming, provocative ways. On the ridges and in the caverns of the Himalayan ranges, Lord Shiva sported with Sati for twenty-five years according to the calculation of the gods. But despite all this play of love, never once did he lose his seed.

Once, with the advent of the monsoon season, Sati complained to Shiva, "O dearest husband, this is a most unpleasant season for wanderers like us who are without a fixed abode. These fearful rumblings and streaks of lightning frighten me. Neither the sun nor the moon is visible. The huge *devataru* trees are falling down with crashing sounds. The day appears like night. See my body, lacerated by cruel hailstones, which fall mercilessly on me. Only the peacocks are delighted with the sound of thunder and dance with delight. In this season even crows and *chakora* birds make nests. We alone are homeless. O my dearest Lord, please make a residence for us without delay."

Hearing these words of Sati, Shiva said, "O my beloved one! Let it be as you wish. Choose the place, in which you would like to stay and a fitting abode shall be made for you. Do you wish to reside in Mount Meru where the gods reside? Or would you prefer to be in Kailasa? Perhaps your preference is for Kasi. Name it and it shall be yours without further delay. Your beauty will rival the beauty of the heavenly damsels and make them blush with shame. Or do you wish to abide in the realm of Himavan, the king of the Himalayas, with the mountain women and the daughters of the *nagas* to attend on you? Even the beasts of prey are peaceful there, for it is the abode of many sages and saints. Perhaps you wish to dwell on my own mountain of Kailasa, close to the abode of Kubera, the god of wealth? Make your choice. It is all yours."

Sati chose to go to the country of Himavan. So the Lord took her there and made a beautiful residence for her and stayed with her for many divine years. He was never bored of her company and she was always enchanted with his. Lord Shiva, who had once delighted only in the *atman*, now delighted only in Sati. Day and night they gazed with delight into each other's eyes, oblivious of the world, wrapped in their own love.

At last one day Sati freed herself from his embrace and started questioning him on many subjects which only he could answer. This she did for the sake of the world for she herself was the divine mother and knew all the answers.

Sati asked, "O great *Yogi*! I wish to know that principle from which all creatures can get release from their misery. What is it that will enable people to free themselves from worldly bondage and attain the supreme region?"

"O goddess Sati, listen carefully for I shall give you that knowledge which shall free all souls in bondage. O goddess, know that the supreme knowledge consists in experiencing the great truth, 'I am Brahman', '*aham brahmasmi.*' In a perfect intellect, nothing else is remembered.

This sort of consciousness is very rare in the world. But, O beloved, remember that I myself am the supreme Brahman, as is Vishnu. Devotion to him or to me is the easiest method of attaining salvation. Supreme devotion is the same as supreme knowledge and is easier to practise. One who is engrossed in devotion enjoys perpetual bliss. Devotion has the power to attract me as nothing else can. I go even to the homes of the outcastes if they are devotees. The nine qualities of devotion are, listening to the glories of God, praising him, remembering him at all times, serving him, surrendering the ego to him, worshipping him in various ways, prostrating to him, dedication to him and friendliness and kindness to all his creatures. The devotee always believes that whatever I bestow on him is for his good. He dedicates everything to me and keeps nothing for himself. One, who attains these nine qualities, attains everything — perfect knowledge and worldly success and eventual salvation. In this Iron Age of Kali, there is no path as easy and as pleasing to me as the path of devotion. In this decadent age, *jnana* or knowledge and *vairagya*, or detachment have become misused and neglected. People who can grasp them are rare. But O beloved! Devotion can give all the benefits of the other two and is most pleasing to me. Remember that both I and Vishnu are subservient to those who are devoted to us."

Hearing this discourse on devotion Sati was very happy. She continued to question him on many matters, relating to the *sastras*, to ethics, morality and religion, the conduct of different people at different times and knowledge of *yantras* and *mantras*.

These wonderful dialogues between Shiva and Sati on all these various topics are the basis of much of the great knowledge, which is found in Hindu philosophy. All the sacred lore, bearing on various sciences like astrology, medicine, herbal lore, palmistry and so on, was given to her. Shiva explained many things with the help of *yantras*, or mystic diagrams and *mantras* or mystic sounds. Thus Sati and Shiva who are intrinsically nothing but the Supreme Brahman, who are omniscient and are always bent on giving help to human beings, carried on their discourses in the Himalayan regions in order to help the afflicted and enable human beings to rise out of the ocean of *samsara*, or the wheel of human existence.

Once Shiva accompanied by Sati and seated on his bull, wandered over the earth. This was the time of the Sri Rama *avatara*, when Lord Vishnu had taken on the form of the prince of Kosala, in order to rid the world of the demon, Ravana. Rama had been exiled to the forest by his stepmother. While they were residing there, his beloved wife, Sita was abducted by Ravana. Rama was bereft and went around lamenting the loss of his wife. It was at this time that Shiva and Sati came to the forest known as Dandaka and saw Rama totally bereft, bemoaning the loss of his wife, like any lovelorn husband.

Seeing Rama and his brother, Lakshmana, Sati asked Shiva, "O Lord, who are these two persons who seem to be greatly distressed over some loss? How is it that you are so delighted to see them and have even gone down and bowed to the blue-complexioned one?"

Shiva smiled and explained, "O goddess! These two are brothers called Rama and Lakshmana. They are the sons of Dasaratha, king of Ayodhya and belong to the solar dynasty. The elder one called Rama is the *avatara* of Vishnu. He is incapable of being harassed. The Lord has incarnated on earth for the welfare and protection of the good. In his human form he merely plays the role of the grief-stricken husband. Actually he is ever immersed in the bliss of the Self." Seeing Rama's extreme sorrow, Sati could not quite believe Shiva's explanation. Seeing her doubt, Shiva told her to go and test Rama. Sati was all too ready to put him to the test. So she decided to take on the form of Sita and go before Rama. "If he is indeed Vishnu, he will be able to penetrate my disguise." So thinking, she took the form of Sita and went in front of Rama.

Rama immediately saw through her disguise and bowed to her and said, "O goddess Sati, obeisance to you. Why have you thrown off your own form and taken on this guise? Where is your Lord, Shiva? Have you come alone?"

Hearing these words of Rama, Sati was delighted and became convinced of his divinity. She told him the whole story of how she had doubted Shiva's word and had wanted to test Rama. But she still had a doubt. She had always thought that Shiva and Vishnu were on par with each other. So why did her husband worship Rama? This was her next question.

Rama answered, "Once Shiva made the divine architect, Visvakarma erect a fantastic hall in which was placed a throne of great beauty. He invited all the gods and sages and celestial beings to congregate there. Then he invited Vishnu from Vaikunta and made him sit on that exquisite throne and at a most auspicious hour, to the accompaniment of *Vedic* chants, he placed the golden crown on Vishnu's head and announced to all that from then on, Vishnu was worthy of equal worship as he.

At that time, Shiva said, 'You are the lord of the universe. You are the one who is supremely worthy of worship by all. You will be invincible in battle even against me. I shall personally give salvation to your devotees.' Thus did Lord Shiva speak and from that time onwards he worships me and I worship him."

Sati was satisfied when she heard this but she was feeling troubled about having doubted her husband's words. When she returned to Shiva she was pensive and sad. Seeing her in this mood, Shiva enquired after the cause of her distress. She voiced her doubt to Shiva and he immediately thought of the promise he had once made to Vishnu, that if Sati ever doubted him or his teachings, he would abandon her. However he did not say a word of this to her. She guessed that some disturbing thought had arisen in his mind. Though he continued to behave with the greatest of love to her, both of them realised that soon some incident would occur, which would enable him to keep his word.

ॐ *Namashivaya*

When all beings are realized as one's a Atman, that seer of oneness has no delusion of sorrow.

ॐ

Rudraya Namaha!

CHAPTER VII

DAKSHA YAGA

"More fiery is He than fire,
More cool is He than water,
None fully understands His mercy.
Aloof He may be but close to His devotees,
More than a mother, tender-hearted is He."

Saint Thirumoolar

Once a great *yaga* or fire sacrifice was performed by the sages who assembled at the sacred confluence of the three rivers, Ganga, Yamuna and Saraswati, which is known as Prayaga. Lord Shiva had also come there, accompanied by his wife, Sati. All those assembled there rose up from their seats and paid obeisance to him. They seated him with great honour and eulogised him with great devotion. Soon after, Daksha came into the hall and everyone rose up to honour him. Shiva however remained in his seat. Daksha, who had become arrogant due to his status in the world, was incensed by this mark of disrespect by his own son-in-law.

Angrily he spoke, "How is it that when the rest of the world gives me respect, only this man who is my son-in-law, arrogantly refuses to honour me? He is totally uncultured and mannerless. But then what can you expect of one, whose attendants are goblins and ghosts? He lives in cremation grounds and wears serpents for garlands! He may be my daughter's husband but I'm going to curse him."

Then turning to the others he proclaimed, "Listen all of you. From this day onwards, let this Shiva, who lacks nobility of birth and pedigree, who frequents cemeteries and burial grounds, be expelled from all sacrifices. Henceforth none of you should give him a share of any sacrifice!" Brighu was one of the sages who acquiesced with these stupid words of Daksha. Shiva said nothing but his beloved attendant Nandi, who could take on the form of his vehicle, the bull, rose up and denounced Daksha in forcible terms.

"O foolish Daksha," he said, "how dare you curse the Lord Shiva, whose very presence sanctifies all the worlds. He is Mahadeva, the great Lord by whom the universe is created, sustained and destroyed. One glance from him is enough to reduce you and your entourage to ashes. The fact that he doesn't do it now shows the extent of his mercy. But beware! You will soon have your pride reduced to ashes!"

Daksha was furious with Nandi for daring to rebuke him publicly, and cursed him as well as all the attendants of Shiva. "All of you will be condemned as heretics and will be cast out of *Vedic* society. Matted hair, ashes and skulls will be your ornaments. You will be expelled from all *Vedic* rites."

Hearing this, Nandi was furious and cursed them all in return. "O foolish people, the great Lord Shiva has been cursed by evil-minded sages like Brighu because of their pride in being Brahmins. But I tell you, these Brahmins who are indulging in lust, anger, covetousness and pride, will become shameless beggars. They will be perpetually poor and will go even to the houses of the Shudras for the sake of money. Due to their greed for money they will fall into hell and be born as *rakshasas*! Daksha's handsome face will soon disappear and will be replaced by the face of a goat."

On hearing this exchange of curses, there was a hue and cry amongst those who had assembled there. Only Shiva was unperturbed. Very sweetly he turned to his follower, Nandi and said, "O dear one, why have you become so angry? Daksha cannot curse me for I myself am the sacrifice, the sacrificial rite, the adjuncts of the sacrifice and very Self of the sacrifice. Who is Daksha? Who are you? Who are all these people? In reality I am all. Knowing this, you should not grieve, nor should you curse anyone. Daksha has done this through his ignorance, for which he will be forced to pay a heavy price. But you are my devotee and should be free from anger and other negative emotions."

Hearing these wise words of his master, Nandi became calm and free from anger. After this unpleasant scene, Shiva returned to his abode accompanied by Sati and the *ganas.* Daksha and his followers also returned to their respective abodes. He was seething with anger against Shiva and waiting for an opportunity to put his curses into practice.

In order to insult Shiva, Daksha started a great *yajna*, or sacrifice to which he invited all the gods and sages and celestial beings. Needless to say, he deliberately avoided sending an invitation to Shiva. Brahma and Vishnu were invited and brought in state to the grand *yajna*, the like of which had never been seen by anyone before. The place where Daksha held his sacrifice was at a place called Kanakhala near modern Haridwar, which is at present known as Kankhal. Since Shiva was not invited, his daughter, Sati was also omitted, though she used to be Daksha's favourite. To house the august assembly of gods and sages and emperors, Viswakarma, the divine architect, created many beautiful mansions.

The sage Dadichi, a devotee of Shiva spoke forcibly to Daksha, "O Daksha! This sacrifice will be incomplete and imperfect unless Shiva is invited. Go immediately with the sages and bring the great Lord along with Sati, to this place. He is the source of all auspiciousness. Without him, everything will be inauspicious and imperfect."

Daksha replied haughtily, "Vishnu, who is the prime cause of this cosmos, who is the source of all virtues, has graced this place by his presence. Brahma, the grandfather of all the worlds has come, along with the *Vedas* and the *Upanishads.* Indra, the king of gods as well as the celestial sages have come with their retinues. What is the necessity of having Shiva here? He is of ignoble birth, the Lord of goblins, ghosts and spirits. I gave my beloved daughter to him only at the bidding of Brahma. He is totally unworthy of being invited to this noble assembly." Dadichi cursed Daksha and told him that his destruction was imminent and stalked out of the *yajna*, followed by some of the other devotees of Shiva.

In the meantime, on the mountain of Gandhamadana, in the Himalayas, Sati was engrossed in sport with her friends. Suddenly she saw her sister, Rohini, going in an aerial car, accompanied by her husband, Chandra, the moon deity. She requested her friend, Vijaya to go and find out their destination. They told her of the details of Daksha's sacrifice to which all beings had been invited and to which they were now proceeding. Now Sati saw that all the rest of her fifty-nine sisters and many other celestial beings were also proceeding in the same direction. "Why has my father not invited me and my husband?" she thought to herself. "It must be an omission on his part. Anyway let me go and ask Shiva about this."

So thinking, she ran to Shiva and told him the whole story. Shiva, who knew everything, looked pityingly at his beloved Sati and took her lovingly on his lap and asked her what was troubling her. She said excitedly, "My Lord, I hear that my father is conducting a great sacrifice to which everybody is going. Why are we not going? Please let us go. I earnestly request you to go with me."

"My dearest one, don't you realise that those who go uninvited to another person's house are sure to be shown disrespect. We have not been invited and so we should certainly not go for the *yajna*."

Sati's normally dark colour became even darker and her black eyes flashed brilliantly at hearing these words of Shiva and she said, "If you, O Lord, by whose presence all sacrifices become auspicious, have not been invited, then my father is surely guilty of a terrible crime. I must go to this sacrifice and ask him, as well as all those present there, why they have gone to a sacrifice to which you, the Lord of all the worlds, have not been invited. So please give me permission to go."

Shiva realised that if he denied her, she would pine and die. He also knew that if she went, death awaited her. Sadly, he gave her permission to go. He told her to mount his own vehicle, the bull, Nandi and sent sixty thousand of his attendants to wait upon her and guard her if need arose. Sati bedecked herself, and set out for her father's home with all the paraphernalia of royalty. The attendants followed her, holding the white umbrella of royalty above her head, waving gaily-coloured banners and yak fans and blaring conchs and trumpets. Sadly, Shiva watched her leave and knew that he would never see her in this form again.

Sati reached her father's mansion abounding with wondrous sights, and descended from the bull, Nandi and went inside alone. Her mother Virini and sisters greeted her with great delight. But Daksha pretended not to see her. Sati looked around and saw all the great souls of the world assembled there. She saw that seats had been allotted to all the deities except Shiva and she became furious. Her eyes burned like red-hot coals and flashed with blue fire. Her tresses that had been tied up became loose and dishevelled. Her third eye that was normally invisible in the middle of her forehead opened and started to throb and quiver. Her aspect was fully that of Kaali or the destroyer.

In a thunderous voice she asked Daksha, "How is it that my husband, whose presence alone can make all functions complete, has not been invited? Any rite performed without him will be impure. I am ashamed to see how senseless and mean my own father has become." Turning to Vishnu, Brahma and the other gods, she unleashed the full power of her anger on them, "Are you all so dense that you don't realise the greatness of Shiva! How could you come to a place which has been defiled by not having his holy feet step on it?"

All of them kept quiet but Daksha retorted, "Who asked you to come here when you were not invited! Knowing Shiva to be a coarse and uncultured type with indecent apparel and rude manners, I deliberately refrained from inviting him here. I rue the day that I gave you to that barbarian. However now that you have come, you may stay. Kindly calm yourself and take your share of the sacrifice."

Sati was filled with anger and sorrow. "I scorn to accept your offer O Daksha!" she flashed at him with fiery eyes. "My husband told me not to go. He warned me that I would be insulted but alas! I did not heed his words for love of you, my father. But now I see that you are despicable. I cannot bear to remain in this body which has come from you. No longer can I bear to be called Dakshayani (daughter of Daksha). Therefore I shall give up my body here and now, in front of all of you. I can never return to my beloved Lord with this body that has now become defiled. All those who reproach Shiva and all those who listen to these reproaches will go to hell, unless they remove themselves instantly from this hall."

Repentently she thought of how she had overridden her Lord's advice of not going to the sacrifice. Turning to her father once again she said, "Shiva has matted hair, carries a skull in his hands and resides in cremation grounds, but even the gods and sages keep the dust of his feet on their heads. You are wicked in every respect. I will have nothing further to do with this body born of you. This body born of your seed, I shall cast off as a corpse. It is worthy of contempt." So saying

Sati retreated into silence. Turning to the north, she sat in *yogic* trance, covering her entire body with her upper garment. She fixed her mind on her Lord, she balanced the different humours within her body, the *prana* and *apana* and lifted the *udana* from the navel and took it through the heart *chakra* and then into the throat *chakra* and finally fixed it in the *ajna chakra* in the middle of her forehead between her brows. Remembering her Lord alone, she left her body and entered the celestial regions.

There was a big hue and cry when Sati left her body. Everybody cried, "Fie on Daksha! Fie on this sacrifice!" and so on. Hearing the loud lamentations, the *ganas* of Shiva, who had been waiting at the door, now rushed in and started to shout and cry. With furious upraised weapons they charged at Daksha and others and started to kill them. Some killed themselves because they feared Shiva's wrath if they returned without Sati. On seeing this, the sage Brighu, invoked many fearful spirits, in order to stop the onslaught. Thousands of powerful spirits, called Rbhus rose up and a terrible fight ensued between the two parties, which ended in the *ganas* of Shiva being routed. They were forced to run for their lives back to Kailasa. At that time, a celestial voice declared that Daksha's sacrifice was doomed to end in a terrible way.

"Since Sati, the mother of the universe and Shiva, the father of the universe, were not propitiated by you, misfortune shall befall you." Hearing this ethereal voice, everyone was stunned and stood aghast. Most of the people left the place. Others advised Daksha to propitiate Shiva immediately before further harm came to him.

ॐ *Namashivaya*

ॐ

Viroopakshaya Namaha!

CHAPTER VIII

THE WRATH OF SHIVA

"O Destroyer of sin and sorrow!
Prostrations to your anger!
And then to your arrow, your bow and your hands."

Sri Rudri. Yajur Veda

The frightened *ganas* ran back to Shiva and begged him to save them. They told him the whole sad story of how Sati had given up her body, because it had been born of a man who had insulted her Lord. Hearing this dreadful news Shiva became filled with sorrow and out of his sorrow was born a terrible anger. He became Rudra, the destroyer. His eyes were frowning and furious. They emitted red and blue sparks of fire. Thus he got the name Virupaksha, the malignant-eyed. Jumping up from the rock on which he had been sitting, he wrenched out a lock of his matted hair and struck the mountain with it. A loud explosive sound, as of a huge rock being cleft in two was heard. From one half of Shiva's locks there appeared an enormous being with the visage of Rudra, having thousands of hands, blazing like firebrands. His name was Virabhadra. From the other half was born the goddess known as Bhadrakaali. She was fearsome to behold, with matted hair falling like a cape over her back, red and fiery eyes, emitting sparks like hot coals, red tongue lolling out, dripping blood, and many hands, brandishing upraised weapons.

In a thunderous voice Virabhadra spoke, "O Rudra of terrific appearance, with sun, moon and fire for your eyes, command me quickly. What should I do? One who is devoted to you will always be victorious. With your favour there is nothing that I cannot accomplish."

Shiva ordered Virabhadra and Bhadrakaali to march with the *ganas* to Daksha's sacrifice and destroy it completely. Virabhadra who had the same features, dress and embellishments as Rudra went ahead in a chariot drawn by lions. Bhadrakaali went with him, accompanied by the nine Durgas (*navadurgas*), Kaali, Kartyayani, Isani, Chamunda, Mundamardini, Bhadra, Mahakali, Twarita and Vaishnavi and many goblins. A host of angry furies, ghosts, ghouls, genies, monsters, dragons, demons, freaks, fiends and spirits accompanied them. Three crores of rabid canine species were born of the hair of Shiva. A virulent type of fever accompanied each of them.

As soon as this awesome contingent set out, many bad omens were noted in Daksha's *yaga*. The whole earth went into convulsions at the very spot of the *yaga*. Falling stars and comets were seen. The sun became spotted and had terrifying circles around it. Thousands of vultures hovered round the spot. Jackals and dogs howled while a fierce tornado tore the *yajnashala* to pieces. Seeing the approach of Virabhadra's army, the earth with its oceans and continents shuddered in terror. Daksha ran to Vishnu and begged for mercy. Vishnu replied that he would have to pay for the insults he had dealt to Shiva, the great Lord — Maheswara. Daksha begged Indra and the other gods to help him and they set out to fight the macabre army. But Virabhadra made short work of them and they had to flee in terror.

Then the horrific army began a methodical annihilation of the *yajnashala*, the place where the sacrifice was being held. Some of them cut the beams and superstructure, while others attacked the inner apartments. One set destroyed the sacrificial fireplace, some the halls and some the kitchens. Others broke the sacred vessels and the sacrificial hearths. Then they bound the officiating priests and chased the gods who were running away. Virabhadra pulled out Brighu's beard, because he had ridiculed Shiva by twirling his moustache. He plucked out Bhaga's eyeballs for he had rolled his eyes and encouraged Daksha to insult Shiva. He knocked out Pushan's teeth for he had laughed, displaying all his teeth when Rudra was insulted. Then he tried to behead Daksha but found it impossible. He thought for a while and then realised that since Daksha had acted in a beastly way, he had to be slaughtered like a sacrificial beast, after being tied to a stake. Bhadrakaali dragged Daksha by the hair to the altar and Virabhadra raised his axe and beheaded the patriarch. His lifeless corpse fell on the ground with a thud. Bhadrakaali drank the blood and Virabhadra made an offering of Daksha's head into the sacrificial fire. Bhadrakaali made a garland of the other heads that were rolling on the ground, while Virabhadra smeared his body with the blood. The two of them danced a macabre dance of victory in the eerie light of the dying embers, accompanied by the shouts and claps of the delighted *ganas.* Then, after setting fire to the whole campus they returned victoriously back to their master. Shiva now came to be known as Hara, the ravisher.

In the meantime, the defeated gods went to Brahma and requested him to help them restore Daksha's sacrifice since he had started it only after getting their promise that they would help him. Brahma as usual went along with them to the abode of Vishnu in order to invoke his aid, "O Lord of Lakshmi! O Lord of gods! We have come to invoke your aid in completing the *yajna* of Daksha."

Vishnu said, "O Brahma, since the gods have committed a sin in taking part in a *yaga* to which Shiva had not been invited, the only thing you can do now is to propitiate him by falling at his feet. Since I have also been guilty of attending the sacrifice, I will also accompany you. I attended the *yaga* only because Daksha is my devotee and I can never let my devotee down."

Thus all of them set out to the abode of Shiva in order to placate him. They saw him seated under the banyan tree with his left leg placed over his right thigh and knee. The garland of *rudraksha* beads was suspended from his left wrist and he was showing the *Tarakamudra* or the teaching pose with his right hand. This was the posture of Dakshinamurti that he had showed Brahma and Vishnu at the time of creation. Seated on a mat of *darbha* grass, he was imparting the knowledge of the eternal Brahman to the sages. The crescent moon peeped through his matted locks and his body was covered with ashes. He looked like the god of peace for all his anger was spent. Friend of the world that he was, he always engaged himself in the practice of austerities for the good of all. Vishnu and the other gods approached him and made obeisance to him.

They said, "Obeisance to the great Lord, who is calm and peaceful, who is the benefactor of the universe. Noble souls always show extreme tolerance and never take revenge against those whose minds have come under the sway of the Lord's *maya.* Therefore O Lord, it behoves you to forgive those who have been infatuated by *maya.* Kindly do what should be done to complete the *yajna* of Daksha, which has been defiled by your *ganas.* May the patriarch Daksha be revived and all those who have been wounded be made whole once again. O Rudra, may the entire remaining portion of the *yajna* be given over to you."

Hearing this Rudra was pleased and said, "I did all this to purify Daksha and not out of revenge. That patriarch whose head was burnt will have the head of a goat in its place, Bhaga whose eyes were gouged out will have to see with the eyes of Mitra, and Pushan who had his teeth knocked out will have to eat powdered rice or eat with the teeth of the master of the *yajna.* Brighu will have the beard of a goat to replace the one he lost. All those priests and others who lost their limbs will have them restored."

Then at the request of the gods, Rudra proceeded with them to Kankhala, the place of the sacrifice. He commanded Virabhadra to bring Daksha's body to him. He did so and Shiva told the gods to bring the head of the sacrificial goat and join it with Daksha's trunk. When Shiva cast his benign glance at the corpse, it came to life. Daksha who had acted like a goat now got the head of a goat. As soon as he saw Shiva standing before him, Daksha's mind, which had been filled with hatred, became purified and he started to extol him, even though his voice choked with emotion at the thought of his beloved daughter, who was no more.

Daksha said, "I thank you for giving me the punishment I deserved or else I would have been condemned to hell for having insulted such a noble personage like you. You are indeed Shankara, the benevolent one."

Daksha was now commanded by Rudra to complete the *yajna* with the help of the priests. All the gods extolled Shiva and Daksha completed the *yajna* with all formality. At the conclusion of the *yaga*, Iswara Himself, in the form of Sri Hari appeared and blessed the participants of the *yaga.*

Sri Hari spoke, "O learned ones! Know me to be the supreme cause of the world, the sole witness of everything, the self-effulgent Being, attributeless and undecaying. I assume different names like Brahma, Vishnu and Shiva for the purposes of creation, maintenance and destruction. This is done through My *yogamaya*, which has the three *gunas* of *sattva*, *rajas* and *tamas*. The ignorant man sees Brahma, Vishnu and Rudra as different even though they are all in Me, the all-comprehensive Brahman. Just as a man will not see the different parts of his body as different from himself, so also one who has taken refuge in Me will see all beings as parts of Me. He attains eternal peace who does not perceive any difference between the three, Brahma, Vishnu and Shiva, who are one in nature and who pervade all beings."

Thus blessing all those who were there, Sri Hari vanished from view and the gods returned to their respective abodes. Though he had forgiven Daksha, Shiva was filled with agony at the loss of his beloved, Sati. Picking up her lifeless corpse, he wandered over the whole universe, carrying the lifeless body in his arms. His *ganas* followed him silently, tears rolling down their cheeks, not knowing how to console their Lord. Their mournful cries rent the galaxies and created havoc in the world. Brahma realised that this had to stop or else the whole universe would be drowned in Shiva's sorrow. He appealed to Vishnu who wielded his discus, the *Sudarshana chakra* and let it fly with great precision towards Shiva. It cut the corpse of Sati into one hundred and eight pieces. Those places where the pieces fell are known as *shakti peethas* and are spots of great psychic power, capable of granting boons to all those who worship there.

When the body of Sati was destroyed there was nothing left but memories, to remind Shiva of his beloved. With his divine insight he knew that Sati could never be destroyed for she was Shivaa, a part of his own being and that she would resurrect herself in another place, at another time. In the meantime he could no longer bear to live in the place where he had enjoyed all types of pleasures with Sati. He isolated himself in the icy mountain caves of the Himalayas and became a recluse once more.

ॐ *Namashivaya!*

ॐ

Kapardine Namaha!

CHAPTER IX

PARVATI

"Rejoices He in having as His life mate, the Mountain Maid,
Whose gait is like the female elephant and the female swan."

Saint Sambandar

As mentioned earlier, Daksha had sixty daughters of whom Svadha was given in marriage to the forefathers. She had three daughters of whom Mena was the eldest, Dhanya, second and Kalavati, third. Once the three sisters went to the abode of Vishnu in order to have *darshan* of the Lord. A great concourse of sages and *yogi*s were there. It so happened that the four boy sages known as Sanaka, Sananda, Sanadana and Sanatkumara also arrived to pay obeisance to the Lord. Seeing them, the entire assembly of sages rose up in respect. Submerged in their own thoughts, the three sisters did not rise. Seeing this lack of respect, Sanaka and the others, though steeped in bliss always, became angry in order to fulfil the inscrutable purpose of the Lord. They cursed the sisters that they would be born as human beings on the earth. On hearing this, the sisters became very sad and fell at their feet and begged for forgiveness.

Sanaka then said, "The curse of a sage is always for the benefit of the world. So you should not worry. Mena will become the wife of Himavan who is actually a part of Lord Vishnu. The goddess Shakti will be born as Mena's daughter and will be known as Parvati. She will become the wife of Lord Shiva. The second, Dhanya will become a great *yogini* and will be the wife of the great saint-king of Videha known as Janaka. Lakshmi herself will be born as her daughter and will be called Sita. She will become the wife of Vishnu in his incarnation as Rama. The third sister, Kalavati shall be born in a Vaishya family of cowherds and will be married to Vrishabhana. Radha will be born as her daughter. This Radha who is now a resident of Goloka will be the beloved of Krishna." The sisters were very happy when they heard this and thanked the sages for their curse, which was actually a blessing, not only to them but also to the whole world.

Along the northern boundaries of Bharathavarsha stands the great mountain, known as Himalaya or the abode of snow. It has a twofold aspect. One is the *achala* or immobile aspect and the other is the aspect with form. In this human form he is the king of all mountains and is known as Himavan. The Himalaya is the storehouse of various gems and medicinal herbs. Many fierce animals live there. Even the gods love to sport amongst the lofty peaks. Sages from ancient times have found that these regions are saturated with spirituality. No wonder that the place came to be called the land of the gods. Himavan, the Lord of the Himalayas, desired to marry and he asked the gods to find a suitable mate for him. The gods approached the manes and requested them to give their daughter, Mena to him since great benefit would accrue to all beings from this alliance. Remembering the words of the sages, they agreed joyfully and the beautiful Mena was given in marriage to Himavan. Vishnu and the other gods attended the grand function.

Soon after that, Shiva married Sati and the divine couple took up their abode near Himavan and Mena. As soon as she saw Sati, Mena wished for a daughter just like her and used to offer her many delicacies. Sati knew of Mena's wish and at the time of casting off her body, she wished that she should be reborn as Mena's daughter.

Seeing Shiva take to the life of a recluse, the gods decided to persuade him to get married once again.

They eulogised Durga, or Shivaa, the feminine counterpart of Shiva and requested her to take birth as the daughter of Himavan and Mena, "O goddess! You are Gayatri, the mother of the *Vedas*, Savitri, the glory of the sun and Saraswati, the goddess of knowledge. To those who perform good actions, you are Lakshmi, the goddess of fortune, to sinners, you are the goddess of ignominy. Your smile brings peace for the universe and your frown — war. You are the divine mother of all creatures."

The goddess appeared before them seated in a divine, bejewelled chariot drawn by lions. Her lustre surpassed that of a crore of suns. Seeing this wondrous form, the gods bowed and begged her to take on a body once more, "O divine Mother! Formerly, you were born as the daughter of Daksha and married Shiva. Ever since you cast off your body, Shiva has been inconsolable. The purpose of your incarnation is still to be fulfilled. So please deign to take birth once again as the daughter of Himavan and Mena so that all may be happy."

The goddess promised to comply with their request and the gods asked Mena to do rigorous austerities in order to have the goddess as her daughter. Mena passed twenty-seven years observing vows and fasts in order to propitiate the goddess who eventually appeared before her and blessed her and promised to incarnate herself as her daughter.

As soon as she became pregnant, Mena shone with a divine radiance. Her husband, Himavan was bent on satisfying her every wish and loaded her with gifts of love. At the time of the divine birth, all the stars and planets were in auspicious positions. The gods rained flowers from above, as Himavan's wife gave birth to the divine child. The whole of Himavan's country rejoiced and the happy father gave many gifts to the poor. The child was called Kaali as well as Parvati. She shone in dark splendour like a blue lotus.

As a child she used to play with her friends on the banks of the Ganga with balls and dolls as any ordinary child. Though the parents had many heroic sons, yet their fond gaze always followed the antics of their beloved daughter. Once the sage Narada went to their abode. Seeing the sage, Himavan was very happy and asked him to look at his daughter's palm and foretell her future.

Narada did so and said, "O Mena! O Himavan! There is no doubt that this daughter of yours has a remarkable future. She has all auspicious signs. She will heighten the glory of her parents and delight her husband. But there is one abnormal sign on her palm. Her husband will be a naked *yogi* without any qualities. He will have neither mother nor father and will be quite indifferent to honour or dishonour. He will be free from lust and his manner and dress will appear inauspicious."

Hearing the words of the sage, the parents were most distressed but Parvati on the other hand was delighted for she knew the description to be true of Shiva, whom she had already wed in her mind.

Seeing the distress of the parents, Narada comforted them with these words, "O Lord of mountains! Don't be unhappy. Lord Shiva will be her bridegroom and he fits in with all that I have said. In him there is neither good nor bad, neither auspiciousness nor inauspiciousness. Let her propitiate him with austerities and no doubt he will agree to marry her. Love such as is found between the two of them will not be found anywhere else. With Parvati as his consort, Shiva will become Ardhanareeswara, or half-male and half-female, with Parvati forming part of his body. By propitiating Shiva by her penance, she will acquire the lustre of gold and will get the name, Gauri."

Himavan had another doubt, "O celestial sage, I have heard it said that Lord Shiva is totally immersed in *tapasya* and abhors all contact with anyone, especially women. I have heard that he made a promise to his wife Sati that he would never take another wife, so how will he agree to marry my daughter, Parvati?"

Narada smilingly replied, "Have no fears O Himavan! This daughter of yours was formerly the daughter of Daksha and was known as Sati. It is she, who has now reincarnated herself as Parvati. There is no doubt that she will become Shiva's wife. You have now placed her on your lap, but her permanent abode will be on Shiva's lap." Thus comforting the Lord of the mountains, Narada took his lute and departed on his perpetual errand of going from world to world, singing the praises of the Lord.

Even though Mena wanted a handsome husband for her daughter, she heeded her husband's advice and encouraged Parvati to do penance in order to get Lord Shiva as her husband.

Himavan said, "The word inauspicious cannot be used in connection with Shiva. He is the soul of all auspiciousness. So advise your daughter to do continuous *tapasya* with the aim of getting Shiva as her husband. Only good will accrue to her out of this."

Mena went to her daughter to advise her but on seeing her slender frame, the mother's heart was filled with pity and she was unable to tell her to perform *tapasya.* The goddess, Parvati, understood her mother's reluctance and said, "O mother, yesterday I had a dream in which a sage came and asked me to perform penance for Shiva."

Himavan also said that he had a dream in which an ascetic, whom he later came to recognise as Shiva, came to his city and stayed there. So the parents decided to wait till the dream came true. Sure enough, soon after, an ascetic, who was none other than Lord Shiva, came to Himavan's territory with a few of his *ganas* in order to do penance. Himavan went to welcome him and told him of his desire to serve him to the best of his ability.

Shiva was pleased and said, "I have come to this mountain to perform penance and the only service you can render me is to see that I am left undisturbed by everyone."

Himavan agreed and gave an order that no one should disturb the Lord. Then he took some fruits and flowers and accompanied by his daughter, he went to the Lord and said, "My Lord, my daughter is very eager to serve you. Please consent to accept her service along with her two maids."

Shiva took one look at Parvati, who was in the first flush of youth, beautiful beyond words, and hurriedly closed his eyes. Her complexion was like a blue lotus; her budding breasts ended in a slender waist that could be spanned by his two hands and her black, curly locks, shone with a divine lustre. Turning to Himavan, he said that in future, he should come alone, without his daughter, "A woman is a phase of illusion. A young woman is a hindrance to ascetics. I am an ascetic, a *yogi*, what use would I have for a young woman as beautiful as your daughter?" Himavan was dumb and did not know what to say. But Parvati spoke up with the courage of love.

"O Lord", she said, "have you considered the fact that all activity comes under Prakriti? Even this activity of *tapasya* can be done only because you are under the sway of Prakriti."

Shiva replied, "I am destroying Prakriti with my penance. In reality I am without the attributes of Prakriti."

Parvati replied, "Don't you know that I am Prakriti and you are Purusha. Without me, you are actionless, attributeless and qualityless. You are also incomprehensible."

Shiva laughed and said, "O Parvati! I see that you are a champion of the Sankhya system, but seem to know little of Vedanta. Know me to be the Supreme Brahman, unsullied by illusion, beyond the workings of Prakriti, comprehensible only through spiritual knowledge. You cannot affect me, even though you are Prakriti."

Parvati replied, "If, as you say, you are superior to Prakriti, then why should you do *tapasya* at all and why should you be afraid of my being near you?"

Shiva was delighted with her quick repartee and said with a smile, "Very well Parvati. See what you can do to me! You may render me whatever service you please."

Elated with her success, Parvati returned home with her father. After that she went daily with her maids and served the three-eyed God, her chosen deity with great devotion. She would wash his feet and drink the holy water and wipe his feet with a cloth, warmed by fire. She would worship him with the prescribed sixteen types of offerings. Sometimes she would sing exquisite songs and sometimes she would dance. After cleaning the precincts with her own hands with a wattle broom, she would return to her own abode. Many years elapsed like this with the Lord being immersed in *tapasya* and never noticing what she was doing. At last one day he came to know of her activities and thought to himself, "She is acting with perfect self-control and great devotion, but there are still some traces of ego left in her. These can be erased only after she herself performs penance."

Thinking thus, the Lord reverted to his state of *samadhi* and did not notice her any more. Parvati continued to serve him, day after day, unperturbed by his apparent indifference.

In the meantime Brahma and the other gods were getting a bit worried. They were being harassed by the demon Taraka and they knew that the only one who could destroy him was the offspring of Shiva and Parvati. But a consummation of their union seemed to be a remote prospect so they decided to employ Kama, the god of love, to aid them.

ॐ *Namashivaya*

ॐ

Kamaraye Namaha!

CHAPTER X

THE DEFEAT OF KAMA

"Dances He while the host of ghouls stand round Him and sing.
A river has He atop the matted coil of His locks.
The *Vedas* set to the notes of music does He sing."

Saint Sambandar

As has been mentioned before, thirteen of the daughters of the patriarch Daksha were married to the great sage, Kashyapa. Of these, the eldest Diti had an evil mind and was the mother of all the demons. Aditi, her sister who was of a noble disposition was the mother of the gods. Once Diti approached her husband and begged him to give her a son who would be capable of defeating the gods who were the sons of her sister, Aditi. Kashyapa was a man who knew that it was useless to try and reason with his wife Diti, who had a crooked mind. So he did not try to argue with her but advised her to perform certain austerities. She did this with alacrity and eventually got a son called Vajranga who had adamantine limbs, as his name implies. At the bidding of his mother, he captured Indra and the other gods and punished them. Aditi, who was the mother of the gods went and complained to Brahma who approached Vajranga and begged him to release the gods. Vajranga was a devotee of Shiva and pleased with Brahma's gentle approach, he released the gods. "I did this only to please my mother," he said, "in reality I have no desire to conquer the worlds. I would rather be instructed by you on the essence of life by which I can always remain happy and free from fear."

Brahma was very pleased with this son of Diti and he created a beautiful woman called, Varangi, whom he gave to Vajranga as his wife. They lived happily for some time and Varangi delighted him with her service and love. He asked her to choose whatever boon she wanted. She immediately asked for a son who would conquer the three worlds and cause misery to Vishnu. Vajranga was in a dilemma when he heard this strange request from his dutiful wife. He certainly did not want enmity with the gods, neither could he afford to displease his wife. He decided to do *tapasya* to Brahma and ask him for the boon of a good son and thus please his wife without harming the gods. At the end of the period of austerities Brahma appeared before him and granted the boon. His wife conceived and delivered in due time. The child had an enormous body and at the time of his birth, many evil portents were seen in the world. Vajranga realised that his son was a demon as wished by his wife and named him Taraka.

The demon performed severe penance for many years to Brahma and when Brahma appeared, Taraka requested from him, two boons. One was that none should equal him in strength in all the three worlds and the other was that only a son of Shiva could kill him. He knew Shiva to be a *yogi* and thought that the chances of Shiva getting a son, was a remote possibility. As usual, Brahma weakly agreed to both requests.

The demon then started his atrocities in all the three worlds and afflicted the gods and humans alike. Whatever he wanted, he took by force, be it from the gods or the sages or from humans. Since he had all the three worlds under his control, he declared himself to be Indra, king of gods. Dismissing the gods, he installed demons in their places. As usual, the gods with Indra as their leader approached Brahma and begged him to do something. Brahma was the cause of all their troubles due to his indiscriminate giving of boons to fiends like Taraka. Brahma said that it would not be proper for him to kill Taraka since he was his own devotee.

"But I have a remedy for you," he said. "The only person who is capable of killing him is the son of Shiva. This is the boon that I myself have given him. But as you know, at the moment Shiva is deep in *samadhi* and refuses to look at Parvati, the daughter of Himavan who is serving him with great devotion. It is up to you to see that he weds Parvati and gets a son. Only the offspring of his seed is capable of killing Tarakasura."

Hearing this, Indra immediately thought of Kama who appeared before him, in all his beauty, accompanied by his wife Rati and Vasanta, the spring season. Indra requested him to go to the Himalayas and use all his wiles in order to persuade Shiva to look on Parvati with favour. "Go and fill Shiva's heart with desire for Parvati. Force him to give up his *tapasya* and embrace the entrancing princess of the mountains," said Indra.

Kama was a very conceited person. He was proud of his prowess and thought himself to be superior to the gods since even they fell a victim to his fatal arrows. He told Indra proudly that he was capable of accomplishing certain things, which even the king of gods could not do!

He proceeded to Himavan's abode and stationed himself at a place close to where Lord Shiva was doing *tapasya.* Spring spread her exquisite carpet of flowers and covered the trees with fragrant flowers and fruits. The warm *malaya* breeze swept across the icy peaks, enfolding them with the fragrance of exotic blooms. The snow melted and turned into gurgling rivers and limpid pools in which lotuses blossomed. All the birds were busy making nests and their excited love-calls filled the air. The cooing of the cuckoos and the buzzing of the excited, inebriated bees, drunk with nectar, caused waves of delight to course through the minds of even the sages who were meditating there. The *apsaras* who had accompanied Kama danced in joy and abandon. The full moon rose in splendour scattering its brilliance, inviting lovers to dally beneath its gentle glow. When Shiva opened his eyes and observed this untimely intrusion of spring into his austere, wintry hermitage, he was a little puzzled but perfect *yogi* that he was, he closed his eyes and slipped into *samadhi* once more. Then Kama who was usually to be felt only in the minds of people, took on his exquisite form and stood on Shiva's left side with Rati beside him. The loving couple then began their dalliance, using all sorts of enticing gestures. With music provided by the celestials, they started to dance in front of the great *yogi* but they could not find any difference in his demeanour. Kama started to feel the beginnings of fear that this might be his first defeat. So far he had never come across anyone other than Shiva, who could resist his wiles. Just then Parvati came along with her maids, bringing various kinds of flowers for her morning worship of the Lord. As usual she approached him timidly, bowed to him and placed the flowers one by one at his feet. Then she stood shyly before him, hoping he would open his eyes and look at her. Shiva opened his eyes for a split second and Kama took the opportunity to shoot his arrow of flowers from his mango bow, straight at the trident-bearing Lord. Usually even if Shiva happened to open his eyes for a few moments, it was his practice to close them again and return calmly back to his meditation. Such was his control! But this time thanks to Kama's intervention, he was unable to tear his gaze away from Parvati's intoxicating form. He stared at her as if mesmerised and Parvati who had been longing and waiting for this day delved deep into his eyes.

Shiva thought to himself, "She is indeed a storehouse of perfection. There is no one to equal her in beauty in all the three worlds. If I feel so much pleasure by just looking at her, think of the pleasure to be derived from embracing her!"

He was on the point of stretching out his hands to touch her when he stopped and thought, "How is it that I have fallen a prey to the pangs of love? Who has caused my fall?" Thinking thus he turned his head and saw Kama standing proudly on his left with Rati beside him. He was holding his bow taut, ready to discharge a second arrow. As the arrow sped fearlessly from his bow, he felt the full blast of Shiva's anger sweep over him. Kama trembled with fear and dropped his bow and mentally invoked the help of Indra. The gods with Indra appeared immediately on the scene but before they could say anything to appease the wrath of Shiva, he opened his third eye and a great flame of fire sprang from the middle of his forehead and shot up to the sky like fiery meteor. It dropped down to the earth and covered the ground, engulfing the trembling Kama and reducing him to a heap of ashes in a trice. Rati, the consort of Kama fell to the ground in a swoon. Parvati was trembling with fright and was led away by her maids. The gods were frightened out of their wits and did not know how to comfort the sorrow stricken Rati. She was grovelling on the ground trying to gather the remnants of the ashes that the wind had not swept away. They begged Shiva to restore her husband to life.

"What have you done to my husband?" cried Rati. "You have

condemned all creatures to live a life devoid of love. Society will collapse if love is destroyed. The bull will forsake the cow, the horse the mare, the bees the flowers and man, his wife. Desire is not just the cause of suffering but it is also the basis of all joy. What is life without desire? It is mere existence alone with no flavour like a flower without perfume. The essence of joy can only be known by one who has experienced suffering. Life has its price which is suffering, but it also has its reward, which is joy and neither can exist without Kama."

Shiva's anger was always short-lived and he admitted the truth of Rati's words. "I destroyed Kama's body but not his spirit. He will live on as Ananga, the bodiless one, in the heart of every creature. He will also be born with form as Pradyumna, the son of Krishna during the time of the Krishnavatara and you, O Rati will once more become his wife." So saying Shiva returned to his austere practices. Parvati did not dare to go there any longer for she was frightened of the consequences of his wrath, which she had just seen.

ॐ Namashivaya

"Prostrations to the one who is in white autumn clouds and the sun. Prostrations to the one who is in storms and deluge. Prostrations to the protector of land and cattle."

Sri Rudri. Yajur Veda

"Prostrations to the one present in cowsheds and houses. Prostrations to the one in homesteads and palaces. Prostrations to the one in thorny bushes and mountain caves. Prostrations to the one in whirl-pools and dew-drops."

Sri Rudri. Yajur Veda

ॐ

Shankaraya Namaha!

CHAPTER XI

PARVATI'S PENANCE

"The pure One who abides eternally in the heart of the soul dear to Him,
And who pays obeisance to Him.
The Lord of the four cardinal points and of the noble Devi."

Saint Thirumoolar

Parvati returned home, highly agitated and disturbed in her mind. Of what use is physical beauty, she thought if it cannot affect my Lord. He is a true *yogi* and I see that the only thing that can affect him is the power of austerity and not that of physical charm. Her parents and brothers tried to comfort her but all in vain. At last the celestial sage Narada came to her and told her.

"O Parvati! Do not be despondent. You will surely win Lord Shiva as your husband. He did not accept you because you still have some traces of ego. In the pride of your youth and beauty, you thought that you could subjugate the three-eyed one by your charm alone. But remember he is the *Mahayogi*. He can only be beguiled by the force of intense penance. I will impart to you the knowledge of the sacred *mantra*, which is especially dear to Shiva. It is the five-syllabled *mantra*, '*Aum Namashivaya*.' Those who repeat this with faith and assiduity will undoubtedly be able to please him."

Parvati then went to her parents to get their consent to go to the forest in order to do penance. Her father gave his consent but her mother, Mena was most reluctant to let her daughter go. "Why don't you perform penance in the house?" she asked. "All conveniences are here. It is not correct for a young woman like you to go alone and perform *tapasya* in the forest. That is meant only for ascetics." Parvati got the name Uma, from these words of her mother. Uma means, "Don't go." Parvati was most crestfallen when she heard this and could not eat or drink for thinking of Shiva. Seeing her daughter in this miserable condition, Mena reluctantly gave her consent.

Discarding all her fineries and jewels, Parvati donned the bark of a tree, tied at the waist with a belt of grass. Accompanied by her two maids she went to the high ridge where Shiva had been doing *tapasya* and where Kama had been reduced to ashes. Seeing that place, where Shiva used to sit, she was filled with sorrow and wept aloud, crying out his name again and again. At last controlling herself with difficulty, she made preparations for her worship. She built an altar in which she kept a *linga* of Shiva. There she sat and repeated the five-syllabled *mantra*, constantly keeping Shiva in mind. In summer she sat in the midst of five fires. In the monsoon she sat in the rain and in winter she sat amidst the snow. All the while she chanted the sacred *mantra* without respite. She bore with fortitude, the heat of summer, the icy cold gusts of the autumn wind and the harsh snowfall of the Himalayan winter. For the first year, she subsisted only on fruits and the next year, only on leaves, thus getting the name Aparna, or the one who existed on leaves. In the third year she gave up even leaves and fasted on ether alone. Clad in bark, with matted hair, restraining all her natural instincts, she surpassed even the sages in her austerity.

Even Nature was thrilled by the power of her penance. Abundant flowers bloomed so that she was never short of flowers for worship. Animals that are natural born enemies of one another became friendly and shed their animosity and roamed about freely in the vicinity of the sacred grove. Year after year passed and still Shiva did not appear. Himavan and his wife Mena came to Parvati and tried their best to dissuade their daughter from continuing this fruitless *tapasya*, but she would not listen to them. She was sure that Shiva would succumb to the power of her penance. Her parents returned and Parvati redoubled her *tapasya* until all the worlds became unbearably heated due to the force of her penance. The gods could not understand the reason for this terrible change of climatic conditions. They approached Brahma and begged him to do something. Brahma went with them to the abode of Vishnu and requested him to help them.

Vishnu smiled and said, "The change in seasons has been caused by the intensity of Parvati's *tapasya.* Therefore I shall go with you to the place where Lord Shiva is sitting in *samadhi* and request him to go to Parvati and grant her desire."

The gods were frightened of approaching Shiva, fearing his anger but Vishnu assured them of his protection and they accompanied him in great trepidation. Shiva was in deep *samadhi.* The gods requested his attendant, Nandi to apprise him of their arrival. Shiva was pleased to grant them audience and they placed their request to him.

Vishnu spoke, "O Lord! All the gods are being harassed by the *asura,* Taraka. Considering you to be a confirmed celibate, he has got a boon from Brahma that he cannot be killed by anyone except a child born of your loins. Parvati, the daughter of the mountains is at present doing severe penance in the hope of getting you as her husband. You alone can save the world from the harassment of the demon, Taraka by accepting Parvati's hand in marriage. Due to her intense *tapasya,* all the three worlds are being heated. Save us all, O Lord! Desist from your penance, for the good of the world."

Shiva said with a sly dig at the gods, "If Parvati were to be accepted by me, Kama would come alive once again and this will prove injurious to all of you as well as the sages for his presence is bound to spoil your meditation! As you know, lust always leads to hell. From lust comes anger, from anger, delusion and delusion destroys penance. Why do you still insist on my marrying Parvati?" So saying, Shiva remained silent.

Vishnu spoke once again, "Don't you know that Parvati is none other than Sati who has been born again as the daughter of the mountains? She is performing intense penance and all the three worlds have been engulfed in the heat of her *tapasya.* We are all anxious to see the consummation of your marriage with Parvati. Only the son of this union is capable of killing the demon, Taraka. So kindly accede to our request and bring joy to us, as well as to Parvati."

Shiva now spoke, "O Vishnu! Marriage is a great fetter for a *yogi.* There are many bondages in the world but association with women is the strongest of them all. Salvation is inaccessible for one who is drawn to worldly enjoyments. My reason tells me not to accede to your request but my heart says otherwise. I have always been a slave of my devotees. I can refuse them nothing. I am willing to give up my own interests in order to serve yours. Although I am not interested in marriage, I shall marry Parvati in order to please you and beget a son."

So saying he lapsed into silence and the gods returned to their respective abodes. Shiva then called the seven celestial sages and asked them to go and test Parvati's resolve. They proceeded to the peak called Gaurishikar, in order to test her. Seeing her emaciated form shining with the brilliance of intense austerity, they bowed to her and advised her to give up her penance, for Shiva would never yield to her request.

"The sage, Narada, who advised you to do *tapasya* is a beguiler. He always tries to turn people off from the worldly path and take to a life of austerity. He stopped the thousand sons of Daksha and forced them to follow the path of asceticism, much to the chagrin of their father who had sent them forth in order to propagate children. He even advised the *asura* boy, Prahlada to be devoted to Vishnu with the result that he was forced to undergo great pain and censure from his father. Now he is doing his best to divert you also. Shiva is indifferent to women and not capable of giving love. In fact he is the enemy of Kama. His looks are most inauspicious and he has neither name nor pedigree. Stop this fruitless task, therefore and return to your parents and marry someone more suited to your gentle nature."

Parvati laughed and replied, "O sages, no doubt what you have said is true according to your understanding but it cannot affect my determination in the least. As you know I'm the daughter of the mountains and I cannot be moved so easily. Hence my name is also Achala. Shiva is the supreme *Yogi*. He is not interested in embellishments. He is the Supreme Brahman and if he does not marry me, I shall remain a virgin. I swear to this. The sun may rise in the west, fire may become cool and mount Meru may be seen to move and lotuses to bloom on rock, but my words shall never be false. I shall continue to worship Shiva until he comes to me. Or else I shall give up my body here and now."

The sages were delighted at Parvati's determination. They returned and reported the whole dialogue to Shiva. Now Shiva himself set out for Parvati's hermitage in order to test her. Actually he was quite convinced of her tenacity but he wanted to have a glimpse of her in her ascetic's garb. He appeared before her in the guise of a very old sage, carrying an umbrella and staff. Parvati rose up to honour the old man and worshipped him with all due reverence. He enquired about her birth and parentage and why she was undergoing such severe penance. Parvati replied, "I am Parvati, the daughter of Himavan and Mena. I am doing penance only with a view to getting Lord Shiva as my husband. But it looks as if my *tapasya* has been in vain for he has not come. I have decided to consign this body of mine into the fire and hope to be born again. In every birth I shall continue to do penance until Lord Shiva accepts me."

Shiva was secretly delighted by her reply but in order to test her resolve further, he urged her to desist from this extreme act. Undaunted, Parvati merely smiled and after saluting him, she jumped into the fire that she had kept ready. But the fire became as cool as sandal paste. The old man smilingly stopped her from making another fire and urged her to repeat the whole story to him. Parvati could not speak due to the tears, which were choking her voice. Her friend, Vijaya narrated the sad tale.

The ascetic then demanded to hear it once again from Parvati's lips. Parvati repeated it and begged the old man to advise her.

The old man said, "O gentle lady, why do you wish to get Shiva as your husband? His body is always smeared with ashes from the cremation ground. His hair is matted and he has snakes twining round his neck. Sometimes he is clad in the hide of a tiger and an elephant and sometimes naked. He moves about either in isolation or is followed by ghosts and goblins. He is a most unsuitable husband for one as beautiful as you are. He had a wife called Sati, the daughter of Daksha who was discarded by her father due to her association with Shiva. At last the poor girl had to give up her life. You are a jewel among women. Why do you want to wed this strange man? Discarding the pleasures of a palace, why do you wish to roam in the forest with such a man? He doesn't have a single quality that could appeal to a woman. He killed your friend Kama and insulted you by going off somewhere else. I advise you to turn your mind away from him and find a more suitable bridegroom."

Parvati was furious when she heard this and retorted, "Why have you come here with these insufferable insinuations against my Lord? You will never be able to turn me away from my course of action. A person devoid of discrimination like you can never know the true form of my Lord, which is that of the Supreme Brahman, devoid of attributes. You say he is full of inauspicious qualities, yet I know that just by thinking of him everything will become auspicious. I have done great wrong in giving hospitality to one, who obviously hates my Lord. Whatever Shiva may be, I love him. He alone is my Lord and I want none other."

Averting her face, she asked her friend to chase away this base prophet who would no doubt continue to pour calumny on her Lord. She turned away in disgust and was on the point of running away from him when Shiva assumed his own form and caught her hand.

"Where are you going, leaving me alone? I will not be discarded by you so easily O Parvati!", he said, teasingly. "I am delighted by your persistence and I've come here only to grant you all the boons you wish for. You have paid the price for my love by your penance. From today onwards, I am your slave. Command me and I shall oblige. You are my eternal companion and have always been so. Forgive me for testing you unbearably like this. But you have passed all the tests and I am your ardent slave. Come with me to my abode in the Himalayas." So saying, he pulled the hand, which was already clasped in his.

Parvati was delighted and said, "My Lord, formerly I was Daksha's daughter but at that time our marriage rites were not properly performed. The planets had not been propitiated. This time I beg of you to approach my father and ask for my hand and let our marriage be performed with all due rites and paraphernalia."

"O sweet Parvati," said Shiva, "this entire world is a world of illusion. I stand above all prophecies and planets. But if it is your wish to perform our marriage rites by propitiating all the planets in the customary way, it shall be done, for there is nothing that I can refuse you. I shall go to your father and beg for your hand as you wish." Parvati returned joyfully to her home and Shiva to his. The gods and *ganas* rejoiced.

Parvati was welcomed back with all due honours after her successful completion of her mission. Soon after Shiva assumed the guise of a mendicant dancer and came to Himavan's court. He sang and danced so beautifully that everybody was thrilled. He blew the horn and played the drum. Mena was entranced. So was Parvati but suddenly he allowed her to see his wonderful form, as Shiva. On seeing this, she fainted and had to be revived. It seemed to her that he was asking her, "Do you want a boon or a groom."

She whispered, "I have already chosen the boon. I want you as my groom." No one else was privileged to hear this intimate dialogue.

Mena was delighted with the dancer and offered him money as well as many precious gems. But he refused all. At last she asked him what he wanted and he replied that he wanted her daughter. She was furious when she heard this and ordered her attendants to drive him out of the town but none could touch him. He was burning to the touch. Suddenly he vanished before their astounded eyes.

The gods were bewildered by Shiva's *lilas* and begged him once again to accede to their wishes and request Himavan for his daughter's hand. This time Shiva went in the guise of a noble Brahmin. He had a garland of crystal beads in his hands and a *saligrama* round his neck and was repeating the name of Vishnu. Only Parvati saw through his disguise and mentally bowed to him and had a good laugh at the joke. The Brahmin strongly advised Himavan not to give his daughter to a mendicant like Shiva. He then left as he had come. Hearing this Mena begged her husband not to give her daughter to such a strange person.

In the meantime Shiva called the seven celestial sages and commanded them to go to Himavan and urge him to give his daughter to Shiva for that was her desire and he had already granted her this boon. They joyfully went to Himavan and said, "Shiva is the father of the universe and Parvati, the mother. Hence it behoves you to give your daughter to him alone. By this gift your life will be fulfilled."

Himavan replied, "I too am anxious to do this but ever since a certain Brahmin came here and denounced Shiva, my wife has been against it and refuses to give her daughter to him."

Then Arundhati, the wife of Vasishta approached Mena and advised her to give Parvati to Shiva for that was the wish of the gods and only by the consummation of this union could the terrible demon Taraka be killed.

The sages told Himavan, "Parvati has been born to be the wife of Shiva. She is the great cosmic intellect, mother of the universe. You will gain honour and glory only if you give her in marriage to Shiva." After hearing all this Mena were pacified and agreed to the betrothal. The sages returned and gave the news to the great God and all preparations were started for the consummation of this joyful event.

ॐ *Namashivaya*

"Prostrations to the one in stones and dust. Prostrations to the one in dry grass and green. Prostrations to the one in deserts and fields."

Sri Rudri. Yajur Veda

"He whose existence and reality shine always and uniformly in all the states of the body, like infancy, etc. And of our mind, like waking, etc. And who reveals the highest knowledge of the Atman by merely showing the jnanamudra, *To that Dakshinamurti, the Supreme Being, embodied in the benign* Guru, *I offer my profound salutation."*

Dakshinamurti Stotram by Adi Shankaracharya

ॐ

Srikandaya Namaha!

CHAPTER XII

THE COSMIC WEDDING

"Shore, sea and mountains and my words as well, He permeates,
The unique one, He of the land of Rudra,
Husband of the handsome hill-maid,
King of the heavenly ones."

Saint Vanthodar

Himavan was determined that the wedding should be the grandest event ever held in the universe. All the gods and the sages as well as the mountains and rivers were invited. The entire city was decorated in a fantastic manner. The roads were swept and watered. Plantain trees, silken festoons and mango leaves lined the streets. Auspicious articles were kept at every street corner and jasmine buds and lotus flowers were strewn on the ground. Himavan invited the divine architect to design a special dais with images of all the gods, to seat the bridal couple. He did this so realistically that everyone thought the gods had already come. Different mansions were made for each of the gods with the best one reserved for the bridegroom, Shiva.

On the appointed day, all the gods assembled at Kailasa in order to accompany the bridegroom. They begged Shiva to dress as befitting a bridegroom. He smiled and complied with their request. The crescent moon took the place of a crown, his third eye became a beautiful jewel on his forehead, the serpents near his ears turned into earrings and the serpents round his neck, into necklaces. The ashes became sweet smelling sandal paste and the elephant hide became a silken garment. Thus they set out with great joy. The *ganas* from all the worlds came and joined the procession, dancing and prancing in front. The gods too were in a very jovial mood and sang and danced. The tumultuous sound of *damarus*, *dundhubhis* and conchs filled the quarters. Vishnu seated on the Garuda accompanied by Lakshmi went in front, Indra on the Airavata followed, as did Brahma on the swan with Saraswati beside him. The Mothers of the universe, the celestial virgins and the wives of the gods all went ahead with great joy to attend Shiva's wedding. Lord Shiva seated on his white bull of crystal purity and beauty, the symbol of *dharma*, shone with a divine lustre in the midst of this auspicious crowd.

When they reached the outskirts of the city of the mountains, Himavan came out with a large retinue to meet them. He was enchanted to see the divine form of Shiva, totally unlike what he had been expecting. The Lord looked wonderful in his form as Sundaramurti, the handsome one. He was smilingly seated on the bull, bedecked with ornaments and clad in delicate silk garments. His smile lit up the whole place with its charm. Himavan was delighted and welcomed the divine entourage with all devotion.

Mena was full of curiosity to see the person for whose sake her daughter had done so much of penance. She went to the balcony and looked down at the bridegroom party that was just coming in. Shiva knew of her pride and in his usual fashion, he decided to play a joke on her. His *lilas* were always directed at reducing the pride of his devotees. He requested Vishnu and the others to go ahead and promised to follow. Mena was delighted to see the splendid procession. First came the Gandharvas, the celestial musicians who were noted for their sartorial elegance. Heavenly nymphs waving banners of brilliant hues accompanied them. Mena thought that one of the Gandharvas must be Shiva and exclaimed in delight but she was told that none of them was Shiva but were only his attendants. Then came the *Yakshas*, the custodians of all treasures and again Mena thought that their chief must be Shiva. Again she was told that these were only his attendants.

"How handsome he must be if his attendants are so fantastic," she thought. Then came Agni, the god of Fire, shining like molten gold and Yama, god of Death of matchless splendour and each time Mena was disappointed to hear that this was not Shiva. When Vishnu came, Mena almost fainted, so handsome was he. She was sure that this must indeed be Shiva, the bridegroom most suited to her lovely daughter but again she was disappointed.

Next came Shiva accompanied by the *ganas*. "Here comes the bridegroom whom your daughter wanted," someone whispered in her ear. Mena stared aghast at the motley crew that now appeared. The *bhutas*, *pretas* and *pishachas* came first, the spirits, ghosts and goblins. Some were in the form of violent gusts of wind, making hissing sounds, some had crooked faces and deformed bodies, some were lame and others blind, some hobbled on one leg and others carried staffs and tridents in their hands. Some had no faces while others had deformed and distorted visages. Some had no eyes and some had many eyes. Mena was terrified when she saw these mutilated and horrible creatures that were supposed to be escorting the bridegroom. She was sure there must have been some mistake and begged someone to point out Shiva to her.

"There is Shiva! There is the bridegroom!" came the shout.

On seeing him Mena trembled and nearly fainted. "Is this the person my dear daughter did *tapasya* for?" she wondered.

He had five faces and three eyes. His hair was matted and had the crescent moon on it. His body was smeared with ashes. He had ten hands with a skull in one, the trident and sword and many other gory weapons in the others. His upper cloth was a tiger's hide and lower one, an elephant's. He was utterly dishevelled and untidy, with odd eyes and wild look as if he was inebriated. In fact, the whole bridegroom party appeared to be intoxicated and was rolling about in a drunken orgy. Now and again they shouted, "Glory to Shiva! Glory to Shiva!" and flung skulls and bones and reptiles into the air instead of flowers.

"This is the bridegroom," whispered a voice behind her. Mena gave one look and fainted. As soon as she recovered she wept and wailed and swore that she would certainly not give her daughter to such a creature.

"What shall I do? Where shall I go?" she wailed. "My family is shamed. My life doomed. Where are those sages who call themselves celestial? I shall pluck out their beards with my own hands. They are the ones who cheated us." Turning to her daughter, she cried out, "Is this the fruit of your penance! Surely your intellect has been deranged. You have cast away sandal paste and smeared yourself with mud. Setting aside cooked rice you are bent on eating the husk! O what have I done to deserve such a fate?" So saying the poor lady wept uncontrollably and bewailed her lot.

Narada and the sages came and tried to reason with her but she would not listen. At last her husband came and told her that this was all a sport of Shiva and he was only trying to test her. Parvati was desperate to see the condition of her mother and said softly to her, "O mother! Why has this delusion overtaken you? Please give me to Lord Shiva. I have wooed him, mentally, verbally and physically. I will never marry another."

Brahma came and spoke to Mena, "Lord Shiva has many forms and names. He delights in indulging in different sports. He is the master of illusion. Knowing this you shouldn't hesitate to give your daughter to him."

Still Mena refused and so Vishnu himself came and said to her, "You are the beloved daughter of the forefathers, yet I'm afraid you have no conception of the greatness of Shiva. He has done this only to test you. He is possessed of all attributes, yet devoid of them. He is both form and formlessness. He is hideous as well as handsome. No one can describe his real form. It is only because of your daughter's great penance that he has agreed to become your son-in-law. Consider yourself to be most fortunate that he has blessed you in this fashion. Hence O wife of Himavan! Stop your tears and accept him as your son-in-law. All will be well."

Hearing these pleasing words of Lord Vishnu, Mena relented a little and said, "I will give my daughter to him only if he assumes a pleasing aspect. Otherwise whatever any of you might say, I will not consent to this marriage. This is my firm resolve." So saying she averted her face and kept a strict silence.

Vishnu went and gave the news to Shiva while Parvati prayed to Shiva with all her heart and begged him to come in a form that would delight her mother. Shiva laughingly agreed and as the palace doors were flung open, he strode in and to Mena's surprise, his form was wondrous to behold.

Every part of his body was exquisite. He was fair and handsome and shone with a divine radiance. His lustrous dark eyes turned towards Mena and penetrated to the depths of her soul. She thought he was the personification of masculine beauty. His dark, silky hair flowed to his broad shoulders. His long, lithe limbs were clad in silk. His neck was adorned with many ornaments. He was wearing a garland of fragrant jasmine flowers. In fact he was Sundaramurti himself. He was the most handsome man she had ever seen. There was a glimmer of a smile on Shiva's face when he saw Mena's discomfiture.

The eight *siddhis* danced in front of him, showering the path with rose petals. The rivers, Ganga and Yamuna walked on either side, fanning him with yak tail fans. Vishnu, Brahma and the other gods followed him.

Mena went forward with Himavan to welcome him and said, "O great Lord, my daughter is indeed blessed. It is only by virtue of her penance that you have now come to our threshold." Thus saying Mena worshipped him with sandal paste and whole rice grains mixed with turmeric. Other married women came with ghee lamps and camphor lights and waved these auspicious flames before him. The Gandharvas sang exquisite songs while the *apsaras* danced in gay abandon.

After this, the wives of the sages ceremoniously escorted Parvati to the temple of their family deity. Her beauty entranced all those present. Her complexion was dark as collyrium; her thick, black hair was plaited and covered with flowers and jewels. Necklaces covered her breasts and bangles and bracelets, her hands. Her lips, which had been coloured with red lac, opened slightly to reveal her lovely teeth that had the sheen of pearls. Sandal paste, musk and saffron had been smeared over her body. Her pink feet tinkled with the sound of anklets as she walked. She carried an exquisite gem-set mirror in one hand and a play lotus in the other. On seeing the fascinating form of the mother of the universe, all the gods bowed. For one split second her eyes met that of Shiva and she gave a small secret smile as an unspoken message of love between them. Then she went out of the city and returned after having worshipped the family goddess. After her return she was given another auspicious bath and bedecked with the ornaments that Shiva had brought for her.

In the bridegroom's house similar rites were being performed for Shiva. After having been bathed and anointed, he rode on the bull to the wedding hall. The white umbrella of royalty was held above him and dancers and singers went ahead. He was followed by the gods and ceremoniously seated on the highly decorated stage reserved for the bridal couple. Then at the auspicious time, Parvati was escorted to the stage and seated on the specially prepared altar. The ceremony began at a time when all the planets were in a favourable position.

Himavan took his daughter's hand in his and repeated these words, "O Lord Shiva, I'm giving this young girl, my daughter to you as your wife. Be pleased to accept her." With these words he placed Parvati's hand in Shiva's hand and repeated the *mantra*, "*Tasmai Rudraya Mahate.*"

Shiva grasped the lotus-like hand of Parvati in his own and repeated the appropriate *mantras*. At the request of the officiating priest, Shiva applied the auspicious red powder on Parvati's forehead. Grasping her trembling hand in his, he took her thrice round the sacred fire and thus plighted their troth. Thus with the chanting of the pertinent *Vedic mantras*, Lord Shiva as Sundaramurti, wed the divine goddess, Parvati. Then they were seated on the same decorated seat while all the guests came and worshipped the cosmic couple who were really two halves of a whole.

After the ceremony was over there were great celebrations and rejoicing in the land. The final rite was when the bridegroom was lead to the beautifully decorated bridal chamber. Parvati was brought by the sixteen celestial mothers and handed over to Shiva. Thinking this to be the appropriate time Rati, the wife of Kama came near them and begged Shiva to resuscitate her husband. Shiva smilingly agreed and much to Rati's delight, Kama appeared before them in his previous form.

As was the custom, after staying four days in the bride's house, the marriage party set out for the bridegroom's abode. Mena wept and begged Shiva to take great care of her beloved daughter. The celestial mothers advised Parvati about the duties of a chaste wife. Parvati bowed to her parents and shed a few tears at the thought of the coming parting. Accompanied by the gods and his *ganas* Shiva returned to Kailasa with Parvati. After ceremoniously leaving the couple there, the gods returned to their own abodes.

ॐ *Namashivaya*

ॐ

Shivaapriyaya Namaha!

CHAPTER XIII

THE COSMIC COUPLE

"I saw Him, I saw Him,
The heart's desire of the beautiful Uma.
He enslaved me, He enslaved me,
I adorned my head with the feet of the Lord."

Saint Sundarar

Parvati was transported from the comfortable palace of her parents to the chilly caves of the Himalayas. Henceforth these caves would serve as her boudoirs. She had no regrets. She had chosen her path and in her eyes everything was perfect. The faultless, brilliant peak of Kailasa was the place chosen by Shiva for his new abode. Close by was the scintillating lake called Manasarovar or the lake of the mind, where celestial damsels sported with their lovers. In these icy waters Parvati would bathe. She was enthralled by the austere beauty of her new residence. The lack of comforts did not put her off in the least. She was prepared for it. With her beauty and wit she conquered the heart of this great *yogi*, this strange ascetic whom she had married. She sported with him on the mountain peaks and slopes of the Himalayas and bathed in the cold waters of the lake Manasarovar amidst the lotuses and the royal swans. She was as gentle and graceful, as he was wild and forceful. Her *lasya* and his *thandava* together enraptured the entire universe. Her beauty inspired him to create all forms of art and song and dance. He became master of all *kalas* or art forms. When they danced together, her movements were soft and slow, *lasya* and his were forceful and masculine, *thandava*.

They danced and made love to the vibrations of the universe. Wrapped in his arms she travelled on the bull, Nandi across the skies.

When it rained he took her above the clouds and when it was hot, he took her into caves. Thus aeons passed while the cosmic couple sported with each other on the peak of Kailasa and in various other celestial spheres.

As time elapsed two demons were born in the world. They were brothers and their names were Shumba and Nishumba. As a result of their *tapasya* Brahma granted them the boon which they requested. They insisted that they should meet with death only at the hands of a woman. She should be a virgin, born of a part of Shiva and she should be so beautiful that they would fall in love with her. Brahma agreed and the brothers became so bold that they began to harass the gods and humans. They were quite sure that no such woman would be forthcoming. The gods went to Brahma and he in turn went to Shiva and begged him to create a woman who would be a part of him and extremely beautiful. Shiva agreed and bided his time to get Parvati into a rage so that she would shed her colour and become the virgin goddess, Kaali, who alone would have the qualifications to kill the demons.

Many years passed while the great *yogi* appeared to be totally tamed by Parvati's exquisite beauty and charm. Her wit and wisdom stimulated him to share with her all the knowledge that he had gained by his intense *tapasya*. Because of her, the whole world gained this knowledge which has come down to us through the *Puranas* and the *shastras* and *tantras*. There was no end to her thirst for knowledge and no end to his wisdom. She was the perfect student and he the perfect teacher, Dakshinamurti. She asked many questions pertaining to society, nature, life, marriage, the duties of all types of people — about music, dance, palmistry, astrology, occult sciences, about birds, beasts and life after death as well as different methods of freeing oneself from mortal coils. There was no subject she did not touch upon and no question that he could not answer. The wealth of their divine discourses has come down to us in various ways through the minds of the sages who have meditated upon him.

Parvati seduced him in subtle ways and he realised that one who ran away from life without dealing with and overcoming the dualities would never attain liberation. On the other hand, one who was totally immersed in worldly pleasures without a thought of the supreme Truth underlying everything, was a fool, who would never attain peace of mind, much less liberation. Harmony or balance between these opposites was what lead to Truth —harmony between Purusha and Prakriti, matter and Spirit — harmony between the cosmic couple, Shiva and Parvati.

Once they had a dance contest. She had to imitate all his poses. She could perform as perfectly as he could, but in order to tease her, he took the difficult posture known as *urdhva-thandava.* In this pose he lifted up his right leg straight above his head. She had to declare herself to be the loser for she could not do this. Then she took a perfectly beautiful feminine pose in front of him. She was so dark that she looked as if she was a statue made out of ebony. Shiva laughed and teased her about her colour. This was a good opportunity to enrage her, he thought.

"You are indeed Kaali," he said, "goddess of the night, goddess of death, goddess who removes all the evils of the age of Kali."

Hurt by his words, she decided to change her colour. Bidding good-bye to him she went to the same forest where she had done *tapasya* in order to get him as her husband. Shiva allowed her to go since he knew that this parting was part of the plan to kill the two demons. In the forest she started rigorous *tapasya.* Once a huge tiger approached her with a view to satisfying its hunger but as it came near her, its body became numb and it could not move. It froze in the crouching position in which it had rested before pouncing on her. The tiger stayed in that position, never taking its eyes off her form. After a long time she opened her eyes and saw it and felt pity for it. She conferred her grace on it. The tiger repented and realised the nature of the divinity on which it had unknowingly meditated for so long, by fixing its gaze on her. The numbness disappeared and from then on, it became her faithful slave and stayed close to her, guarding her from attacks by other wild animals.

Seeing her engaged in rigorous penance, Brahma arrived on the scene and eulogised her. He begged her to take another form and rid the world of the two demons, Shumba and Nishumba who were terrorising everybody.

"O Mother! I have granted a boon to these arrogant demons and only you are capable of vanquishing them. I beg you to destroy them.

You alone can do this."

Hearing this, the goddess, Parvati cast off her dark skin and became fair in colour and got the name, Gauri or the radiant one. The dark outer skin took the form of Kaali, the virgin goddess, with the lustre of a black rain cloud. She held the conch and discus of Vishnu as well as the trident of Shiva in her various arms for she had the strength of both. She had three eyes and was moon-crested like Shiva. She had three natures, gentle, terrible and a mixture of the two. She was a virgin, beautiful and invincible. Parvati told her to go with Brahma in order to slay the demons. Kaali took a huge tawny lion that appeared on the scene, as her vehicle. Bowing to her mother, Parvati, she rode on the lion and went to the Vindhya mountains that was to be her abode. The two demons, Shumba and Nishumba came to the place where she had taken up residence and were smitten by her beauty. They tried to molest her but she killed them easily as prophesied by Brahma.

Part of Parvati's dark colour is said to have gone into the river Yamuna, or Kalindi as it was later called, when it made its way from the Himalayas to the forest of Vrindavana where Krishna was to sport with the *gopis* in an age, which was yet to come, the age of Dwapara.

Gauri returned to Kailasa and delighted her lord once more in her new role as the goddess with the colour of molten gold.

Seeing that she was still a bit put out with him for having allowed her to go to the forest, without protest, he said, "O my beloved one! Don't you know that we can never be parted from each other? It was only for fulfilling the request of the gods that I ridiculed your colour. This universe of forms is known only through words. You are the form of the words and I am the meaning of the words. How can meaning be separate from word? You are the form of knowledge and I am the object of all knowledge. Who can separate us?" Thus by his gentle teasing and rational talk he won her over until she became her usual happy self. Once again they indulged in all their favourite sports.

Sometimes they would play dice in their mountain retreat. At one of their games, Shiva wagered his trident and Parvati, her jewels. He lost and then staked his serpent and lost again. Parvati seemed to be on a winning spree and soon Shiva lost everything. He pretended to be quite disgruntled and walked off by himself into the forest. Vishnu met him there and promised to help him win if he could entice Parvati to another game.

Parvati agreed since she was sure her luck would hold but she began to lose steadily and Shiva was able to win back all the things he had lost previously. Parvati was highly suspicious of this sudden change of luck and warned him of the consequences of cheating. In the middle of their heated argument, Vishnu appeared and pacified Parvati by telling her the truth. He admitted that he had entered the dice, thus ensuring that Shiva won. He also reminded them that life was like a game of dice. Sometimes we win, sometimes we lose, but both life and dice games are unpredictable. We should not set much store by either gain or loss but should carry on with the game. This bit of salutary advice pacified both Shiva and Parvati. Shiva pronounced a blessing on all those who chose to play dice on that particular day. This day came to be known as Diwali, the festival of lights.

Once, the cosmic pair had an argument about the reality of the world. Shiva, the perfect renouncer held the *advaitic* view that the world was only an illusion and nothing existed except Brahman. Parvati advocated the Sankhya view and insisted that Prakriti was equally real. She, herself was Prakriti. So nothing could exist without her. To prove her point she chose to leave the icy peaks of the Himalayas and withdraw into her own subtle nature. Naturally her disappearance caused havoc in the world. Everything came to a standstill. The earth became barren, the seasons did not change and there was no food for anyone. Animals, humans, demons and gods, all had to starve. They cried to Prakriti to save them from this cruel fate. Even the sages declared that without food nothing was possible, least of all the realisation of Brahman. The divine mother was unable to resist the pleas of her children and chose to manifest herself in the holy place called Kasi or Varanasi. There she set up a kitchen to feed her hungry children and all of them came in different forms and were given in plenty by her. Even Shiva, the perfect *yogi* came to her in the form of a *bikshu* or beggar and begged for alms. She fed him with her own hands. Thus she came to be known as *Annapurna*, or the giver of food.

Many are the *lilas* enacted by the cosmic couple in order to enthrall the world. Once it is said that Shiva got fed up of all this conjugal bliss and went into the forest and resumed his *tapasya*. Parvati followed him but he took no notice of her. She prayed to Vishnu to help her. He came and advised her to take on the form of a tribal woman and entice her husband. She did so and Shiva got distracted and followed her back to their own cave. Inspired by her beauty he composed many tunes on his favourite instrument, the Rudra Veena.

Another time when Shiva was teaching her, he found her attention wandering to the fish in the lake. "If contemplation on the fish is of more interest to you, than my words, you might as well become a fisherwoman," he said.

His words came to pass and Parvati was born as the daughter of a fisher chief. She was wild and beautiful and could fish and handle boats better than any other man. Her father was delighted with her and wondered how best he could find a husband to match his beautiful daughter for she was quite unlike the rest of the fisher folk. From the peak of Kailasa, Shiva watched the progress of his beloved with interest and wondered how he could get her back. One of his *ganas* called Manibhadra decided to help his master. He took on the form of a shark and began to harass the fisher folk, in the ocean, off the coast where Parvati lived. He upturned boats and ate all the unwary fishermen who ventured into the water. The fishermen were dejected for they could not go fishing for fear of this terrifying creature. At last the fisher chief declared that his daughter would be given as the bride of anyone who could kill the shark. Shiva took the opportunity to disguise himself as a fisherman. He came to the village and volunteered to kill the shark. He did so with ease and married Parvati and took her back to their Himalayan retreat.

It was Shiva and Parvati who taught the world the secrets of the *Kundalini Shakti*, the coiled up serpent of spiritual power that lies at the base of the spine. Parvati herself was the energy of the *Kundalini*, the primary spiritual energy in all humans, which seeks for union with Shiva, the pure Spirit. It lies coiled at the base of the spine at the bottom of the passage called the *Sushumna*. Shiva, the pure Spirit is stationed at the top of this passage at the energy vortex or *chakra* called the *Sahasrara* on the crown of the head. Parvati is *shakti*, the manifestation of all energy and Shiva, the manifestation of pure Spirit. She is matter or Prakriti, and he, Consciousness. He is known as Bhava, or eternal Being and she, Bhavani or eternal transformation. They are the opposite and complementary poles of existence. When they join with each other in cosmic union, the individual soul or *jivatma* ceases to exist and melts into the *Paramatma* or cosmic soul. Parvati uncoiled herself and rose up through the *Sushumna nadi* like a snake that unwinds itself and darts towards its prey. Piercing the six *chakras* or the whirls of spiritual energy situated in the spinal column, known as *Mooladhara*, *Swadishtana*, *Manipura*, *Anahata*, *Vishuddhi*, and *Ajna*, she rose to join her Lord, the pure cosmic consciousness, in the seventh *chakra* known as the *Sahasrara* or the thousand petalled lotus on the crown of the head. These seven *chakras* are the psychic centres for fear, desire, hunger, anger, communication and introspection and one who has pierced all these, rises beyond these emotions and becomes the Pure Consciousness, which is Shiva. As Parvati touched each of these *chakras*, they bloomed like lotus flowers with petals of different hues. When she reached the last *chakra* she no longer existed as a separate being. In that state of perfect union, there was bliss alone. There was no duality. Only unity — *Shivoham, Shivoham.* Thus aeons passed while the cosmic couple was submerged in this blissful union of the Purusha with Prakriti which would be totally unproductive as far as progeny went. In that state there was neither creation nor destruction. Everything was bliss alone. When there is neither lust nor desire, how can offspring be begotten? The gods were troubled. They were anxious that their union should produce a son who would kill the *asura*, Taraka. It looked as if Shiva and Parvati had completely forgotten the purpose of their marriage. The gods approached Vishnu and begged him to intercede on their behalf and remind Lord Shiva of his promise.

ॐ *Namashivaya*

ॐ

Laladakshaya Namaha!

CHAPTER XIV

KARTHIKEYA

"I bow to Subramanya, the son of Shiva, the general of the gods,
Who has six faces, and is adorned with sandal paste,
And who has the peacock as a vehicle."

Subramanya Pancharatnam

Creation and destruction are the opposite poles of existence. They are complementary to each other and both are necessary for living a complete life. Duality is the very nature of existence. It is essential for a total understanding and appreciation of life. Without having experienced darkness we will never be able to appreciate light. Thus we see that the *Puranas* are filled with stories of the wars between the gods and the demons, the *devas* and the *asuras*. The *devas* are creatures of light and the *asuras*, of darkness. Their mutually antagonistic roles ensure their eternal enmity. At times the gods are victorious and at times the demons. This seesaw provides the dynamism by which this dualistic cosmos sustains itself. The prayers and sacrifices of human beings sustain the power of the gods and on the whole they manage to maintain the cosmic balance between good and evil. Sometimes however when the world is passing through a particularly negative period, when the evil propensities of human beings tower above the good, then a demon of extraordinary power and wickedness will be born. When this happens, the gods are forced to take recourse to Vishnu and Shiva to help them. However we notice that even the gods never had direct approach to these cosmic Beings. They could only approach them through the mediation of the Creator, Brahma. The *asura*, Taraka was born at such a period in cosmic history when negativity was at its peak. He was a demon of extraordinary might whom the gods could not defeat by themselves so they went to Brahma who approached Vishnu and that is how the union of Shiva and Parvati came to pass. Now, once again they approached Brahma who placed their request before Vishnu and all of them went to Kailasa to ask Shiva to fulfil his promise to beget a son who alone could kill Taraka.

The *ganas*, who were stationed outside the cave where Shiva and Parvati were consorting, had orders not to let anyone enter, so they forcibly stopped the gods. Standing outside the entrance, the gods started to eulogise Shiva. Shiva and Parvati had been in cosmic bliss for many aeons and neither of them was aware of the passage of time. At last Parvati roused herself from this cosmic embrace and the thought darted into her mind that it would be wonderful to have a child by Shiva. Shiva guessed Parvati's desire and was prepared to fulfil it. At this point of time the gods came to their doorstep. When Shiva heard their distressed cries, he controlled himself and went outside. As soon as he heard their request, he discharged the seed that he had been withholding for so many aeons. The fiery seed fell on the earth. The earth could not bear the heat and begged Agni, the God of fire to help her. Agni took on the form of a dove and swallowed the fiery seed.

In the meantime Parvati was left, totally bereft. She came out angrily and cursed the gods, "O you selfish ones! You are only interested in getting your own ends and never think of the unhappiness of others. Thanks to you, I have become barren. I curse all of you that all your wives will also be barren!"

Agni found the heat of the potent seed to be unbearable. He discharged it on to the mountain, Himalaya in the midst of the snow and ice, in the hope that it would cool down. But it continued to scorch the mountain. Himavan, the king of the mountain was unable to bear the fierce heat of the seed and hurled it into the river Ganga. The river transported the seed to its banks and deposited it on a clump of grass. This grass became the womb for the seed of Shiva and nurtured the foetus. On the sixth day in the bright half of the lunar month called, *Margashirsha*, the son of Shiva was born. The gods played celestial music and rained flowers on the divine child who was as bright as a flame.

At this time when the divine child was gurgling and kicking his legs in the clump of grass, the great sage Visvamitra came upon him and was amazed to see his brilliance. The sage understood that the child wanted him to perform the purificatory rites. These rites are essential and have to be performed soon after birth. The sage grasped the message, which was transmitted mentally, and he forthwith did all that had to be done. The child blessed him and said that in future he would be known as a Brahmarishi. On being asked about his parentage, the child replied, "Know me to be Guha (the mysterious one) and let this be kept a secret." He also came to be known as Sarabhu (born among reeds).

Soon after, Agni came to the spot and recognised the boy to be his son, since he had carried the seed within himself. He presented him with a spear or vel, which became Guha's weapon from then on. Thus he was known as Velayudha (the one with the spear-weapon). He was also known as Pavakatmaja (son of fire).

Meanwhile six ladies known as the Krittikas, who are really the constellation known as the Pleiades descended to the earth and saw the boy and were enchanted by him. All of them wanted to nurse him and started an argument among themselves as to who should suckle him first. Knowing their desire, the child assumed six faces and drank milk from all their breasts. Hence he came to be known as Shanmukha (six-faced). The Krittikas took him to their own abode and fed and fondled him to their heart's content. Since they were his virtual mothers, they called him, Kartikeya. He became their dearest treasure and they never let him out of their sight even for a minute.

In the meantime, Parvati went to her Lord and begged him to find out what had happened to his seed, which had fallen on the ground. She knew that it could never be destroyed. Shiva called the gods and told them to find out what had happened to it and who was concealing it. Agni confessed that he had swallowed it, since the earth could not support its heat. But he himself had been unable to bear the heat and had deposited it on the mountain, which in turn had thrown it into the Ganga. Even Ganga could not cool the fiery seed and she had deposited it on the banks amidst a clump of *Saras* reeds. The wind god now took up the tale and told Parvati that the maidens known as the Krittikas had taken the child to their abode and at the moment, he was in their custody. They were nurturing him as lovingly as if he was their own son. Hearing this, Shiva sent his *ganas* to the abode of the

Krittikas. These emissaries of Shiva surrounded the residence of the Krittikas, who became terrified at the sight of these extraordinary creatures and begged Kartikeya to save them. He told them not to be afraid since he could easily conquer them. Before he could confront them, Nandiswara, the commander-in-chief of the *ganas* stood before him and recounted the whole story of his birth and urged him to return to Kailasa where Shiva and Parvati and the whole concourse of gods were awaiting him. Kartikeya agreed and took leave of his foster-mothers, the Krittikas and went with Nandiswara to Kailasa. A huge entourage was there, ready to welcome him and escort him into the assembly. Eulogising him, they took the boy also known as Kumara, to the presence of his divine parents. As he strode into the assembly everyone was astounded to see his amazing personality. He was the colour of molten gold and had the brilliance of the sun, with a halo round his head. Both Shiva and Parvati were filled with joy when they saw their son and embraced him with great love. Parvati kept the boy on her lap and gave suck to him and fondled him. Then Kumara sat on Shiva's lap and played with the snakes round his neck.

After a while the gods urged Shiva to crown the boy. So Shiva seated him on a jewel-studded throne. The sages worshipped him with *Vedic* chants. Jewelled pots filled with water from all the holy rivers of the land were brought. These pots of water were consecrated by *mantras* and poured over the boy's head to the accompaniment of *Vedic* chants. Brahma performed his *upanayanam* ceremony and gave him the holy thread, a water pot, the invincible arrow called the Brahmastra and the famous the Gayatri *mantra*. He also gave him all knowledge of the *Vedas*.

Vishnu presented him with a crown, and many bracelets. He also gave Kartikeya his own Vanamala. Shiva gave him a trident, the bow called the Pinaka, an axe, and the missile called Pasupata. Indra, the king of the gods gave Kartikeya, his own weapon, the thunderbolt and a royal elephant. Varuna, king of the waters gave him the white umbrella of royalty and a necklace of gems. The sun gave him a chariot that was as swift as the mind and a coat of invincible armour. The moon gave a vessel filled with nectar. Kubera gave him a mace and Kama, the weapon of love. His mother, Parvati blessed him with all power and prosperity. Lakshmi, the goddess of wealth gave him divine wealth and Savitri, the goddess of *siddhis*, or supernormal powers gave him the knowledge of these powers. The powerful rooster was given to Kartikeya as his insignia and became the emblem on his flag and the peacock, his vehicle.

Thus blessed by all the gods, Kartikeya was ready to face the demon. Shiva told the gods to take him as their general and kill the demon, Taraka. Thus he is also known as Devasenapathi (general of the gods). Seated in a celestial, aerial car, Kartikeya led the gods to the region of the *asuras*. The demons led by Taraka came out, fully armed with all types of weapons. Virabhadra, leader of the *ganas* rushed at the *asura* and fought a terrific battle with Taraka. At last Virabhadra was defeated and the *asuras* exulted. Then Indra came forward and fought with Taraka and was defeated. The apparently invincible Taraka defeated all the gods one by one. When Vishnu set out to fight with him, Brahma came and advised him not to fight for only the son of Shiva could kill him. That was the boon that Brahma had given Taraka. The gods eulogised Kartikeya and begged him to save them from the scourge of this terrible demon. Thereupon ensued a terrific duel between Kartikeya and Taraka. Both of them had spears as their weapon and charged at each other like maddened bulls. As they grappled with each other, the wind held its breath, the sun became dim and the earth quaked. At last when the specified time for his death had come, Kartikeya brandished his spear and struck Taraka hard on the chest. The *asura* fell down with a tremendous roar and died before the gaze of all the astounded spectators. The rest of the *asuras* fled in fear. Shiva and Parvati came to congratulate their beloved son and the whole world rejoiced.

Bana was another demon who had fled from the battle. He now started harassing the mountain Krauncha who came to Kartikeya for help. Kartikeya killed Bana and delivered the mountain. In order to commemorate the killing of all these *asuras* Kartikeya installed three *lingas* of Shiva. He then delivered Kumuda, the son of the serpents from harassment from the *asura*, Pralamba. After this, the jubilant gods escorted Kartikeya back to Kailasa, the abode of his father, Shiva. He was received with great delight by his parents and stayed with them for a while on the mountain.

The esoteric meaning of Kartikeya's personality is worth investigating.

He was born to destroy the demonic forces of the world; therefore he had to come from the seed of Shiva, who personifies the destructive aspect of the trinity. The seed was strengthened by contact with fire and then cooled in the purity of the Ganga. The baby was nurtured by the heavenly constellation called the Krittikas. His six faces represent the six seasons and thus he was master of time. He sucked from the breasts of these heavenly damsels and was thus sustained by the power of the heavenly bodies. His weapon is the spear with which he routs all demonic forces. His vehicle is the peacock, which is noted for its vanity. Kartikeya is the eternal youth, most handsome to behold but his vanity is totally under control for he rides on it. His insignia is the cock, which is noted for its virility and arrogance. The man of strength and beauty who has mastered himself has no pride in either of these personality traits and is ever immersed in the bliss of the Supreme. He is wedded to a tribal girl for he sees all humans as the same. Such a person is rewarded by the king of gods who gives him, his own daughter as consort. Heaven itself rewards one who is above the lure of physical beauty and strength and who concentrates only on the Supreme Truth, which is the source, from which all of us have come.

ॐ *Namashivaya*

"The moving and non-moving universe is but the manifestation of His subtle and unmanifest form. He by whose grace all these manifestations disappear with the realisation, Nothing exists except the Supreme Brahman: To that Dakshnamurti, the Supreme Being embodied in the benign Guru, *I offer my profound salutations."*

Dakshinamurti Stotram by Adi Shankaracharya

ॐ

Sharvaya Namaha!

CHAPTER XV

GANESHA

"I bow to the single-tusked, Lord Ganesha,
Who has a huge body, shining like gold,
And a large belly and beautiful eyes."

Gananayakashtakam

One day while Parvati was taking a bath, Shiva entered the premises without permission. Parvati felt rather shy and rebuked Shiva in a soft manner for having entered without permission. Soon after, her two friends, Jaya and Vijaya came to her and urged her to keep an attendant for herself, who would be totally subservient to her and to no one else. In view of the previous incident she decided that this was just what she should do. Moreover she longed to have a child of her own since Kartikeya was always busy with wars. The next time she went for a bath, she smeared herself with tumeric and saffron powder and then scraped it all off her body and shaped the ball into the form of a little boy and breathed life into it. The child was big and handsome, filled with strength and valour. She named him Vinayaka, the leader and gave him clothes and ornaments and said, "You are my son and from now on you will be my bodyguard also."

The boy was very happy to hear this and asked his mother to command him. She told him that his first job would be to guard her door, while she took her bath or wanted to be alone in her apartments. She also presented him with a staff to ward off intruders. The next day when she went for her bath, she stationed the boy outside and told him that no one should be allowed to enter. Soon after, it so happened that Lord Shiva came on the scene and tried to enter. The boy blocked him with his staff. Shiva could not believe that a small boy could be so audacious and asked him sternly, "Who are you and who gave you permission to stop me from entering my wife's apartments?"

The boy replied, "Sir, my mother is taking her bath and she has kept me here and asked me to keep off all intruders."

Shiva replied, "Don't you know me? I'm Shiva, and Parvati is my wife. Now let me go." The boy politely refused and barred the way once again. At first, Shiva was quite amused by this and tried to move the staff and enter. At this point the boy hit him with the stick. This was too much. Shiva controlled his temper and went back to his apartments and told his *ganas* to go and forcibly remove the boy. The boy confronted the *ganas* fearlessly and told them that he would not let any one inside, even if he were Brahma, the Creator himself. The disgruntled *ganas* returned to Shiva and informed him of the proceedings. They were forced to retreat since they did not feel like killing such a charming boy. Shiva told them to return and try all their arts of persuasion but Vinayaka could not be subdued with words. Hearing the altercation going on outside the bathroom, Parvati sent her maids to enquire into the matter. They reported that Vinayaka was bravely confronting the whole regiment of *ganas*. She was delighted when she heard this and told them to encourage Vinayaka.

He was also happy to hear these words of encouragement and told the *ganas* fearlessly, "Look! You are the *ganas* of Shiva and I am the *gana* of Parvati so we are both equal. My mother has told me that no one should enter this apartment either forcibly or humbly. So you may all go back."

They returned to Shiva and asked him for further orders. Shiva was not too happy at having to admit defeat at the hands of his wife's single *gana* so he accompanied his guards back to the spot and there ensued a terrific war between Vinayaka on one side and Shiva and his *ganas* on the other. Seeing that his *ganas* were all being defeated, Shiva hurled his trident and neatly severed the boy's head from his shoulders.

When Parvati came to know of this, she was furious and created many *shakti*s and ordered them to go and fight with the *ganas*. The gods now entered the fray and came to help the *ganas*. The war that ensued was terrible and at last the gods begged Parvati to forgive them and cease the fight.

She replied, "My son has been killed and I shall never forgive, unless he is revived." The gods gave this message to Shiva. He told them to go in a northerly direction and chop off the head of the first creature they saw and affix it to the body of Vinayaka. It so happened that the first creature they met was an elephant. They promptly cut off its head and affixed it to the headless body. They chanted *mantras* for the resuscitation of the body and sprinkled holy water on it and immediately the body rose up. He had the body of the original boy, Vinayaka and the head of an elephant. Parvati was happy to see her son come back to life even though he had the head of an elephant. It is said that once long ago she had gone to an art gallery of the gods. When she came to the glorious figure of ॐ, she was entranced and stood spellbound in front of the *mantra*. It was at that moment that the figure of Vinayaka came to her mind and she being the mother Goddess, naturally the figure came to be created. Thus Vinayaka's figure is a dynamic, anthropomorphic representation of the mantra of ॐ, the symbol of Brahman. She was delighted to see how closely her conception tallied with his form.

She kissed Vinayaka and blessed him and told the gods that he would in future be the remover of all obstacles in worldly life and in spiritual undertakings and hence he should be worshipped first, before the commencement of any other worship. Shiva and the others agreed and thus it is that to this day Vinayaka has to be worshipped before the commencement of any ritual. Parvati also insisted that he should become the leader of the *ganas* and thus he came to be known as Ganesha or Ganapati. Since he was born on the fourth day of the dark half of the month of *Bhadra*, Shiva declared that from then onwards that day would be celebrated by all as Ganesha's birthday and the fourth day of each lunar fortnight would also be known as a special day for him. Shiva, Parvati and all the other gods showered many other boons upon Ganesha.

Once the child Ganesha was playing with a cat. He pulled its tail and rolled it in the mud. The irate cat gave a pained howl and dashed off. He ran back to his mother and climbed on her lap but found to his dismay that she was quite muddy and had tears in her eyes. Anxiously he asked her for the cause of her distress and she taught him an important lesson about the unity of all life. "You alone are the cause of my distress," she said,

"How can that be? I never did anything to harm you."

"Didn't you pull my tail and roll me in the mud?" she asked. Then Ganesha realised this great truth that any harm done to any creature was tantamount to harming his mother, who was also the cosmic mother.

Before going further into the story of Ganesha it would be good for us to find out the meaning of his form and origin. Parvati is *Shakti*, or the power of Lord Shiva, the Supreme. Ganesha's origin is from the dirt and other material things scraped off from her body. Thus he represents the consciousness that evolves from matter and expands to its highest state of spiritual freedom. In the form of Ganesha we find the symbol of the emergence of life from earth and the unfoldment of consciousness from matter. He represents the initiating spiritual power that underlies everything; hence he has to be worshipped first. If we look closely at his figure with the curling trunk you can see the figure ॐ. He is also Ganapathy or Ganesha, Lord of the *ganas*, which are the subtle, obstructive forces of this universe. Since he is their overlord, he is also Vigneswara, the Lord who clears all impediments or obstructive forces that act as an obstacle in the way of our spiritual progress. In the human being he is situated in the *mooladara chakra* situated at the bottom of the spine, potent with spiritual powers.

Ganesha's vehicle is a rat. This is really surprising. Imagine the mighty figure of the elephant seated calmly on a tiny rat. What is the meaning of this? A rat is born of the earth and has its existence in burrows and holes in the earth. Consciousness, according to Indian belief is ingrained even in the grains of sand. It merges into an intelligent state after passing through the rudimentary forms. The rat is a fitting symbol for this. It has a primitive intelligence encased in ignorance and is thus restless, avaricious and worried. On the other hand, the elephant is the symbol of strength and wisdom. It is said to have remarkable memory and power of discrimination. The elephant's trunk is a symbol of discriminating wisdom that can separate grain from chaff. Its trunk can pick up a tiny pin lying on the ground as well as lift the heaviest logs in the forest. The elephant's head therefore suggests the strength, expansion and reverence of the mighty powers lying hidden in nature. The figure of Ganesha on the rat thus suggests that the human being has both characteristics within him. The elephant is normally calm and composed. It is a majestic creature with immense potential power. The rat on the other hand is a restless animal, constantly running here and there in its frenetic quest for food. The human being has the power to be calm and majestic with ever expanding consciousness stretching to the infinite but he continues to be a rat and rush about in the "rat race" of life, fighting and squabbling over trivialities. These two animals symbolise the two stages of consciousness, the primitive state and the expanded state. The human body is in between these two and connects them.

The noose in Ganesha's hand is for controlling the senses that run hither and thither like unbridled horses. In another hand he holds the hook which is generally used by *mahouts* to control elephants on the rampage. Our passions can be compared to mad elephants and the hook alone can subdue them and bring them to order. The snake round Ganesha's belly suggests the arousal of the *kundalini* energy in the human, the psychic energy that rouses itself when certain techniques of *yoga* are used. The two tusks represent the pairs of opposites in life and the broken tusk shows that the man of perfection is not under the sway of these opposites. He holds this tusk in his right hand like a pen, denoting the creative capacity of the man of wisdom. The *modaka* or round sweet which he holds in another hand indicates, the bliss and real sweetness of life which the enlightened person alone can savour.

One day the sage, Narada came to visit the cosmic couple and see the divine children. He brought a pomegranate fruit and offered it to the children. But since this was a very special fruit, the fruit of cosmic wisdom, it could not be cut. Only one of them could have it. So Shiva told the children that the one who took a round of the universe and returned first, would get the fruit. Kartikeya immediately set off on his peacock mount, quite sure of getting the fruit. Ganesha's mount was the lowly rat that could never outdistance the peacock but he was not in the least put out. He calmly circumambulated his parents and held out his hands for the fruit.

"In what way have you qualified for this fruit?" asked the amused parents.

"Both of you together constitute the entire universe. Why should I go round the material universe?" he enquired.

Shiva and Parvati applauded him for his wisdom and presented the fruit to him. When Kartikeya returned he was shocked to find his brother eating the fruit. He angrily questioned his parents about this and was told the reason for their apparent partiality. Kartikeya was quite angry at this trick which his brother had played on him and declared that he would leave Kailasa and go and meditate somewhere in order to get supreme wisdom. He asked Shiva's permission to go and in Tamil literature it is said that Shiva gave the answer, "*Palam nee*" which means,' "You yourself are the fruit". This is the great *Upanishadic* statement, "*Tat twam asi*" or "That thou art." Legend has it that Kartikeya left Kailasa and went to the hill known as Palani in the South where he practised penance in order to discover this truth.

There is another story that explains Subramanya's departure. When their two sons had reached marriageable age, Shiva and Parvati wanted to get them married. Now the question arose as to who should get married first. Shiva declared that the one who went round the world first would have first choice. Kartikeya immediately set off on his peacock whereas, the intelligent Ganesha, took his purificatory bath and solemnly circumambulated his parents thrice and demanded that he should have first preference. When questioned about the propriety of his conduct he declared that Shiva and Parvati contained within themselves the whole universe of movable and immovable things and hence going round them was tantamount to going round the universe.

Prajapati Viswarupa had two daughters called Siddhi and Buddhi and he requested Lord Shiva to accept them as wives for his son, Ganesha. Thus Ganesha's marriage was celebrated even before his brother returned. Kartikeya was quite angry with his parents and he departed to the mountain known as Palani despite his parents' earnest request not to go.

The esoteric meaning of Ganesha's two wives is as follows. Ganesha represents the liberated human, the *sthitha prajna* of the Bhagavad Gita and such a person is wedded to Buddhi or the discriminative intellect and acquires Siddhi or super-conscious powers. The evolved person will be blessed by having both these as consorts. Both the wives of Ganesha had offspring. Buddhi's child was called Kshema or well-being and prosperity and Siddhi's child, Labha or gain — the attainment of a higher state of consciousness. One who has realised the Supreme Self, lacks for nothing, not even material prosperity.

Kartikeya in the meantime lived on the hill called Palani, in the Southern range of mountains. There he came to be known as Muruga or the divine youth. While living amongst the tribals, he fell in love with a beautiful tribal girl, called Valli and married her. Later, Indra, the king of the gods gave his own daughter, Devayani to the great hero who had won the war for the gods.

Once when Shiva gave a discourse on *yoga*, every creature in the world rushed to Kailasa. As a result of this mass exodus, the whole world started to tilt towards the Himalayas. All wisdom and knowledge had gone to the North. There was nothing to keep the balance of the world. Shiva told Agastya, the wisest of his disciples to proceed south, carrying with him all the sacred and secular lore that he had taught him. Agastya agreed but begged Shiva to give him something that would remind him of the Himalayas. Shiva gave him two huge mountains to take to the South. The demon, Ettumba was designated to carry them. He made a huge bow and tied the hills on either side and carried them across his shoulders. When he reached Palani, he kept the mountains down and went to the river. When he returned he could not pick them up again. He looked around and found a beautiful young boy sitting on one of the hills. The demon became very angry and told the boy to get off the hill so that he could carry it to its destination. The boy refused and Ettumba was furious. Just then Agastya came on the scene and recognised the boy to be none other than Kartikeya. He bowed low before him and Kartikeya said, "I shall keep these mountains here for they remind me of my home in the North." Agastya agreed and thus Kartikeya resides on the hills and Agastya on the plains. The balance of the cosmos was restored.

It is said that Parvati was so unhappy at the separation from her eldest son that she begged Shiva to go South. He agreed and they came to the famous *jyotirlinga* at Sri Shaila, called Mallikarjuna. From this place it was easy for them to go and visit their son, Kartikeya.

Descriptions of the marriage of the sons of Shiva vary from North to South. In North India, Kartikeya is supposed to be the elder son and in the South, Ganesha. In the North, Kartikeya is supposed to be a celibate because he saw his mother in every woman. In the South, Ganesha is the *Nitya Brahmachari* or the eternal celibate because he never found a woman anywhere to compare with his mother. In the South, Kartikeya or Muruga is worshipped everywhere. He is seen as the personification of masculine beauty and virility and is always flanked by his two wives, one from Heaven and one from the earth. This again has a lesson no doubt. In the North the worship of Kartikeya hardly exists any more. Ganesha however has a special place both in North, and South and his wives Siddhi and Buddhi are considered an essential part of him. The two sons of Parvati, the cosmic mother, denote the two aspects of the evolved human being — strength and wisdom.

ॐ Namashivaya

"I bow to Sri Dakshinamurti, Lord and teacher of the three worlds, Who cuts asunder the painful shackles of birth and death and who is to be meditated upon, As sitting beneath a banyan tree and bestowing His grace, of supreme knowledge on the sages."

Dakshinamurti Stotram by Adi Shankaracharya

"I am not the prana *or the five vital forces, I am not the seven elements of the body nor the five sheaths, I am not the organs of speech, or procreation or excretion, I am the essence of consciousness and bliss —* Shivoham! Shivoham!*"*

Nirvanashtakam by Adi Shankaracharya

O Shiva! O Pashupate! Thou Lord of Parvati!
Kindly rescue me, helpless as I am,
From the trackless forest of this miserable world.

ॐ

Tripurantakaya Namaha!

CHAPTER XVI

THE THREE DEMONIC CITIES

"Prostrations to the great Lord, the master of the universe, the great God, the three-eyed one, the destroyer of the three cities, the extinguisher of the three fires as well as the fire at the time of death, the blue-necked one, the conqueror of Death, the Lord of all, the ever peaceful one, the glorious God of all gods!"

Sri Rudri. Yajur Veda

The three sons of the demon, Taraka were called Tarakaksha, Vidyunmali and Kamalaksha. Furious at their father's death, they decided to propitiate Brahma and get some boons from him, by which they could annihilate the gods. They did *tapasya* for many years and at last Brahma appeared and promised to give them the boons they craved for. With true *asuric* mentality, they immediately asked for immortality of the body. Brahma said that it was not in his power to grant this. Everything that had a birth, had to have a death at some time or other so he advised them to ask for something else. Having pondered a while they came up with another brilliant scheme. They each asked for a wonderful city of their own which would be impregnable and which would never be destroyed by any one. Tarakaksha asked for a golden city which would traverse the heavenly regions, Kamalaksha asked for a silver one, which would go about in the skies, and Vidyunmali opted for a magnetic, steel city that could move about freely on the earth. But in order to comply with Brahma's decree that no one and nothing could be totally indestructible, they agreed that the three cities could be destroyed when they came in line with each other. This phenomenon would happen only once in a thousand years at midday, when the constellation Pushya was in ascendance. They also insisted that only a single arrow which could pierce all three cities at the same time could destroy them. This arrow had to be discharged by Shiva alone.

Brahma, in his usual weak fashion, agreed to all these conditions and the divine architect, Mayan built three impregnable cities and gave them to the three brothers. *Asuras* are egoistic and cruel by nature. When their strength was enhanced by the acquisition of these miraculous cities, it was only to be expected that the three brothers started playing havoc in their respective regions — the earth, sky and heavens. At last the frustrated gods went to Brahma and asked him to rescue them as well as the earth and the terrestrial regions from the rampages of these cruel brothers. Brahma of course could only give these absurd boons. He was quite incapable of undoing them. So they went to Shiva as usual and placed their request before him. Shiva told them that he would not be instrumental in destroying his devotees. The cunning demons, who knew that Shiva was the one ordained to kill them, had started the worship of Shiva in all their three cities.

So the gods with Brahma at their head went to Vishnu, the saviour of the world. Vishnu told them that he was powerless to destroy the devotees of Shiva. Every time the *asuras* committed some crime, they immediately propitiated Shiva through some sacrifices, and thus eliminated the effects of their *karmas*. In this way they became invincible. The only way to make them weak was to stop them from performing these rites. Vishnu created an ascetic who went to the three cities and spread a heretic lore, totally at variance with the ancient *Vedic* cult. The sage advised them to stop worshipping gods like Shiva who were really weak when compared to the *asuras*. He initiated the demons into this dogma and soon all worship of Shiva was forbidden in the cities. The rites of the virtuous came to an end and evil conduct reigned supreme. In each of the three regions, where they dominated, the demons swooped down on their hapless victims and ground them to death. Once again, the gods approached Shiva and told him about the latest developments and begged him to rescue them from their plight. Shiva agreed but there were many obstacles to killing the demons of the cities. Brahma reminded the gods that the demons could be killed only with a single arrow, which would have to pierce all three cities at the same time.

This was quite a difficult task since they were always flying about in different spheres. The gods were sorely perplexed by this dilemma. Vishnu as usual came to their aid and told them that the cities would be aligned once in a thousand years and that time was soon to come. Shiva agreed to kill them if he was provided with a suitable chariot and arrow. Vishvakarma, the divine architect made a cosmic chariot incorporating all the forces of nature. It was golden in colour and brilliant to behold. The right wheel was the sun and the left, the moon. The right wheel had twelve spokes for the twelve months of the year and the left had sixteen, corresponding to the sixteen digits of the moon. The six seasons were the rims of the wheels. Time itself was its velocity. All the great *mantras* hung as bells on the spokes. Lord Brahma was the charioteer and the gods with Indra at their head, held the bridle. Vishnu penetrated the arrow and Agni, the spearhead. The *Vedas* were the four horses. Shiva or Sharva was the cosmic archer.

As he got into the chariot, the earth quaked and the mountains trembled. All the gods eulogised him. Brahma drove the chariot with the speed of the mind, with the gods following. Shiva chased the three cities from sphere to sphere but they did not come in one line. Then came a celestial voice, which told him to worship Ganesha if he wanted victory. Shiva duly recalled to his mind, his own son, Ganesha and requested him to remove all impediments from his path. As soon as he did this, the three cities were seen to come in alignment. A thousand years had passed and the time specified by Brahma had come. Shiva stood up in the chariot and fixed the arrow on the bow and drew the string taut. At the auspicious moment called Abhijit he discharged the arrow which flew with a tremendous, hissing sound. Since Vishnu himself was in the arrow and Agni, its steelhead, the arrow blazed forth like a meteor and burnt the cities with the demons within. Thus Shiva got the name, Tripurantaka, the slayer of the three cities. The gods eulogised him but Shiva's face was stern. Taking the ashes from the charred remains of the flying cities, he drew three horizontal lines across his forehead and proclaimed, "Mark my words! One day, the whole world will become as corrupt as these three cities. On that day, I shall wield my bow once again and destroy the whole cosmos. Let these ashes on my forehead remind everyone of Death, the destroyer. In future, all my devotees shall have this mark on their forehead."

The story of the Tripuras is the story of human redemption from the demonic to the divine life. The three cities represent the three sheaths, the body, mind and intellect. They also illustrate the three *gunas* or modes of Nature — *sattva*, *rajas* and *tamas*. Shiva is the divine archer or the Supreme Spirit, residing within this fortress. The golden city stands for *sattva*, the silver for *rajas* and the iron for *tamas*. They have to come to a state of equilibrium, in a straight formation before the divine archer can shoot the arrow of knowledge and kill all three and thus give redemption to the *jivatma* or the embodied soul. When the time is ripe for such liberation, all the gods, or the cosmic forces will come to our aid and the human soul imprisoned within the fortress of the body will be liberated.

Once Shiva and Parvati went to the Mandara mountains and sported among the peaks. Parvati playfully closed Shiva's eyes with her lotus like palms. As soon as she did this, a deep darkness spread over the whole universe. Since his eyes had the scorching heat of fire, her hands started to perspire. Drops of sweat dripped to the ground. Out of this heat and sweat there appeared an inhuman and terrible being. It was black, deformed, and blind. It had matted locks of hair all over its body. It howled, danced, and flicked its tongue here and there like a serpent and roared like a lion. Parvati removed her hands from Shiva's eyes and light came to the world, once again. She was terrified at the sight of this strange creature and asked her Lord what it might be.

Shiva replied, "When you closed my eyes O beloved, your sweat flowed to the ground and combined with the heat of my eyes and produced this creature. So you are the cause of this creature. He shall be called Andhaka, or the blind one and you shall care for him like your own son."

Parvati agreed and the boy was brought up by the *ganas*. At this time the *asura*, Hiranyaksha was doing *tapasya* to Shiva in order to get a son. At the end of his *tapasya* Shiva appeared before him and Hiranyaksha asked him for the boon of a son. Shiva was pleased with his austerities but told him that he was not fated to have a son but he, Shiva would present to him, Andhaka as his son. The asura was delighted and returned to his kingdom with Andhaka in tow.

Later on Lord Vishnu killed Hiranyaksha and his brother Hiranyakashipu. Prahlada was the son of Hiranyakashipu. Though the son of an *asura*, he was a great devotee of Lord Vishnu and became the king of the nether-world, after the death of his father. Hiranyaksha was the elder brother but since his son was blind, he could not become king. Andhaka was teased by his cousins for his inefficiency and inability to rule his father's kingdom. Unable to bear these taunts, Andhaka set out to the forest and started doing severe penance, swearing to cut off parts of his flesh and sacrifice the pieces into the fire if Brahma did not appear. At last Brahma appeared and asked him to choose a boon.

Andhaka immediately asked for immortality and invincibility in warfare. Of course, Brahma was powerless to grant him immortality. He could only give him a choice as to the method of death. Andhaka thought for a minute and came up with a brilliant idea. He agreed that death could befall him if ever he coveted a woman like his mother, who was the fairest in the whole world. Brahma agreed and touched his emaciated body, which immediately became strong and handsome. He also gained his sight. Andhaka was delighted. He roamed about all the quarters from the heavens to the nether-worlds and conquered every region and made Indra and the gods subservient to his will. Proud of his prowess, he slighted the *Vedas*, the gods and the Brahmins. He indulged in sexual sports with diverse, beautiful women of all types. Once, as luck would have it, he decided to spend some time in the Himalayas on the Mandara peak. His ministers came and told him of a wonderful sight that they had seen.

"O Lord of demons," they said, "living in a cave not far from here, we saw a sage in deep meditation. His matted hair was topped with the crescent moon and he wore an elephant hide round his hips. Serpents were twined round his body and a necklace of skulls adorned his neck. He was smeared with ashes. But what is of interest to you, is the fact that the most divinely ravishing lady was seated close to him. What is the use of your having gained eyesight, if you are unable to feast your eyes on her? However, we should warn you that two creatures guard their cave. One is an old bull and another, a creature with simian features."

On hearing this, the demon was thrilled and ordered his emissaries to go and ask the sage to give his wife to him peacefully or else be prepared to fight. The *yogi* was none other than Shiva and the emissaries of the demon went and told him that it was not befitting for a *yogi* to keep a young woman by his side. They ordered him to relinquish her immediately and hand her over to the king of the *asuras*.

Shiva smilingly told them to go back to their master and tell him to mind his own business. Shiva then announced to Parvati that he was going to an impenetrable forest in order to perform severe penance. While performing this, he would have to be a celibate and so it would be better if Parvati did not accompany him. Leaving his *ganas* to guard her, the Lord left for the dense forest. Precisely at this time Andhaka came with his army and fought a fierce battle with the *ganas* who were stationed at the door of the cave. When Parvati saw that the battle was going against them, she prayed to Vishnu to come to her rescue. Vishnu took numerous forms of thousands of ravishing women who immediately surrounded Parvati so that Andhaka was unable to distinguish which was Parvati. He didn't know what to do and beat a hasty retreat. Soon after this Shiva returned and once again a fierce battle ensued between the *ganas* and *asuras*. At last Shiva decided that the hour for Andhaka's redemption had come, for he had coveted his own mother, Parvati, who was the fairest in the whole world. Shiva impaled Andhaka on his trident and hoisted him in the air. Shiva's trident is known for its cleansing qualities and as soon as Andhaka was impaled on it, he came to his senses. All the evil was wiped out of him and he begged Shiva and Parvati to forgive him. Shiva was never one to bear a grudge, so he readily forgave him and asked him to choose a boon. Andhaka begged Shiva to make him, his constant companion. Shiva agreed and made him chief of the *ganas*. The *ganas* as we have seen were a motley crew composed of the forlorn, the ugly and the unwanted, so Andhaka was a fitting candidate for this post.

ॐ *Namashivaya*

ॐ

Shoolapanaye Namaha!

CHAPTER XVII

JALANDARA

"O Lord with matted locks on which is kept the Ganga,
O Lord of ghouls, and death to Death!
O destroying fire of Cupid.
O Lord with throat filled with poison,
O Lord of the elements,
Be gracious unto me."

Saint Sundarar

Once Indra and the other gods, accompanied by Brihaspati, the preceptor of the gods went to Kailasa to see Lord Shiva. The latter wanted to test them and assumed the form of a huge *yaksha* and lay in their way. When the giant refused to move, Indra, with the arrogance born out of power, raised his weapon, the thunderbolt in order to kill him. The *yaksha*, who was none other than Shiva, wanted to humble his pride. He held up a blade of grass in his hands and asked the gods if any of them could dislodge the grass from his hands. The gods were quite scornful of this childish request and each of them thought it would be a simple matter to squash the grass. One by one they tried to dislodge it. The wind god, Vayu, tried first, but blow as he might he was not able to make the blade of grass sway in the gust. Next, Agni, the god of fire tried his best to burn the little blade with his flame but it remained unscorched. At last Indra hurled his thunderbolt at the blade of grass but neither the *yaksha* nor the grass seemed in the least affected.

The gods were perplexed and asked the *yaksha*, "What is the meaning of this. Who are you?"

The *yaksha* replied, "Have you forgotten that there is another power above you. Without the support of that power none of you can do anything."

Indra was enraged and raised his *vajra* once more and hurled it at the *yaksha.* Shiva opened his third eye. The fierce flame that shot out of his eye would have reduced Indra into cinders had not Brishaspati intervened and begged Shiva to forgive Indra. Shiva forgave him but the fire that had emanated from his third eye would have scorched the world had it dropped on the earth so Shiva cast it into the sea at the confluence of the Ganga and the ocean. Here the flame took on the form of a handsome, demon boy. Hearing the fierce howls of the child, all the three worlds quaked in fear. The gods ran to Brahma and told him to do something about this strange creature. Brahma went to the ocean and took the boy in his lap. Immediately the demon put his arms round Brahma's neck and tried to throttle him, till tears started to come out of the Creator's eyes. He had hard work to extricate himself from the demon boy's strangling embrace. The ocean, which appeared to have a parental interest in the boy, now asked Brahma to perform the post-natal rites for the child and give him a name and foretell his destiny.

Brahma, whose eyes were full of tears caused by the demon's stranglehold, replied, "Since he was able to make my eyes water, he will be known as Jalandara. This name is doubly appropriate since he took birth in the water. He will be invincible, heroic and majestic like the ocean itself and he will become the emperor of the demons. No one except Shiva will be able to slay him. He will have a wife who will be exquisitely beautiful and noble in all ways."

The ocean was very pleased and took the boy to his own abode and nurtured him with great affection. He grew up into a handsome and splendid youth. The ocean requested the *asura*, Kalanemi to give his daughter, Vrinda to the young man in marriage. Jalandara became king and ruled over the demons for many years. Once he decided to conquer the gods and sent Indra an order to submit to him or else be prepared to fight. Indra decided to fight but was routed by Jalandara. As usual Indra rushed to Brahma for aid but the latter told him to go to Vishnu and seek his help. The gods approached Vishnu but Vishnu said that Jalandara was his brother-in-law and so he could not kill him! Vishnu's consort the goddess Lakshmi, was born of the ocean just as Jalandara was and Jalandara claimed that Lakshmi was his sister and

Vishnu, his brother-in-law. Thus Jalandara had got a boon from Vishnu that he would not kill him. The gods now requested the celestial sage, Narada to go to Jalandara and try to persuade him to infuriate Shiva; otherwise the great Lord would not agree to kill him.

Narada immediately proceeded to Jalandara's abode, stringing his lute. He lauded him and congratulated him on his great good fortune in having subdued all the three worlds. Narada continued, "I see that there is no one to equal you in all these worlds but I have just come from Kailasa, the abode of Lord Shiva and I have to confess that Lord Shiva's wife is the most beautiful lady I have ever seen. I know you to be a connoisseur of feminine charms and I am sure you will want to possess her."

Hearing this Jalandara was terribly excited. If there was one thing that all demons had in common, it was their lust for beautiful women and invariably, unbridled passion was what brought them to ruin. Jalandara was no exception to this even though his own wife, Vrinda was a paragon of all virtues. He sent his emissary to Shiva and demanded that he surrender his wife willingly to him or face the consequences of his wrath! Shiva was amused at his audacity and sent the emissary away with a stiff reprimand to his master. When Jalandara heard this he sent his army to fight with Shiva.

There now ensued a fierce battle between the *ganas* and the *asuras*, which ended in the former being routed. Then Jalandara roared to Shiva to come and fight with him. Shiva caught hold of the advancing *asura* and sent him flying a hundred miles away with his arrows. Realising that he was no match for Shiva, Jalandara created an illusion by which Shiva was surrounded by wonderful Gandharva singers. Shiva was immersed in the music of these celestial singers and lost all interest in the battle.

Taking this opportunity, Jalandara took on the form of Shiva and entered Parvati's private apartments where she was seated with her attendants. Seeing her Lord enter, she came forward. When he looked at her divine beauty, Jalandara could not control himself and his disguise fell off. Parvati immediately transported herself to the banks of the lake Manasarover and prayed to Vishnu to come to her aid. The gentle Lord came to her and asked her what she wanted of him. She recounted the tale of how the *asura*, Jalandara had tried to flout her modesty and capture her. She begged Vishnu to do the same to Jalandara's wife, Vrinda. Vishnu promised to help her and went to the forest near Vrinda's palace in the guise of an ascetic. While Vrinda was walking in the park, she was frightened by the sudden appearance of two fierce looking monkeys. The ascetic, who was none other than Vishnu, saved her. Later the ascetic assumed the form of her husband Jalandara, just as Jalandara had assumed the form of Shiva, in order to confuse Parvati. He went near Vrinda and put his arms round her. When Vrinda realised that this was not her husband but Lord Vishnu, she cursed him that one day, his wife would be abducted by a *rakshasa* in the guise of an ascetic and he would have to roam about in the forest searching for her. Monkeys and bears would be his only helpers. The Lord laughed and accepted the curse for he knew that all this was bound to happen in his *avatara* as Rama. Vrinda then immolated herself in the fire. Her spirit rose up in a flame and joined the aura around Parvati. All the gods rained flowers round her and applauded her for her great chastity and purity.

In the meantime, unable to see Parvati, Jalandara returned to the battlefield and challenged Shiva to battle. Shiva started to churn the ocean with his big toe. As he rotated his toe, a huge wheel came out of the waters. This was the famous *Sudarshana chakra* which he later presented to Vishnu.

Shiva now told the demon, "O Jalandara if you wish to fight with me you will have to lift this wheel with your toe. Only then will you be deemed competent to fight with me."

Jalandara laughed in scorn and insulted Shiva and boasted of his own prowess. But try as he might, Jalandara was unable to lift the wheel. Shiva's eyes emitted sparks of red and blue flames and taking up the wheel, he whirled it in the air and cut off the head of the arrogant monster. The splendour that came out of Jalandara's body merged in the splendour round Shiva, just as Vrinda's spirit had merged in Parvati's aura. The entire universe now returned to its former state of normalcy and the gods and other celestial beings returned to their own abodes fearlessly.

Another similar story about Shiva concerns the demon called

Shankachuda. An *asura* called Dambha had no sons. He went to his preceptor, Shukra and asked his advice. Shukra gave him the great *mantra* of Lord Krishna and told him to repeat it and perform austerities at the lake called Pushkara. Lord Vishnu was pleased with his devotion and appeared before him and asked him to choose a boon. Dambha asked for a son. Soon after, his wife conceived and a baby was born to them. In his previous birth this soul had been a close comrade of Lord Krishna and had been called Sudama. He had been cursed by Radha and was now forced to take birth as a demon. He was named Shankachuda. When he came of age he followed his father's example and went to the lake of Pushkara and performed severe *tapasya* in order to propitiate Brahma. The Creator appeared before him and asked him to choose a boon. Shankachuda said that he wanted to be invincible and be able to defeat the gods. Brahma agreed and presented him with the divine amulet of Sri Krishna to wear on his arm. He advised him to go to the holy spot called Badrikashrama in the Himalayas, where he would meet a lady called Tulasi who would be the perfect match for him. Shankachuda followed his advice and married Tulasi. Shankachuda now became the chief of the *asuras*. With the blessings of his *guru*, Shukra, he defeated the gods and took over the heavens. He took over all the three worlds and became a great emperor. Everyone was happy for he was a wonderful ruler. Only the gods were unhappy for they had been ousted from Heaven. They went with their complaints to Brahma who went with them and requested Lord Vishnu to help them.

Vishnu spoke to them, "Listen O gods!" he said. "This Shankachuda was a great devotee of mine in my *avatara* as Sri Krishna. He was called Sudama and was a great friend of Sri Krishna. He was cursed by Radha and has now taken on the form of an *asura*. Krishna has ordained that he will be killed by Shiva's trident, so you should approach Shiva and request his help." The gods went to Kailasa and asked Shiva to help them. The Lord agreed and sent his emissaries to Shankachuda and ordered him to give Heaven back to the gods. Shankachuda refused to do so and told them that they would have to fight for it. Thus war was declared and Shiva's *ganas* marched to Shankachuda's kingdom.

At this point Shankachuda started to remember his previous birth and knew that the appropriate time for his release had come. He installed his son on the throne and parted lovingly from his beloved wife, Tulasi before proceeding to the battlefield. A mighty battle ensued between the opposing armies in which Shankachuda showed himself to be invincible. At last Lord Vishnu approached Shiva and told him the secret of Shankachuda's invincibility. He had been given impenetrable armour. Moreover he had a spotlessly pure wife who was constantly praying for his safety and as long as she did so, he would not die.

Shiva requested Vishnu to delude Shankachuda with his *maya*. Vishnu forthwith took on the disguise of an old beggar and went and requested Shankachuda to give him his armour. Shankachuda could never refuse a mendicant and immediately ripped off his armour and gave it to him. Wearing this armour, Vishnu approached Shankachuda's wife, Tulasi and made love to her, pretending to be her husband. Immediately, Shankachuda was bereft of all his powers and could easily be killed by Shiva's trident. Shankachuda was released from his curse and regained his previous form and returned to Goloka to be with his beloved, Sri Krishna. It is said that all conches in the world that are used in the worship of Vishnu are made of Shankachuda's bones. When Tulasi heard of the deceit that had been practised by Vishnu, she was totally bereft and decided to give up her own life. She cursed Vishnu that he would be turned into a rock. At that time Shiva appeared and told her not to worry, for Vishnu had done this only to aid the gods who were his devotees.

"O gentle lady," he said, "cast off this body of yours and you will be given a most virtuous form. On this earth you will become the holy basil plant known as Tulasi. You will be beloved by Krishna and Vishnu and worshipped by all. The conch and Tulasi leaves will be essential parts of the worship of Krishna and Vishnu. Your body will also take on the form of the river called Gantaki. Due to your curse, Vishnu will become a rock in this river. Crores of sharp toothed worms will penetrate and erode this rock and the pieces will be known as *saligramas* and will be used in the worship of Vishnu. One who keeps a *saligrama*, a conch and Tulasi leaves in his house will be loved by Vishnu." With this pronouncement Shiva vanished from view and Vishnu took Tulasi with him to his abode. She cast off her body, which became the river, Gantaki and Vishnu became a rock on its banks.

The great sage, Atri was the son of Brahma. He was married to the most perfect of all women. She was called Anasuya. Since the couple had no children, they went to the forest and meditated on the great God, whoever he might be, in order to get progeny. After many years of penance, a brilliant flame emanated from Atri's body, which threatened to consume the whole world. The gods as usual approached Brahma and he in turn went to Vishnu and they all went to the abode of Shiva. Since Atri had not mentioned the name of any one God in his *tapasya*, all three of them decided to go to him in order to grant his request. The sage was rather surprised to see all of them and politely asked them the reason for their visit.

They replied, "You have meditated on the great God and since we are all equally great, we decided to grant you three sons, each of whom will have a part of our glory." Thus saying, they returned to their own abodes. Very soon Anasuya conceived. The child, who was a part of Brahma, became the moon, Chandra. The part of Vishnu, who was born as their son, was famous in the world as Dattatreya. He taught the world the greatness of the path of renunciation. That part of Shiva, who was born as their son, was known as Durvasa and became a great sage. He was famous for going round the world, testing people. It is true that he was known for his bad temper but one will notice that every time he lost his temper it was for some good reason and the person whom he cursed, gained something thereby. The sage king, Ambarisha became famous for his piety due to Durvasa's temper. At the end of Sri Rama's life on earth, Durvasa tested even Rama in order to show the world how the king was prepared to renounce his beloved brother in order to keep his word.

There is another interesting story concerning Anasuya, the wife of sage Atri who as we have seen was a model of chastity. Once the three gods, Brahma, Vishnu and Shiva, decided to test her chastity. They took the form of mendicants and went to her hermitage, to beg for alms. She came out to give them some food but they said very politely that they had taken a vow that they would be served only by a naked woman. Anasuya was in a dilemma. It was considered most improper to refuse to give food to a holy man. Moreover they looked very noble and would perhaps curse her if she refused. On the other hand it would be totally against the vows of chastity for her to go naked in front of three men. She thought for a while. Then by the power of her great chastity, she turned the three gods into three small babies and took them inside the house. She then took off her clothes and calmly proceeded to feed them. Thus they were forced to remain in her *ashrama* for a long time. In the meantime Lakshmi, Saraswati and Parvati, who were the consorts of the three gods, began to get rather worried at the prolonged disappearance of their husbands. At last they discovered that they were in Atri's *ashrama.* When they went to the hermitage they found three babies playing with Anasuya. When questioned, she admitted that the three were not real babies but wandering mendicants who had come for food. The three goddesses shamefully confessed that the mendicants were none other than their husbands. With her *yogic* powers, Anasuya turned them once again into their original forms. They were very pleased with the success of their test and blessed Anasuya and Atri and returned to their respective abodes.

ॐ *Namashivaya*

"I don't gain any merit by the performance of good, or do I lose anything by the performance of evil. I have neither happiness nor unhappiness. I gain nothing by chants, pilgrimages, yajnas *or the study of* Vedas. *I am not the eater, the food or the act of eating. I am the essence of consciousness and bliss* — Shivoham! Shivoham!"

Nirvanashtakam by Adi Shankaracharya

"I have no death, or doubt or caste. I have no father or mother for I am unborn. I am neither friend, nor relation, neither guru *nor disciple. I am the essence of consciousness and bliss* — Shivoham! Shivoham!"

Nirvanashtakam by Adi Shankaracharya

ॐ

Neelakandaya Namaha!

CHAPTER XVIII

THE CHURNING OF THE OCEAN

"O Dispenser of mercy,
Who consumed the strong poison
So that the dwellers of Heaven might regain their youth,
Have mercy on me and restore my eyesight."

Saint Sundarar

Once it happened that Indra, the king of the gods was cursed by the sage, Durvasa. The sage who had got a divine garland from Vaikunta had presented it to Indra. Not realising the profound value of this gift, Indra threw the garland carelessly over his elephant's head. The elephant shook its head and the garland fell to the ground and was trampled in the mud by its foot. When Durvasa saw this, he was furious and cursed Indra that he, along with his retinue of gods would become old and decrepit. Immediately all the gods lost their youth and supernormal powers. As usual they ran to the Creator, Brahma and requested him to intervene with Lord Vishnu on their behalf. They went en masse to Vaikunta and begged Lord Vishnu to help them.

The Lord appeared in all his glory and spoke to them. "O gods," he said, "time is the master controller of all things. At the moment, time is favourable to the *asuras* who are your arch enemies. The wheel of time turns slowly but one day it will turn in your favour. That will happen only if you churn the milky ocean and get the elixir of life, called '*amrita.*' Anyone who drinks it will gain eternal youth. But in your state of decrepitude, you will never be able to do this by yourselves. You will have to get the help of the *asuras*. In desperate situations, there is no harm in taking the help of even your confirmed enemies! After you gain your objective, you can return to your original state of enmity!

One who drinks *amrita* will become immortal, so waste no time in doing this. Go immediately to the *asuras* and solicit their help. You have no option but to agree to whatever terms they suggest. Many precious objects will come out of the ocean when it is churned. Have no attraction or repulsion to whatever comes. Take only what is given to you and don't lose your temper if you are prevented from possessing any of them. You may use the Mandara mountain as the churning rod and the serpent Vasuki as the rope. Consign all types of medicinal plants and shrubs and creepers into the milky ocean in order to curdle it. Only then will it yield the desired benefits." So saying Vishnu vanished from view.

The gods went and solicited the demons, who agreed to help them, provided they were given a fair share of the *amrita*, the nectar of immortality. Imbued with confidence in their own ability, both parties went and lifted the mountain, Mandara and started to carry it to the ocean. Very soon they could not bear the weight and the golden mountain came crashing down, killing many gods and demons alike. Lord Vishnu appeared on his eagle vehicle and lifted it up with one hand. Balancing the mountain easily on the eagle's back, he took it to the ocean and placed it in the correct spot. The gods then requested Vasuki, the Lord of snakes to act as the rope for churning the rod, on the understanding that he too would get a fair share of the *amrita*. With great enthusiasm the gods and demons wound the snake round the mountain and started to pull this mighty churning rod this way and that. Since the gods were too old and weak to do much, Lord Vishnu himself caught hold of the snake's head while the demons were told to take the tail. The demons were quite mortified at this apparent insult. They refused to touch the tail and declared that it was most demeaning for noble people like them, to be forced to catch the posterior of the snake! Lord Vishnu smilingly gave up the head and lifted up the tail with the gods behind him. Thus both sides started to churn the mighty ocean with great vigour. Unfortunately since the mountain was not supported beneath, it started to sink down. A great cry rose up in the ranks of the *devas* and the *asuras*. Lord Vishnu comforted them and took the form of an enormous tortoise and swam below the mountain and lifted it up so that it had a firm base. This was Lord Vishnu's incarnation known as the Kurmavatara. This primeval tortoise of infinite length and strength bore that huge mountain on its back as easily as if it was a mere pebble. It is said that the Lord, as the tortoise, was delighted with the pleasant sensation of scratching on his shellback as the mountain rotated rhythmically over it, while the two teams churned vigorously. Despite their best efforts, the work was still proceeding very slowly so Lord Vishnu took a dual form, that of a *deva* and of an *asura* and entered both their ranks in order to encourage both sides to greater efforts. He also entered the snake, Vasuki in the form of a type of anesthesia in order to shield it from the torturous churning which it had to endure. When the vigorous rotating movement seemed to upset the balance of the mountain, the Lord took a gigantic form and stood on top of the mountain and maintained the balance, pressing down each side as and when needed. Thus the Lord took on various manifestations in order to strengthen the resolve of all those concerned. The fumes and hot breath coming out of the tired snake were now scorching the *asuras* who had stupidly opted for the head. The *devas* too got their fair share of the fumes which began to spread everywhere. Then the Lord made rain pour down on them, cooling both sides and giving relief to the snake also.

However, despite their best efforts, no *amrita* appeared, and both parties began to lose hope. In order to encourage them, the Lord took an enormous form, with thousands of hands and stood in the middle of the two parties and started to churn the ocean with five hundred hands on either side. It was a wonderful sight and both *devas* and *asuras* watched spellbound. At last things seemed to be moving. Many aquatic creatures began to surface.

By now the poor snake was quite sick of the whole affair and started to throw up the dreaded halahala poison, also called Kalakuta. Its fatal and penetrating fumes started to spread everywhere. Crying loudly in terror, the gods, urged by Lord Vishnu and lead by Indra, ran to Shiva and begged him to save them from this new horror. If it fell on the ground, the whole universe would be destroyed. Shiva, the ever-merciful one, immediately appeared on the scene along with Parvati and caught the lethal poison before it dropped to the ground and drank it without hesitation. He was prepared to sacrifice his own life in order to save the universe. Parvati knew only too well that his powers were immeasurable and that nothing could harm him, yet her love for him made her weak. She exclaimed in horror and caught her husband's throat in order to stop the poison from slipping down. The poison thus stuck in his throat and made it blue in colour. Lord Vishnu extolled Shiva as Neelakanda or the blue-necked one while the gods and demons joined in praising him.

The ability to sacrifice one's own welfare for the sake of others is the highest form of the worship of the Supreme and all the *devas* and *asuras* extolled Lord Shiva. It was a common belief that one who ate poison should not be allowed to sleep during the night so all of them remained awake through the different watches of the night, singing the praises of Lord Shiva. Even now, this night is celebrated as Mahashivaratri or the great night of Shiva, and all devotees of Shiva keep watch during this night, singing hymns to the all-merciful Lord. The few drops of poison that happened to drop from the Lord's hands turned into snakes, scorpions, and other poisonous plants and creatures.

The next day, the *devas* and *asuras* once more enthusiastically began to churn the milky ocean. The first to appear was the heavenly cow called Kamadhenu. This was presented to the *rishis* for their ritualistic purposes. Then came the white horse, Ucchaisravas. Though the *devas* eyed it greedily, the Lord urged them to give it to the *asura*, Bali. Next emerged the four-tusked, white elephant, Airavata, which was grabbed by Indra. Then came the jewel Kaustubha, which was given to Lord Vishnu to adorn his neck. Next came the celestial, wish-fulfilling tree, known as the Parijata as well as the celestial nymphs called the *apsaras*. Both these were taken by the gods.

Finally the goddess, Lakshmi, seated on a shining, red lotus, rose out of the ocean. She was the personification of beauty, filled with auspiciousness. Seeing her dazzling appearance, both the *devas* and the *asuras* stopped their work and ran after her and stood gazing at her with great admiration. The gods of all the quarters brought precious articles for her adornment. When she was elaborately adorned as befitting a bride, they begged her to choose a husband from amongst them. Clad in royal raiment, she carried the wedding garland in her tender hands and made her undulating gait round the host of august personages who were crowding round the banks of the ocean. But she did not find anyone who appealed to her! According to her all the gods had some defect. At last she spied Lord Vishnu, seated nonchalantly on the banks of the ocean, dabbling his feet in the water, totally unconcerned about her. She realised that he alone was the fitting consort for her and shyly went towards him and placed the beautiful garland of lotus flowers round his neck. The Lord graciously accepted her and gave her a most coveted position in his heart, from which position she casts her gracious look on all his devotees and blesses them with all worldly and spiritual goods. Thus it is said that Lakshmi, the goddess of wealth does not go to those who run after her but only to those who run after her husband!

Next came Vaaruni, the deity of intoxication. The *asuras* happily took her into their midst. After more strenuous effort, there suddenly emerged the handsome figure of a man holding the pot of nectar, the divine *amrita*, in his hands. He was known as Dhanwantari and was a partial *avatara* of Lord Vishnu. He is the father of the science of Ayurveda. As soon as the *asuras* saw him, they realised that this was the immortal drink for which they had been waiting. They greedily decided to appropriate the whole thing for themselves and immediately grabbed the pot and ran off with it. The *devas* were too weak and stunned to do anything. After having gone through such back-breaking labour, they were bereft to find that their efforts were in vain and the *asuras* as expected, had not kept to their part of the bargain. They rushed to Lord Vishnu with their tale of woe.

He comforted them and promised to help them. "All those who worked for the accomplishment of the task must get their just reward and a share of the nectar but since the *asuras* have greedily grabbed the whole pot for themselves, they will be punished and will get nothing. This is the eternal law of *dharma* which cannot be gainsaid." Saying this he vanished from their view and in his stead there appeared a most fascinating woman, lovely beyond description. With undulating movements of her broad hips, she glided into the midst of the *asuras* who were now quarrelling amongst themselves as to who should get the maximum *amrita.* When they saw the beautiful damsel they left the pot of nectar and rushed to her and enquired who she was and why she had come and begged her to distribute the nectar impartially amongst them and thus put an end to their quarrels.

She said that her name was Mohini and with a seductive side long glance of her lovely eyes she said teasingly, "I'm actually a woman of a very low type, a harlot as you might say. How can you possibly trust me?"

The *asuras* laughed merrily at her pleasantries and swore that they trusted her implicitly. Mohini said, "I shall divide the nectar amongst you only if you promise to abide by my decision, whatever it may be and not start quarrelling afterwards."

They agreed happily and the maiden made them sit, facing east on mats of *kusa* grass. She called the *devas* and asked them to sit on the opposite side, facing the *asuras*. The *asuras* did not dare to murmur a word since she had already made them swear implicit obedience. When both parties were ready and sitting meekly in two neat rows, Mohini entered, carrying the golden pot of nectar. All eyes were fixed on her as she appeared. They were so fascinated by her looks and flirtatious behaviour that they forgot to look at what she was doing. Vishnu did not want to give the nectar of immortality to the *asuras* who were cruel by nature. To give them immortality would have been fatal. As Mohini passed through the ranks of the *asuras*, all she gave them were loving glances. The nectar, she gave, only to the *devas*. The demons did not even notice what was going on for they were mesmerised by her looks and deportment. Each one thought that she had fallen in love with him. At last when the whole of the nectar had been consumed, Mohini reassumed her original form, to the consternation of the *asuras* who realised that they had been neatly tricked.

Immediately they started to attack the *devas*. The latter had by now gobbled up the nectar and regained their lost youth and they fought back with redoubled vigour and eventually defeated the *asuras* who returned home to lick their wounds, plotting all the while for further ways to defeat their arch enemies.

This story as most of the stories of the *Puranas*, has an esoteric meaning. The milky ocean is the mind. The gods and the demons are the negative and positive thoughts in our mind, which churn it so forcefully. The Mandara mountain is the load of nescience that we carry from birth to birth. The rope of the snake is our pride. When we try to subdue this mind by some form of *sadhana* or spiritual practice like meditation, the first thing to emerge is the accumulated poison of passions like lust, greed, anger, fear and so on. That can only be removed by the Lord himself. Only then will the ambrosia of wisdom arise. Even at this point, great care has to be taken to keep our ego in check or else this wisdom will be snatched from our mouth by our negative emotions. Our *asuric* ego will grab this opportunity to declare itself to be supreme. Once again it is only the Lord who can save us. Sincere prayer and effort can help us to regain this lost wisdom and only then can we become liberated beings.

Lord Shiva had returned to Kailasa after having saved the world by swallowing the poison. There he heard how Vishnu had saved the day by taking on the form of Mohini, the most fascinating woman in the world. He became very desirous of seeing this alluring form of the Lord. Accompanied by Parvati and his host of goblins, he went to Vaikunta in order to see this enticing form.

Shiva said, "I have had occasion to see many of your wonderful incarnations but I have never seen you as a woman. I'm most anxious to see this, so please show yourself to me as Mohini."

Vishnu smiled and said, "Are you sure you want to see it? It is a form which is calculated to arouse passion in every person but of course you are a perfect *yogi* so perhaps it might not do harm to you." So saying, the Lord vanished from view. Suddenly Shiva felt that he was in a beautiful garden into which spring had just come. There in the midst of the riotous blooms, he beheld a most charming young woman playing with a golden ball. Her doe-like eyes darted hither and thither after the movements of the unpredictable ball, which was flying around as if bewitched by her beauty. The ball was not the only one to be thus bewitched. Shiva found that he had even forgotten the existence of his spouse standing beside him. He forgot everything except the entrancing young lady playing with the ball before him and started to chase her. The damsel cast him a bashful, side long glance as she darted past him, trailing her transparent garments that seemed to be slipping off her tantalising breasts. She made a show of trying to hold up her slippery clothes with her left hand while bouncing the ball with her right and danced off with a provocative glance at Shiva. Even Shiva the great *yogi*, was totally carried away by Vishnu's *maya*, the great illusory power of the Lord, so how can ordinary mortals be blamed for falling under the spell of this *maya*. Before the astonished gaze of Parvati, Shiva ran after Mohini. At last, tiring of the game, Vishnu as Mohini, allowed herself to be caught in a fierce embrace by Rudra, whose passion had been inflamed by her beauty. She broke free and ran on and Shiva's divine seed dropped on the ground as he followed in hot pursuit. Wherever Shiva's seed dropped, gold and silver mines sprang up. Suddenly, Shiva came into possession of his senses and realised how he had been duped by the great Vishnu-*maya*. He became serene once more and Mohini resumed her original form as Vishnu.

Vishnu congratulated Shiva on having been able to overcome his *maya* that was so difficult for anyone to overcome. "Who but you can overcome the infatuation of my *maya* by his own efforts and come back to his original senses."

It is said that out of this union of Hari and Hara, or Shiva and Vishnu, the *avatara* of Dharma Shasta was born. The boy was supposed to have been born from the thigh of Lord Vishnu and combined in him the qualities of both these deities.

Even Hanuman is supposed to be a manifestation of Shiva. The rest of the divine seed of Shiva was taken up in a leaf by the seven sages and given to Vayu, the wind God to deposit in a suitable womb. Vayu carried the seed with him to the Southern mountains. There he saw the maiden known as Anjana who belonged to a family of monkeys. He deposited the seed in her and the child she got from this came to be known as Hanuman. He is the one who helped Lord Vishnu in his incarnation as Sri Rama to defeat the demon king, Ravana.

ॐ *Namashivaya*

ॐ

Gangadaraya Namaha!

CHAPTER XIX

THE ADVENT OF THE GANGA

"O eyes of mine,
Behold Him,
With the throat which swallowed the sea-spawned poison,
The Lord who eternally dances,
Swinging rhythmically His eight arms,
O eyes of mine,
Behold Him!"

Saint Appar

There was once a king of the solar race called Sagara who performed the *Aswamedha yaga* or the horse-sacrifice in order to worship the Supreme Being. The sacrificial horse for the *yaga* was normally let loose to wander over the country. It had to be followed closely by the king's army. Anyone who wanted to question the king's prowess would have to obstruct the horse and fight with the king's men. It is said that anyone who performed a hundred *Aswamedha yagas* would be able to rule over the gods. When Sagara started his hundredth *yaga*, Indra, the king of the gods became afraid that he would oust him from his position. He stole the sacrificial horse and hid it away in the nether regions next to the place where the great sage, Kapila was meditating. When the horse disappeared, Sagara sent his people to search for it but it was nowhere to be found. The hundred sons of the king now went forth to look for the horse and dug up the entire earth in their efforts. At last they found the horse in the nether world, grazing happily beside the great sage Kapila. Their minds bewildered by their own evil propensities, they thought the sage to be the thief and pounced on him. Kapila opened his eyes and the fire of austerity that blazed from his eyes, immediately consumed them. Hearing this news, the king's grandson, Amsuman went forth to reprieve his grand-uncles. He came to the place where the horse was tethered. He saw the sage and immediately recognised him to be an enlightened soul and begged him to release the horse and forgive his grand-uncles. The sage blessed him and told him to take away the horse and complete his grandfather's sacrifice.

"Your grand-uncles can only be purified by the holy waters of the river Ganga which resides in the heavens," said Kapila. Amsuman returned and completed the *yaga* but he was not able to do anything about getting the Ganga in his lifetime. His son Dileepa also performed great *tapasya* but was unable to get the Ganga to the earth.

Next in the line of the glorious Ikshvaku dynasty was Prince Bhagiratha, son of Dileepa. When he heard of the great efforts made by his father and forefathers, he was determined that he would succeed where the others had failed and force the celestial Ganga to come to the earth and thus give salvation to his ancestors. Filled with determination, the young prince went to the Himalayas and performed rigorous penance for many years at the place, which is now known as Gangotri.

At last the goddess, Ganga was pleased and told him that she was willing to come down to the earth. "I'm pleased with your penance O Bhagiratha," she said, "but if I come down, the force of my descent will crush the earth down and she will not be able to survive the impact of my tremendous weight. So you will have to find someone who is capable of breaking my fall and bearing my weight. Moreover, when I come to the earth, all human beings will wash off their sins in my pure waters and I will become polluted. Who will be there to purify me?"

Bhagiratha humbly replied, "O goddess, whenever a holy man comes and takes a bath in your waters, he will cleanse you from your contact with sinners. A holy man is a repository of all purity. The Lord who is the essence of purity ever lives in the hearts of the holy and no impurity can remain in their presence. As for your first difficulty, Lord Shiva alone is capable of breaking your fall. He is the epitome of compassion. When he hears of the great benefit which will accrue to all humankind if you were to come to the earth, he will surely agree to help me."

Thus saying, Bhagiratha started on another bout of terrible penance by which he propitiated the compassionate Shiva and begged him to help him in this endeavour. Shiva agreed and Bhagiratha once more begged Ganga to come down. The celestial Ganga is normally retained in the *kamandalu* or water pot of the Creator, Brahma. In his *avatara* as Vamana, Lord Vishnu took on a universal form in which one of his feet thrust its way into the world of Brahma. The Creator was overjoyed to see the lotus feet of the Lord and reverently poured the Ganga water over the feet of Vamana. This was the holy water, purified by washing the feet of Lord Vishnu that now came dashing down with all its force on to the earth. Playfully Ganga decided to test Shiva's strength and bore down with all her might on to the planet. Shiva opened his locks and caught her in her impetuous fall so that not a drop remained, thus subduing her pride. She disappeared completely into his hair. Struggle as she might, not a drop could manage to squeeze out of Shiva's hair, which he calmly knotted up again. Poor Bhagiratha! Once again he was forced to meditate on the three-eyed Lord and beg him to release at least one portion of the heavenly Ganga so that his ancestors could gain peace. Having curbed Ganga's pride, the Lord was pleased to grant Bhagiratha's request and allowed a small trickle to escape from his topknot.

This is the Ganga we see today. What was only a small trickle to Shiva is a mighty torrent to us. The Ganga came out of the glacier known as "Gomukh" which is in the form of a cow's mouth, in the lofty regions of the Himalayas. Since she was brought down by Bhagiratha, her name in those regions, is Bhageerathi. Since she is kept in Shiva's hair, she became his second wife and Shiva came to be called Gangadara.

Bhagiratha rode his horse swiftly down the Himalayan slopes with the river following closely behind. He had a long way to go before reaching the sea, where the ashes of his ancestors lay. On the way it is said that he passed the hermitage of the sage, Jhanva and since the river was about to destroy his *ashrama*, the sage calmly took her into himself through his left ear. Bhagiratha looked back to find that Ganga had disappeared and guessing the cause, he returned and begged the sage to release her. Jhanva was only too happy to oblige and he allowed

Ganga to come out of his right ear. Thus she got the name, Jhanavi or daughter of Jhanva.

The stories of the sages are only meant to give us an inkling of the greatness of these holy men who were in such perfect control of themselves that they could manipulate the forces of nature. These sages were one with the supreme centre of the universe and thus there was nothing that they could not command. Ganga was reminded of the assurance of Bhagiratha that if any pure soul touched her, all the sins she had accumulated, due to the sinners who had washed their sins off in her waters, would in turn be destroyed. Thus the Ganga surged after Bhagiratha purifying everything on her way until she reached the ocean near modern Calcutta. The ashes of the sons of Sagara were lying there and she flowed over them and redeemed Bhagiratha's pledge of giving salvation to his ancestors. Despite their sin in having insulted a most holy person, these princes attained heaven through the indirect contact of their ashes with the holy waters of the Ganga. Bhagiratha's name has come to be synonymous with superhuman effort and valour in order to achieve impossible ends. It is to his glory that the Ganga is here with us today, ready to bless all those who bathe in her waters or pray to her with devotion. All devout Hindus hope that their ashes will be immersed in the heavenly Ganga by their children, after death, for in that lies ultimate salvation.

ॐ *Namashivaya*

"I am formless and without any modification or attributes. I am all-pervading and free. I am ever the same all the time, neither bound nor liberated. I am the essence of consciousness and bliss — Shivoham! Shivoham!"

Nirvanashtakam by Adi Shankaracharya

ॐ

Somaya Namaha!

CHAPTER XX

THE DEMON, BHASMAKA

"Henceforth O Father!
Instead of contemplating on Thy divine feet day and night,
I shall brood on shedding this body on earth,
And enter the haven of your feet.
This is my serfdom."

Saint Manikkavachakar

Once there was a demon by the name of Bhasmaka who wanted to get control over the whole world. He decided to propitiate Lord Shiva by his *tapasya.* After practising severe austerities for many years, Shiva was pleased to grant him any boon that he might choose. Bhasmaka who had only one thought in his mind immediately said, "Grant me the boon that anyone on whose head I place my hand will instantly become a heap of ashes. The very word *bhasma* means ashes and perhaps his name might have prompted him to ask for this strange boon. Shiva, who is noted for his love of his devotees, granted the boon without thinking of the consequences of such an act. With the true *asuric* nature which does not hesitate to bite the hand that feeds it, the demon immediately decided to try out the efficacy of the boon by placing his hand on his benefactor's head! He took two steps forward before Shiva realised his intentions. The only thing to do was to take to his heels and this he did with Bhasmaka in hot pursuit. Shiva rushed to Vaikunta and begged Vishnu to help him. Vishnu immediately took on the form of Mohini, the temptress of the entire world and stood before the advancing demon who held his hand aloft in eager anticipation of the kill. When he saw Mohini blocking his way, he forgot his intentions and begged her to marry him. Vishnu, the arch deluder, who can entice the whole universe with his *maya*, looked coyly at the lusty demon and hung her head in apparent bashfulness.

"I have taken an oath O noble one, that I will bestow my favours only on the person who can defeat me in the art of dancing."

"O I'm an expert dancer," cried the infatuated *asura*, even though he was as 'graceful' as a buffalo!

"Very good," said the damsel. "I will take some poses and you should follow them as best as you can."

"Certainly!" said the demon, "but please make it short since I'm in a hurry to gather you up in my arms!"

Mohini smiled her secret smile. Without wasting time in further talk, she started to take pose after pose. She looked so ravishing when she stood in these beautiful statue-like poses that Bhasmaka could hardly restrain himself from grabbing her. But he managed to control his ardour and tried to imitate her as best as he could. He was in such a hurry to get on with it and so bemused by her beauty that he hardly looked at what she was doing but simply tried his best to copy her. At last Mohini took a pose and placed her right hand on her own head. Without thinking Bhasmaka did the same and was reduced to a heap of ashes!

Shiva is noted for his impetuosity, generosity and gullibility. He is said to forget his own safety in his anxiety to serve his devotees. He blesses everyone and does not try to curb anyone, not even the demons. He is quick to get angry and as quickly appeased. Vishnu on the other hand is noted for his shrewdness and his ability to contrive all situations so that he was always the master of the situation and never the victim. Thus Vishnu saved Shiva and he was very grateful.

ॐ *Namashivaya!*

ॐ

Sadashivaya Namaha!

CHAPTER XXI

STORY OF MARKANDEYA

"O Pure One, O Virtuous One!
O Lord with the proud bull of bloodshot eyes!
O limpid honey!
O water of life!
O Lord of beautiful eyes!
O Lion among the immortals!
Pray tell me who is my kin here?"

Saint Sundarar

There was once a poor Brahmin called Mrikandu who was childless. He and his wife prayed to Lord Shiva to give them a son. Shiva appeared before them in a dream and asked them, "Would you prefer to have a child who is brilliant in every way but who will die at the age of sixteen or would you prefer a long-lived fool?"

After much consideration, the parents opted for the noble child. The baby who was born to them was indeed an exceptional child. Everyone who saw it was struck with wonder and delight. But as the child grew older, he noticed that his parents were always overprotective about him. At last he questioned them about their extraordinary anxiety and they told him the reason.

The boy answered, "Lord Shiva is said to be the cause of both mortality and immortality. Isn't he the one who granted your desire for a son? Will he not be able to grant me the boon of immortality if I pray to him?"

The parents were amazed by the young boy's faith. They encouraged him to do daily worship of the *linga* which was installed in their little temple. The boy faithfully performed the worship of the *linga* in the prescribed manner. At last the day of his sixteenth birthday dawned. The anxious parents were loath to let the boy out of their sight. The child was not in the least bit worried. He proceeded as usual to their family temple followed by his anxious parents. Just then he saw the frightening figure of Yama, the Lord of Death, striding beside him, carrying the noose in his hand. The boy ran towards the *linga* and it is said that in each one of his footsteps a Shiva *linga* sprouted, blocking the path of the god of Death. The boy ran into the temple and clasped the *linga* tightly with both his arms. Yama came forward and swung his noose round the boy but since he was clutching the *linga* the noose went round both the child and the *linga*.

The frightened boy cried aloud, "O Shambho! Save me! Save me! I'm alone and helpless!

Immediately the lord appeared out of the *linga* and spoke to him. "Fear not," he said gently, "I will not allow Death to take you away." Then turning to Yama he said, "O Yama! You may now return to your abode. The child was given only sixteen years of life and you have come at the appointed time to do your duty. You may take it from me that it has been done. Now I will take over."

Yama bowed to the Lord and said, "O Lord! You are the giver of both mortality and immortality. You are the Creator, Preserver and Destroyer. What can I do but obey your commands?" So saying he departed.

Shiva lifted up the child who had closed his eyes since he was too frightened to open them and watch the proceedings. "My dear child," said the Lord. "Have no fear. My devotee can never fall. Death himself will be helpless against my devotee. Your faith and devotion will not go unrewarded. I grant you a very, very long life. You will live for the whole of this *Manvantara.* You will be acclaimed as a great sage. You will take up your residence in the Himalayas in the Kedar Kanda, at the holy spot of Badrikashrama. There you will live and do *tapasya* for the whole of this cycle of creation and then join the formless essence at the end of that time. Have no fear. No one can harm you any more."

Thus saying the Lord departed. After staying with his parents for some time Markandeya, as he came to be called, left for the Himalayas, for he realised that the sole aim of life was to contemplate on the Supreme

Lord. Many aeons passed with the sage in deep contemplation. As usual, Indra, the king of gods became jealous of him for he thought that Markandeya's desire was to usurp his own position. In order to entice the sage and make him fall a prey to passion, Indra sent his retinue consisting of Kama, the god of love, the *apsaras*, and other celestial maidens. Everywhere that Kama went, spring would follow, accompanied by the perfumed *malaya* breeze. They went to the holy spot known as Badrikashrama where the sage had his hermitage and transformed that bleak spot into one of beauty. The vernal season set in. The crescent moon decorated the evening sky. Flowers bloomed in profusion. The thick creepers were laden with flowers dripping with honey. Inebriated bees buzzed around, intoxicated with the nectar that flowed in abundance. The atmosphere was enough to arouse pangs of love in the heart of the sternest ascetic. Kama arrived, carrying his bow of sugar-cane and followed by a troupe of *apsaras* strumming their lutes and singing sweetly.

The sage was sitting in meditation, with half-closed eyes, after having finished offering his oblations into the flames of the sacrificial fire. He looked as lustrous as the fire itself. The *apsaras* came forward and started to dance. The musicians strummed their instruments softly as Kama drew his five-pronged arrow taut on the bow. The heavenly dancer, Punjikasthali advanced in a slow and sensuous fashion and swayed in time to the music just in front of the sage. Her transparent clothes were coming loose and her whirling hair trailed over his face. It was at this opportune moment that Kama shot his arrows.

Markandeya opened his eyes. Indra and his companions who were discreetly watching the proceedings from behind the safety of a bush, turned pale, for they had not forgotten what had happened to Kama when he had dared to do such a thing to Lord Shiva, at their own behest. This time Kama was trying the same stunt on one of Shiva's devotees and they were a bit uncertain of the consequences of his action. They were ready and poised for flight if things appeared to be getting out of hand but strangely enough, the sage was the gentlest of all souls. He saw the dancers standing bashfully in front of him and smiled at them. He was one with the Supreme and he knew what was passing through their minds. He beckoned to Indra who was peeping from behind the bush. Indra came forward shamefacedly and prostrated before him and asked Markandeya to forgive him.The sage assured Indra that he had not the slightest desire to usurp his position and that his only desire was to worship God without interference.

When Indra departed, the incarnations of Vishnu known as Nara and Narayana approached Markandeya in order to bless him. They told him to ask for any boon and after much persuasion, the sage asked to be shown a glimpse of the Lord's divine *maya.* This was indeed a strange request. All of us are in the habit of asking the Lord to take away the veil of *maya* but Markandeya, who was ever immersed in *atmic* bliss, did not know the meaning of *maya.* The Lord smiled at this surprising request and agreed to comply.

As soon as they left, Markandeya found that black and glowering clouds were beginning to gather in the sky. Torrential rains came pouring down and though he was sitting on the peak of a mountain it appeared as if the ocean was rising up from all sides. Markandeya found his *ashrama* to be in danger of being washed away by the flood. He was unable to save himself from drowning in the waters and for the first time in his life he felt the emotion called fear. He floated for an infinite length of time on the waters of the deluge, tortured by pangs of hunger and pain, unable to find any hope of reprieve. He felt as if he had been swimming in this ocean of *samsara* for all time. He lost all recollection of his former life. At times he would be totally submerged and at times he would be afloat.

He cried out piteously to the Lord to help him and suddenly he saw a delicate banyan leaf floating on the waters. Lying on the leaf was a glorious infant, blue in colour and eyes filled with love. The baby had taken up one of its own, tiny feet with its two hands and was sucking his big toe. It was a silent message to Markandeya that the only recourse for those who were drowning in the ocean of *samsara* was the lotus feet of the Lord. At the sight of this wondrous infant, the sage forgot his woes and was irresistibly drawn towards the babe. As he stretched forth his arms to embrace it, he felt himself to be drawn into the child, through its breath. Within the child he saw the vision of the universe as he remembered to have seen it before the deluge. The sky with all the galaxies, the heavens, the earth, the oceans, the forests and the mountains were all there inside the heart of this wondrous infant. His own *ashrama* was also there. As he watched the scene in wonder, he was forcibly expelled from the child's stomach through his breath. Once again he was floating on the floodwaters and the wondrous infant was lying on the water, cradled on the banyan leaf, just out of his reach. Overpowered by the loving side-long glances of the infant, the sage swam forward to embrace him but just as he stretched his arms out, the Lord disappeared and Markandeya found himself back in his *ashrama* in the Himalayas and realised that the enormous passage of time that he had imagined to have passed, was nothing but an instant. He had just experienced the glory of Vishnu's *maya.* All Time is but an instant to the Lord. For Him there is neither past nor future. There is nothing but a glorious present.

Seeing his devotee in this exalted state, Lord Shiva and his consort, Parvati came down to bless him. The sage was sitting with closed eyes, meditating on the form of the divine baby when he found the vision to have been replaced by the forms of the divine couple. He opened his eyes and saw them standing before him. Shiva was the colour of lightning. His matted locks were adorned with the crescent moon and he was clad in an elephant hide. He was holding the trident, club, shield, sword and bow as well as the rosary of *rudraksha* beads. Parvati, the mother of all the worlds was standing beside him. Rising up in haste Markandeya prostrated before them and extolled them. Shiva asked him to choose any boon.

Markandeya, who had just suffered from the effects of one boon, replied, "I have just experienced the drastic effect of Vishnu's *maya.* I want nothing more from this world. All I want is firm devotion to your feet and to the feet of Lord Vishnu and to all your devotees."

Lord Shiva replied, "O great and noble soul! All that you have asked for will be given to you. You will be free from the trammels of old age and death. Your lifespan shall extend to the length of the cosmic dissolution, as I have already told you when I saved you from Yama's noose. You shall have knowledge of the past, present and future as well as complete renunciation and total illumination. The very sight of a holy man, filled with renunciation is enough to purify a soul. The gods themselves yearn to have the sight of a holy person. Just by having your vision, all people will become purified. Your fame shall last for all time."

Thus blessing him, Lord Shiva and Parvati left the place. The sage Markandeya is said to be still meditating in the lonely regions of the Himalayas to this day, ready to bless all devotees of the Lord.

On the banks of the river Narmada was the beautiful city of Dharmapura. A Brahmin by the name of Visvanara lived there with his wife Suchismati. They were both great devotees of Lord Shiva and prayed to him for the boon of a son. In fact, they begged that Shiva, himself would be born as their son. The Lord agreed and a son was born to the couple and was named Grahapati. When the boy was in his eleventh year, the celestial sage, Narada came and read the boy's hand and foretold that some doom would come to him in a year's time and it would be in the form of fire. The parents were grief- stricken but when he heard the cause of their sorrow, the young boy comforted them and told them to stop lamenting for he would propitiate the Lord and thus avoid the doom that was awaiting him. Taking leave of his parents he proceeded to the famous town of Kasi or Varanasi which is supposed to be Lord Shiva's favourite resort. There he bathed in the famous Manikaran ghat and worshipped the *linga* of the Lord for one full year. The time foretold by Narada came. Indra, the king of the gods approached him and told him to ask for any boon. The boy refused and said that he would ask for boons only from Lord Shiva. Indra became furious and raised his thunderbolt in order to make an end of the impudent boy.

The boy raised his arms in supplication to Lord Shiva and begged him to save him. Shiva appeared before him and said, "O child, don't be afraid. It was I who appeared before you in the form of Indra in order to test you. No one can molest my devotee— not Indra or his thunderbolt or even death. I shall now give you the name of Agniswara. You will be made the guardian of the quarter of the Southeast. One who is devoted to you will never have fear of fire or lightning or premature death." Fire is said to be another form of Shiva. It is the third eye of the Lord.

ॐ *Namashivaya*

ॐ

Kripaanidaye Namaha!

CHAPTER XXII

THE MANIFESTATIONS OF SHIVA

"O Heart of mine! Meditate on the immaculate one,
With upstanding golden locks,
The consort of Devi,
Daughter of the cloud-capped mountain,
O heart of mine! Meditate on Him."

Saint Appar

Normally one does not associate Shiva with incarnations but it is a fact that he has taken many manifestations at the behest of his devotees. We shall now try to describe a few of them. One of the incarnations of Lord Vishnu was the man-lion, Narasimha. After he had killed the demon Hiranyakashipu, it is said that his fury did not abate and the entire world trembled with fear at the fire of destruction that was emanating from the Narasimha's mouth. The gods approached Shiva and begged him to intervene. So Shiva took on the fierce form called Sharabha. He looked like a gigantic bird with an enormous, curved beak and huge wings. His fangs jutted out and his neck was black. He had powerful arms and four legs and adamantine claws. His three eyes were wide and blazing like the fires of destruction at the end of the world. Like a vulture seizing a serpent, the creature caught hold of the Narasimha in its claws and killed him. Then all the gods eulogised him.

Shiva assumed his own form and said, "Just as there is no change in constitution when milk is poured into milk or water into water or ghee into ghee, so also Vishnu and I are one and it makes no difference whether I kill him or he kills me. In actual fact we are both immortals and neither of us can be killed. It is only our *lila*. Like actors who don different costumes to amuse the spectators, we play different roles for the sake of our devotees."

ॐ ॐ ॐ ॐ ॐ ॐ ॐ ॐ ॐ

Once there was a sage named Shilada. He did *tapasya* to Indra to be blessed with a son. When Indra appeared, Shilada asked for the boon of a son who would be immortal. Indra said it was impossible for him to grant immortality. The only person, who could grant him such a boon, was Shiva. So Shilada started to meditate on Shiva. After many years when his body was reduced to a mere skeleton, Shiva appeared and told him that he himself would be born as his son. Shilada now started a *yajna*. At the end of it, a child emerged from the fire. He had three eyes and four arms and held a trident and mace. He wore armour made out of diamonds. The gods showered flowers on this new incarnation of Shiva. Since the child had brought joy to everyone, he was named Nandi, which is the short form for *ananda* or joy. However, as soon as the child was taken to Shilada's hermitage, his divine appearance vanished and he became an ordinary human child. He also appeared to have forgotten his divine origin. Though Shilada was disappointed, he controlled himself and concentrated on giving the child a good education.

One day the two gods, Mitra and Varuna appeared in the hermitage. They looked carefully at the boy and told the father that though he appeared to have all auspicious signs, yet the fact was that he would not live beyond the age of eight years. Shilada was naturally most upset at this bit of news and started to weep. When Nandi heard the reason for his father's grief, he prayed to Shiva. The Lord appeared and told Shilada not to cry, for the child was immortal. He promised to keep the child with him always. Shiva took off his necklace and put it round the child's neck. Immediately Nandi resumed his divine form and Parvati adopted him as her own child. He was elected as one of the *ganapatis* or the leaders of the *ganas* of Shiva. Thus you find that Nandi, in the form of a bull, is always seated in front of Shiva.

ॐ ॐ ॐ ॐ ॐ ॐ ॐ ॐ ॐ

Countless are the manifestations which Lord Shiva is said to have taken to test his devotees and bless them. We will only narrate a few here. Once in the village of Nandigrama, in the Mathurai district, there lived a prostitute called Mahananda. She was very beautiful and was a great devotee of Shiva. She was an adept in all the arts, especially the art of love. Despite her nocturnal activities, she still found time to dance and sing for the Lord of her heart, who was Shiva. Out of the bedchamber she would don only simple clothes and wear *rudraksha* beads, which are loved by Shiva and smear ashes on her forehead. She had as pets, a monkey and a cock that she used to decorate with *rudrakshas.* She had taught them to dance when she sang songs to the Lord. Her strange vocation coupled with her devotion to him, intrigued Shiva and he decided to test her. He went to her house in the guise of a merchant, called Vaishyanatha. Wearing a necklace of *rudraksha* beads, he entered the house, chanting the names of Shiva. Mahananda was delighted to receive him, not only because he was a handsome man but also because he seemed to be a devotee of her Lord. As she seated him and paid all honour to him, her eyes were drawn to the beautiful gold bangle on his wrist, studded with gems.

"What a beautiful bangle you have," she said, eyeing it greedily.

The merchant guessed her desire to possess it and said, "You can have it if you want but let me warn you that it is a very valuable bit of jewelry. What price can you pay for it?"

She answered, "I come from a family of harlots. How else can I pay you but with the coin of love?"

"Very well," said the merchant. "How much do you think this is worth?"

She answered, "If you give it to me, I will be your wife for three days and three nights."

The merchant readily agreed and asked her to repeat the oath three times with the sun and the moon as witnesses. She did so and the merchant handed over the bangle to her. He also gave her a *linga* of Shiva covered with scintillating gems and told her to keep it in a very safe place since it was most precious to him. She took the image and kept it devoutly on an altar, in the centre of the stage where she used to dance. The cock and the monkey were kept to guard it. Mahananda and the merchant spent the night together but at midnight they were woken by the crowing of the cock and the crying of the monkey. A big fire was blazing across the stage and the whole place was consumed, along with the image.

The merchant was bereft when he saw this and bewailed his loss. "I have no desire to live after having lost my precious idol," he said, "Prepare a pyre for me immediately and I shall jump into it and end my useless life."

Though Mahananda cried and pleaded, the merchant was adamant and going round the fire thrice, he took a flying leap into the flames. The woman was desperate when she saw this. Though she was only a prostitute she was a great devotee of Shiva and she had given her word to the merchant to be his wife for three days and three nights and now she could no longer keep her faith.

"Greedy for a mere jewel, I had taken an oath that I would be his wife for three days and three nights. Now that he is dead I can no longer keep my word. My only recourse is to keep to the vow of a chaste wife and enter into the flames with him."

Despite the pleas of her relatives, she was firm in her resolve and prepared to jump into the fire after her husband. Fixing her mind on the feet of her Lord, Shiva, she took a step back in order to jump. Just then Shiva appeared before her, in all his glory and stopped her.

Catching hold of her hands he consoled her, "It was I who came to you in the form of a merchant in order to test your piety, courage and devotion to me. It was I who produced the burning fire that consumed your stage and the *linga.* You have passed your test admirably. Now you can ask for any boon you wish."

The prostitute was overwhelmed by the Lord's grace and said, "I have no desire for the pleasures of this earth or the heavens or any where else. All I desire is the touch of your lotus feet. My servants, maids and relatives are all your devotees. Please take them along with me to your holy abode and take away from us the terrible fear of repeated births." Hearing this the Lord was very happy and took her along with her kinsmen to his abode.

This story shows us how the Lord is more aware of our intentions than our actions. The woman was a prostitute by birth. To her, prostitution was a job like any other job but her private life was dedicated entirely to the Lord. She had no choice, where her work was concerned, but her heart was always fixed on Shiva. The Lord who sees into our hearts judges us, not by our external show but only by our internal purity.

ॐ ॐ ॐ ॐ ॐ ॐ ॐ ॐ ॐ

Another delightful manifestation of Lord Shiva is Kirata, the hunter. The Pandavas and Arjuna in particular, were all devotees of Shiva. Their cousins, the Kauravas, exiled them to the forest. At that time Lord Krishna came to them and advised Arjuna to make the best use of his time in the forest by placating Lord Shiva and asking for his powerful missile, the *Pasupata.* With this weapon Arjuna would be able to defeat the Kauravas in the battle which Krishna knew to be inevitable.

Thus advised by Krishna, Arjuna went to the mountain called Indrakila, in the Himalayas, near the place called Badrikashrama. While he was meditating with closed eyes and matted locks and subsisting only on leaves and berries, his wicked cousin Duryodana instigated a demon called Muka, to go and molest Arjuna and distract him from his *tapasya.* Muka took the form of a wild boar and charged into the forest. But Lord Shiva never forsakes his devotees. Taking the form of a hunter or Kirata, he went into the forest and chased the boar. Parvati accompanied him in the form of a huntress or Kirati. Hearing the tremendous sounds made by the boar and the hunter, Arjuna opened his eyes and saw the boar rushing into the clearing where he was sitting. Immediately Arjuna strung his bow and shot the beast as it charged towards him. He was seated before a mud *linga* of Shiva that he had made for his worship. At the same moment, the Kirata also shot the boar. Both arrows found their mark simultaneously. Arjuna went forward to retrieve his arrow. At the same time Shiva in the form of the Kirata, strode out of the thickets into the clearing. Shiva always enjoyed teasing his devotees and Arjuna was especially beloved by him. In an angry voice Shiva said, "Halt! Don't touch the beast. It's mine. Shot by my arrow."

Arjuna was quite indignant when he heard this and retorted scornfully, "Do you know who I am? I am Arjuna the famous archer. How can you, a mere forest dweller ever hope to equal my prowess in archery? Of course, it was my arrow that shot the boar."

The heated verbal argument soon led to a fight and they decided to test their prowess with bows. A dreadful battle ensued between the Lord and Arjuna in which Shiva mentally applauded his devotee's dexterity. But despite all his skill Arjuna was no match for the divine archer. Arjuna was amazed that a low-born tribal could beat him in archery. He did not know what to do and asked for a short respite. This was granted and Arjuna quickly made a garland of wild flowers and adorned the neck of the *linga* which he had been worshipping faithfully for many months and begged Lord Shiva to save him. Fortified with renewed hope and courage, he turned round to face his opponent and was astonished to see the garland that he had just placed round the *linga*, adorning the neck of the fake hunter! It was only then that Arjuna understood that it was all the Lord's play and ran forward to prostrate at the divine hunter's feet and beg pardon for the great offence he had done in daring to fight with him. Shiva now revealed his true form with Parvati by his side and the *ganas* frisking around. Arjuna prostrated again and again and begged Shiva to forgive him.

Shiva laughingly declared, "It was a great experience to fight with you. I'm proud of your prowess. You may now ask me for any boon you wish."

Arjuna was so ashamed that he did not dare to ask for the weapon for which he had been doing *tapasya*. "All I want is to have devotion to your holy feet all my life," he said. Shiva who could see into his heart insisted that he could ask for anything he wished and it would be granted to him. At last Arjuna asked for Shiva's weapon, the *Pasupata*.

Lord Shiva spoke, "I shall certainly present you with my own missile, the powerful *Pasupata* by which you will become invincible. You will be able to defeat your enemies and regain your kingdom." After having thus blessed Arjuna, the Lord returned to his own abode and Arjuna rejoined his brothers and Draupadi in the forest.

ॐ ॐ ॐ ॐ ॐ ॐ ॐ ॐ ॐ

The beautiful temple of Kanyakumari is situated at the southernmost tip of the Indian subcontinent. It is dedicated to the virgin goddess and has a beautiful story connected with it. At the request of the gods, Parvati the consort of Shiva was once forced to take birth on earth in order to kill some demons. Her name in her earthly form was Punyakshi and she was naturally, a great devotee of Lord Shiva. She longed with all her heart to marry him. However, the gods did not want her to marry, since only a virgin had the power to kill the demons. She begged Shiva to intercede with the gods on her behalf and come and take her as his bride. Ever ready to comply with the wishes of his devotee, Shiva asked the gods to allow him to marry her. The gods could not refuse the request but they thought of a trick by which they could stop the wedding.

"Anyone who marries her will have to pay the bride price," they said.

"What is this price?" asked Lord Shiva.

"The bride price is a sugar-cane stem without rings, a betel leaf without veins and a coconut without eyes," they said.

Shiva laughed at their tricks and conjured up these gifts in a trice. "Now you can fix the time for the wedding," he told the astonished gods.

They were determined to thwart him somehow so they said, "You will have to marry her before the cock crows tomorrow or else you will have to wait till the end of this age." This was quite a challenge since Punyakshi lived at the very tip of the Indian peninsula and Shiva at the very top, in Kailasa. Shiva agreed and set out immediately for the South. Just before he reached Kanyakumari, he heard the cock crow. The gods had duped him by making the cock crow at midnight. Thinking it to be dawn, Shiva decided that there was no point in proceeding further since he would not be able to reach his bride before the appointed time. He broke his journey and decided to stay in the form of a *linga* in the town called Suchindram close to Kanyakumari. There he remains waiting for the end of this epoch in order to keep his promise to his beloved Punyakshi.

Punyakshi was told of the time of the nuptials and she decked herself out in all her bridal finery and waited for the Lord to appear. The guests arrived and even the food had been prepared, for the feast that would follow the wedding. Unfortunately, Shiva was unable to keep his promise since the gods had seen to it that he was obstructed on the way. The cock crowed as the sun rose and there was no bridegroom.

Punyakshi was terribly disappointed. She burst into tears and kicked the pots of food into the sand and threw away her ornaments.

The demons teased her and said, "Why don't you marry us instead!" She was so furious that she picked up a sickle and threw it at them and killed the whole lot of them, much to the delight of the gods who had gleefully planned the whole coup. Punyakshi took up her abode at the very tip of the subcontinent of India and came to be known as the virgin goddess — Kanyakumari. There she waits to this day for Shiva, her betrothed. The gods promised her that at the end of this cycle of cosmic evolution, she would be united with her Lord. The food that she had overturned mixed with the sand and even today we find sand of many different types of colours and shapes on the beach of Kanyakumari.

ॐ ॐ ॐ ॐ ॐ ॐ ॐ ॐ ॐ

Meenakshi was the princess of the ancient Tamil kingdom of Madurai. She was born with three breasts. The astrologers foretold that she would lose her middle breast only when she came face to face with the man who would marry her. It seemed most improbable that Meenakshi would marry at all since she had a very masculine temperament and preferred to learn the art of warfare than the accomplishments of a princess. She became the general of her father's army. She lead them north, south, east and west to all four corners of the country, conquering the whole land right up to the Himalayas and overcoming all the intrepid kings who dared to oppose her.

While in the Himalayas she heard of a hermit who was very powerful and who refused to bow to the dictates of the kshatriyas. No king had been able to vanquish him so far. She was determined that she would be the one to do so. She charged ahead of the rest of the brigade but was suddenly accosted by a handsome hermit who blocked her path. She ordered the man to move out of her way. He merely smiled and refused to budge. Infuriated by his behaviour, she jumped off her horse and ran towards him with upraised sword. He laughed in her face and did not flicker an eyelid. As she raised her indignant eyes to glare at this upstart, she was startled into immobility. Her third breast dropped of its own accord and she felt as if she was melting in the penetrating gaze of the ascetic. Her upraised arm came down and the sword dropped to the ground. She bent low at the feet of the handsome hermit who was none other than Lord Shiva. She herself was Parvati, who had taken on the form of Meenakshi in order to play out the divine *lila.* The gods rained flowers on the couple and the wedding of Sundareswara, as this manifestation of Shiva was called, and Meenakshi was presided over by Vishnu himself. To this day the divine couple is worshipped in the temple of Meenakshi in Madurai in Tamil Nadu.

ॐ ॐ ॐ ॐ ॐ ॐ ॐ ॐ ॐ

There was a time when the sages who lived in the forests and practised severe austerities became filled with ego and thus fell from their high code of conduct. To teach them a lesson Shiva took on the form of a handsome young hermit, which apparently was a role, he loved and went into the forest. When they saw him, the sages and their wives ran after him and begged him to stay with them, promising to change their ways and do whatever he wished them to do. Shiva laughed contemptuously at their request. They were furious at the lack of respect shown to them by the young hermit and with their magic powers they created a tiger, a serpent and a goblin and set them on the young man. Shiva killed the tiger and took the skin for his garment, twined the serpent round his neck and jumped on the goblin's back and started to dance. It was a macabre dance, shaking the very foundations of the earth. His flying locks crashed into the heavenly bodies, his footstep split the mountains and his arms whirled amongst the stars. The gods descended from the heavens and the demons abandoned the nether regions in order to watch this awe-inspiring dance. As the dance went on and on to the accompaniment of celestial music, the sages realised that what Shiva had done was to flay the tiger of their ambition, tame the serpent of their passion and crush the goblin of their ego. His wild dance was the very essence of life, the cosmic cycle of creation, organisation and destruction. It was the mad dervish dance of the protons, neutrons and all the energy particles that make up this world of matter, throbbing with energy. He was the creator, the preserver and the destroyer. In his right hand he held the rattle-drum which produces the sound which emanates from the throat at the point of death and also the reverberation at the onset of birth. In his left hand he held the fire that burns and destroys, yet illuminates and cooks the food which supports life. Around him, revolved the huge wheel of time, the wheel of *samsara*, the roundabout of infinite births and deaths. The gods and sages and other celestial beings watched spellbound at this awesome spectacle of the Lord as Nataraja, the cosmic dancer. It was this dance which inspired the great treatise on Natyashastra or the science of dance, by the sage Bharata. This event is immortalised in bronze, in the awe-inspiring figure of Shiva as Nataraja, in the temple of Chidambaram in South India.

ॐ *Namashivaya*

ॐ

Bhaktavalsalaya Namaha

CHAPTER XXIII

SHIVA — THE BELOVED

ॐ ॐ ॐ ॐ ॐ ॐ ॐ ॐ ॐ

"I am not the intellect, mind, ego or perception,
I am not the sense of hearing, taste, smell or sight,
I am not the sky, earth, fire or air,
I am the essence of consciousness and bliss — *Shivoham! Shivoham!*"

Nirvanashtakam by Adi Shankaracharya

The tales of Vishnu and Shiva intermingle with each other so that sometimes Vishnu is said to be worshipping Shiva and vice versa. Once it is said that Vishnu promised to worship Shiva with one thousand and eight lotuses. Lotuses are normally used in the worship of Vishnu himself. Vishnu said that he would repeat the thousand and eight names of Shiva and offer one lotus for every name. In order to test Vishnu, Shiva removed one lotus from the bunch so that at the end of the *puja* there was one flower short. Not in the least put out, Vishnu, the lotus-eyed one, plucked out one of his own beautiful eyes and placed it on the *linga.* Shiva was so pleased with this gift of love and sacrifice that he presented the *Sudarshana Chakra* to Lord Vishnu.

Ravana, the demon king was a great devotee of Shiva. Every day he would travel in his aerial car from his island city of Lanka, which lay off the coast of India in the extreme South, to Shiva's abode in Kailasa, which was in the Himalayas, in the extreme North. After a time he got fed up of these daily trips and hit upon a master plan. He decided to bring Shiva, along with his entire entourage to Lanka. The easiest way, thought Ravana, was to uproot the whole mountain of Kailasa and bring it to his own city. He put his hands under the mountain and started to shake it. Parvati was quite annoyed at this outrage and begged Shiva to stop Ravana's impudence. Shiva simply pressed the ground down with his big toe and the mountain crashed on Ravana's hand. Ravana howled with pain and begged Shiva to release him. Shiva refused to listen. It is said that Ravana then composed the famous *Shiva Thandava* hymn that impressed Shiva so much that he released Ravana's hand and allowed him to go with his blessings.

Ravana next designed a musical instrument known as the Rudra veena and presented it to Shiva. The latter offered him a boon. The demon king, true to his nature, immediately asked for Parvati herself!

Shiva laughed and said, "So be it. Go and get her. She is bathing in the lake of Manasarovar." With his usual impish humour, he wanted to know how his wife would deal with this situation.

Ravana rushed to the lake, but Parvati's attendants had already informed her of these odd happenings so she was quite ready for Ravana. She picked up a frog or *manduka* and transformed it into a beautiful female and called her Mandodari. When Ravana arrived he found this fascinating woman sitting on a rock beside the lake. Never having seen Parvati before and having no occasion to doubt Shiva's words, he thought the woman to be Parvati and carried her off to Lanka as his wife.

ॐ ॐ ॐ ॐ ॐ ॐ ॐ ॐ ॐ

Kubera was a great devotee of Shiva. He was actually Ravana's brother. Kubera, Ravana and Vibhishana were the three sons of the sage, Vaisravana. Lanka had originally belonged to Kubera. Ravana defeated him and threw him out of the city and appropriated all Kubera's possessions including his marvellous aerial vehicle called Pushpaka. Kubera roamed about the world, unhappy and forlorn. At last he came to the city of Kasi which is famous for the temple of Shiva and there he meditated on the three-eyed Lord, who appeared before him and gave him many boons. Shiva fell for Kubera in a big way since he was short and misshapen, with only one eye and a big pot-belly. Shiva delighted in helping those whom everybody else shunned. He told Kubera that he could go and live in the city of Alakapuri, which was in the Himalayas, near Kailasa and made him the overlord of the *Yakshas* and *Kinnaras* and the custodian of all the wealth of the nether-world.

Kubera was so fond of Shiva that he wanted to do something for him and thought that he could please him by giving him gifts. Being the guardian of all wealth he wished to present Shiva with a lot of money and jewels. Shiva laughed at the enormity of Kubera's pride in thinking that he could actually please Shiva, the Great Lord of the worlds, with wealth! When Kubera insisted, Shiva told him that if he was so anxious to do something for him, he could feed his son, Ganesha, who was never satisfied with the food he got in Kailasa! Kubera agreed and decided that this was an easy task. The next day Ganesha went to Alakapuri where a huge feast had been specially made for him. Kubera welcomed him with all honours and placed an enormous repast before him consisting of every type of delicacy one could imagine, all prepared in gargantuan quantities. Ganesha polished off all that was put before him and asked for more. A lot more was prepared and served, but that also disappeared in a trice. Kubera was frightened that Ganesha's belly would burst open.

Ganesha guessed what was passing through his mind and pointed to the snake that was encircling his stomach and said, "Look at this snake. It will ensure that my stomach will not burst so you don't have to worry about that. Please prepare more food since my hunger has not been appeased. You promised my father that you would satisfy my hunger and now you seem to be backing out of your bargain."

This feast went on till Kubera exhausted all his wealth and still Ganesha's appetite could not be appeased. At last he realised his mistake and fell at Ganesha's feet. Kubera begged Ganesha's pardon for having been so presumptuous as to suppose that his wealth was so great that he could buy anything with it, including the gods. Ganesha is known for teaching people to keep their egos in check.

ॐ ॐ ॐ ॐ ॐ ॐ ॐ ॐ ॐ

The demon, Bana, was another great devotee of Lord Shiva. He had thousand hands and he used to please Shiva by playing on a thousand percussion instruments while Shiva danced the *Thandava*. Shiva was pleased with Bana's devotion, which took the form of this unusual accompaniment to his dance and told him to choose a boon. Bana with true demonic guile immediately asked Shiva to be the watchman of his palace!

One day Bana came to Shiva and told him that his thousand arms were itching for a good fight! He could not find anyone in all the worlds who would be able to defeat him!

"The thousand arms which you have given me have become a burden to me. I'm dying to have a good fight with someone but the moment I go near anyone, they run away as soon as they see my arms. Longing for a fight, I have powdered mountains, sent elephants to their quarters and smashed the earth into bits but still I'm dissatisfied. I want a worthy opponent!"

Shiva said, "O Bana! Know that when your flagstaff breaks in two, you will find someone to match your mettle but remember that he will also be the one to extinguish your pride!"

Bana was delighted to hear that he would find someone who would be able to grapple with his thousand arms. He watched his flag-staff daily to see if there was any sign of breakage. He did not pay much attention to the second half of Shiva's prophecy.

Bana had a beautiful daughter called Usha, who fell in love with Lord Krishna's grand-son, Aniruddha. They had a clandestine affair and the prince stayed in her private apartments without the knowledge of anyone except her close friend. However, after some time the news leaked out. When Bana heard this, he was furious and had Aniruddha caught and put into prison. When he heard of his grandson's fate, Krishna marched with the Yadava army to Bana's capital and there ensued a glorious combat between Bana and Krishna in which Bana was helped by Shiva and his *ganas* since Shiva had promised to guard him. Bana's flagstaff came crashing down as soon as Lord Krishna arrived and Bana realised that he would soon meet his match, as foretold by Shiva. After a terrific fight in which Bana's army was completely routed, Krishna had Bana at his sword point. Krishna spared his life but methodically proceeded to chop off all Bana's arms since it appeared that they were directly responsible for his inordinate pride. When only two pairs were left, Shiva intervened and begged Krishna to spare Bana's life and the remainder of his arms since Bana was his devotee.

Lord Krishna said, "O worshipful Lord! Whoever is dear to you is dear to me. I will never kill this *asura.* No doubt I chopped off all his extra arms which were proving a burden to him but I will spare the four which are left and give him the boon that these arms will never age and will retain their adamantine strength till the end of his days."

Bana was delighted when he heard this and was happy to give his daughter Usha to the handsome Yadava prince, Aniruddha.Thus we see that in the *lilas* of Shiva and Vishnu, at times one defeats the other and at other times the roles are reversed, thus enabling them to keep both their devotees happy!

ॐ Namashivaya!

"The Atman is all-pervading and self-revealed. It has no support. The universe of name and form is insignificant and is separate from Me, who am the one Atman, without a second, attributeless and indestructible, even when the whole creations is destroyed. It is of the nature of supreme bliss and purity."

Dasasloki by Adi Shankaracharya

"O Resident of the mountains and giver of all good, Make your arrow peaceful; do not destroy the people of the material world."

Sri Rudri. Yajur Veda

From Food all creatures are produced, as many as on earth are found.
By food they live and food they become when at last they are buried in the earth.
There is another Self than this one consisting of food.
That is the one consisting of vital energy.
There is still another Self than this one consisting of vital energy-
The one consisting of Mind.
Verily there is another Self than this one consisting of Mind-
The one consisting of Consciousness-
The one consisting of Bliss.

Taittiriya Upanishad

ॐ

Haraya Namaha!

CHAPTER XXIV

THE JYOTIRLINGAS

"O Destroyer!
The burning ghat is your playground,
Your companions are monsters,
Besmeared are you with the ashes of funeral pyres,
Your garland is a string of skulls,
Your name and nature seem inauspicious.
Yet, O Giver of Blessings!
Those who meditate on you,
Are supremely auspicious."

Shiva Mahima Stotram

The thirteenth night of the dark half of every lunar month is special to Shiva and is known as Pradosha or Shivaratri. Normally gods are not worshipped in the dark half of the lunar month. The period when the moon is waning is usually considered inauspicious for starting anything. Demons and ghosts move about at this time and only Shiva can control them. As we have seen, Shiva always proved that to the *yogi*, the word inauspicious has no meaning. So on those days when the crescent moon is out, people pray to Shiva to keep off all evil from them. The thirteenth night of the waning phase of the moon, which comes in the month of Phalguna, February/March is known as Mahashivaratri. This was the day when Shiva drank the dreaded *halahala* poison during the churning of the milky ocean. It is said that all the gods kept vigil with him, singing his praises. So on this particular day in the month of Phalguna, when the winter mists are melting into spring, all the devotees of Shiva keep awake, chanting and praying to the great Lord and offering worship to him. Ganga water is poured on the *linga* to cool him from the heat of the poison!

On one such Mahashivaratri day, a tribal who had none of this esoteric knowledge, lost his way in the jungle. Frightened of wild animals, he took shelter on top of a *bel* tree. The leaves of this tree have three segments corresponding to the three eyes of Shiva and they are very special in his worship. To keep himself from falling off the tree, the tribal kept plucking the leaves of the tree and throwing them to the ground. It so happened that there was a *linga* just below this tree so that without his knowledge he worshipped the Lord on that particular night, fasting and keeping awake and offering the leaves of the *bel* tree to the *linga.* In the morning Shiva appeared before him and blessed him. Adoration of Shiva on Mahashivaratri day, even though performed without knowledge, brings its own reward.

This story as given in the Mahabharata about this festival concerns a king called Chitrabhanu who was said to have observed the fast with great enthusiasm. In his previous birth he had been a hunter called Suswara. Once as night fell over the forest the hunter could not return home. He climbed to the top of a *bel* tree and took shelter. Tormented by thirst he started to cry and his tears fell on a *linga* of Shiva, which was beneath the tree. In order to keep awake and not fall off the tree, he started to pluck the leaves of the tree and drop them down. *Bel* leaves are very important in the worship of Shiva and without his knowledge these leaves were falling on top of the *linga.* That night happened to be the night of Mahashivaratri and the hunter had accidentally worshipped the Shiva *linga* throughout the night, fasting and keeping vigil. As a reward for this he was born as the king Chitrabhanu in his next life.

In a dialogue between Shiva and Parvati, the latter asked him which was the ritual that pleased him most.

Shiva replied, "The fourteenth night of the new moon, in the dark fortnight of the month of Phalguna is my favourite day. My devotees who fast on this day and worship me during the four periods of the night with *bel* leaves are most pleasing to me. These leaves are more precious to me that jewels. *Abhisheka* or ritualistic bathing should be done in the four watches of the night. During the first watch, I should be bathed in milk, during the second watch in curd, in the third, in ghee and in the fourth in honey. Next day the devotee should break his fast only after feeding the poor. O Parvati! There is no ritual which pleases me more than this!"

The cosmic primeval condition of the divine before creation is a state appearing like night or darkness. This is Siva's night or Shivaratri and this is the state of Shiva. Therefore he is worshipped during the night and is known to be the representative of *tamas.* This darkness or *tamas* is due to the excess of light and not to the absence of light. When the frequency of light is intensified to a very high level, it is incapable of being seen by human eyes. Some lights are called blinding lights. This is because when we look at such a light, our eyes see only darkness. God is really the light of all lights and thus, it is invisible to the human sight. The owl cannot look at the sun. It can only seek darkness. So the human soul, which has not realized the greatness of God, cannot see the blinding light of god. Shiva, the compassionate one thus takes the form of night and extols us to worship him as darkness in order to train our mystical eyes to develop and see Him in all His splendour! This is the esoteric significance of Mahashivaratri, the night of Shiva..

Worship of the *linga* is one of the most important aspects of devotion to Shiva since it is believed that he is present in the *linga.* The word *linga* actually means a sign or characteristic. The Absolute Brahman is formless and has no attributes; so it has no "*linga*" but since the human being needs some form, which makes it easier for the mind to concentrate, the *linga*, which is a rounded, upright, stone, is used as a symbol of Brahman.

Once Shiva is said to have stood for thousands of years on one foot making himself into an axis for the revolving universe. This figure has no beginning and no end and is the cosmic *linga* of Shiva. The Shiva *linga* is also considered to be the divine phallus, containing within it the seed of the universe. From it all life is created. Together with the *yoni* or seat on which it rests and which corresponds to the female vulva, the *yoni-linga* represents the union of man and woman, Shiva and Shakti, the cosmic Spirit in union with the cosmic Prakriti, which brings everything into existence.

Once it is said that the sage, Brighu went to Kailasa and found Shiva and Parvati lost in love. They did not even notice his presence. The sage cursed Shiva that in future he would be worshipped without form, as a *linga* trapped within a *yoni.*

Another story describes how Shiva, the handsome hermit roamed amongst the *devataru* forests of the Himalayas. Seeing his irresistible body, the wives of the hermits ran after him. The sages cursed Shiva that he would lose his handsome form. Shiva immediately turned into a fiery *jyotirlinga* which threatened to annihilate the entire universe. The sages were terrified and ran to Parvati to save the world. She immediately took the form of a receptacle or *yoni* and captured the *jyotirlinga.* Shiva's fury abated. He asked the sages and their wives to worship the *linga-yoni* and curb their lust and anger. The *yoni* represents the divine mother. It has a utilitarian aspect also. It acts as the base for the *linga* and collects the water, milk, etc. which are poured over the *linga* during *puja.*

There are thousands of *lingas* all over India but some of them have a special importance. The most important of these are called *jyotirlingas* and they are twelve in number. They are : Somnatha, Mallikarjuna, Mahakala, Omkara, Kedara, Bhimshankara, Vishvanatha, Tryambaka, Vaidyanatha, Nagesha, Rameshwara and Ghushnesha. Most of them have sprouted up on their own accord. Others have been installed by human hands.

1. Sommnatha

We have already seen how Chandra or Soma as the moon-god is called, was one of Daksha's sons-in-law. Daksha had cursed him that he would wane away to death and Soma had appealed to Lord Shiva to save him from this curse. The place where Soma prayed to Shiva is known as Somanatha. It is the first of the *jyotirlingas.*

2. Mallikarjuna

We also heard the story of how Shiva's son Kartikeya left Kailasa and decided to go and live on a hill in the Southern regions. Parvati was bereft at the departure of her son and she begged Shiva to take her to her son. Kartikeya refused to have them live on his own hill so Shiva and Parvati took up their residence on the hill of Mallikarjuna, and this is the second *jyotirlinga.*

3. Mahakala

The ancient city of Avanti, modern Ujjain, is situated on the river Kshipra. There were four Brahmins in that city who were great devotees of Shiva. On one of the hills opposite the city there lived a demon called Dhushana. He used to kill all those who practised *Vedic* rites or worshipped Shiva. When he heard of the four Brahmins of Avanti, he went there to kill them. Not a whit put out, the brothers continued praying to the *linga.* Suddenly the *linga* split open with a tremendous sound and Shiva leapt out brandishing the weapons of destruction. His form was that of Mahakala, the great destroyer. Dhushana was burnt to ashes and his men took to their heels. The Brahmins begged Shiva to stay there forever. The Lord agreed and this is the *jyotirlinga* known as Mahakala.

4. Omkareshwera

Once the celestial sage Narada had gone on a visit to the mountain Vindhya. The mountain offered worship to the sage but Narada knew that Vindhya was puffed up with pride and so in his usual bantering fashion, he told Vindhya that the mountain, Sumeru was superior to it. Vindhya decided to become the equal of Sumeru and started doing *tapasya* to Lord Shiva. When Shiva appeared, Vindhya begged him to remain there all the time so that it would be the equal of Sumeru. Shiva agreed and this is the fourth *jyotirlinga*, which is known as Omkara, situated on the banks of the Narmada river.

5. Kedarnatha

There are two stories connected with the fifth *jyotirlinga*, which is known as Kedara, in the Himalayas. One is associated with the Pandavas. At the end of their sojourn on earth, the five Pandava brothers along with Draupadi proceeded to that part of the Himalayas, which is known as Kedarkanda. On their way they found that a wild-looking dog and a noble buffalo had joined their party. Realising the buffalo to be none other than their personal deity, Lord Shiva, the Pandavas chased him. Eventually Shiva allowed himself to be caught. Each of the five brothers caught one part of the animal and to their consternation it came apart into five pieces in their hands. They threw the pieces far and wide and the places where the pieces fell came to be known as the Panch Kedars, which are all very important places in the Himalayas, for the worship of Shiva. The hump of the buffalo fell at the most important of these places and this is the *jyotirlinga* known as Kedara. Unlike other *lingas*, the *linga* at Kedara is in the shape of the hump of a buffalo.

The second story pertaining to Kedara is connected with the dual incarnation of Vishnu, known as Nara-Narayana. These two sages are supposed to be constantly meditating in Kedarkanda in the place called Badarikashrama, which is an important place of pilgrimage for the devotees of Vishnu. After a long time, Shiva appeared to the sages and offered them a boon. They requested that he should always be present as a *linga* on the peak of Kedara.

6. Bhimshankara

During the time of the *avatara* of Vishnu as Rama, he had killed both the demon king Ravana and his brother Kumbakarna. The latter's wife was called Karkati and she had a son called Bhima. After Kumbakarna's death she lived alone with her son on a mountain. Once her son, Bhima wanted to know who his father was and why they were staying on that mountain, in solitude. His mother told him the whole sad story of how his father had been killed by Rama. Bhima swore vengeance on all the devotees of Vishnu. His first target was the king, called Kamarupa who was a great devotee of Vishnu. Bhima attacked the city and destroyed everything and threw the king and his wife into a dungeon. They prayed to Shiva to save them. When he heard this, Bhima rushed to the dungeon with sword upraised to cut off the king's head. At that moment, Shiva jumped out of the *linga* and killed Bhima by the mere utterance of the word "*hum*". This is the sixth *jyotirlinga*, known as Bhimshankara.

7. Visvanatha

The seventh *jyotirlinga* is known as Vishvanatha and is located in the most holy city of Varanasi. Brahma himself is supposed to have performed *tapasya* at this spot. It is said that Varanasi will not be destroyed even at the time of Mahapralaya, when the rest of the world goes into dissolution. Shiva is said to raise the city on the point of his trident and protect it while destruction rages all around. There is another story connected with Varanasi. Once Shiva and Parvati had gone to Brahmaloka. Brahma began reciting hymns through all his five faces in praise of Shiva. But one of the mouths was making mistakes and so Shiva who was a perfectionist where music was concerned, plucked off the head which was making mistakes. But since this was a crime against a Brahmin, Shiva found that he could not shake off the head, which had stuck to his back. It was only when he went to Varanasi that the head fell off. So Shiva decided that he would stay there in the form of a *linga.* This *linga* is called Vishwanatha or the Lord of the Universe. The first humans to worship there were Swayambhu Manu and his wife Shatarupa who were the first couple ever to be created by Brahma.

8. Tryambakeswara

The eighth *jyotirlinga* is known as Tryambakeswara. It is situated on the banks of the Godavari river. This place is associated with the sage Gautama and his wife Ahalya. They prayed to Shiva for a long time. When he appeared, Gautama asked him for a boon. He begged that the Ganga would flow beside his hermitage so that he could bathe in her purifying waters and thus expiate for his sin in having killed a cow by accident. Shiva granted the boon but Ganga insisted that she would go there only if Shiva took up his residence there. Thus Shiva agreed to stay there in the form of a *linga.* Ganga flowed beside him and took the name, Godavari.

9. Vaidyanatha

The ninth *jyotirlinga* is known as Vaidyanatha. Ravana, the king of the *rakshasas* was a great devotee of Lord Shiva. He started practising *tapasya* in the Himalayas. Shiva did not appear, so Ravana came down to the foothills of the Himalayas. He dug a pit and placed a *linga* inside and started doing *tapasya* there. When Shiva refused to appear, Ravana, being a *rakshasa* decided to sacrifice his heads in the fire. He had ten heads. He lit a fire and started throwing his heads one by one into the flames. When the ninth head had been chopped off, Shiva appeared and asked him to choose a boon, since it was pretty obvious that if he sacrificed his last head, there would be no one left to give the boon. Ravana prayed for superhuman strength and for the restoration of his nine heads. Shiva granted this boon for he was Vaidyanatha, the Lord of healers. He also gave him a wonderful *jyotirlinga* and told him to take it straight to Lanka and never to put it on the ground. Ravana started on his journey back to his capital, Lanka, carrying this radiant *linga.* The gods feared that he would become invincible if he took the *linga* to his island. They asked Ganesha to thwart him in his attempt. Ganesha took the form of a young *brahmachari* and appeared before Ravana just as he felt a terrible urge to answer the call of nature. Ravana gave the *linga* to the boy and told him to hold it till he returned. However, Ravana took such a long time that Ganesha put the *linga* down. When Ravana returned he found no trace of the *brahmachari* and try as he might he could not budge the *linga.* It was rooted to the spot and this *linga*, which Ravana installed, is known as Vaidyanatha.

10. Nagesha

The tenth *jyotirlinga* is known as Nagesha. There was once a merchant called Supriya. He was a great devotee of Lord Shiva. He had to travel through a forest, which was owned by a *rakshasi* called Daruka. She kept harassing him all the time. He begged Shiva to help him. Shiva came with his serpents or *nagas* and drove Daruka away. Daruka appealed to Parvati who gave her a dense forest of her own, where she could reside peacefully without troubling anybody. The *linga* worshipped by Supriya is known as Nageshvara, Lord of serpents and Parvati's name here is Nageshwari.

11. Rameswara

The eleventh *jyotirlinga* is in the south of India and is known as Rameshwara. In Lord Vishnu's incarnation as Rama, Ravana, the demon king, had abducted his wife, Sita and taken her to his island fortress off the coast of India, known as Lanka. Rama built a bridge to cross the straits, which separated India from Lanka. But before he crossed, he made a *linga* of Shiva and worshipped it. Shiva appeared and blessed him with all success and Rama requested Shiva to stay there forever. This is the *linga*, on the banks of the ocean, which is known as Rameswara, and it is one of the most famous places of worship in India.

12. Gushnesha

The twelfth and last of the *jyotirlingas* is known as Gushnesha. A very charming story is connected with this *linga.* Once there was a Brahmin called Sudharma. He had a wife called Sudeha. They were very unhappy because they had no children. Sudharma decided to conduct an experiment to find out if they were fated to have a son. He plucked two flowers and mentally associated one with a son. He asked his wife to choose one flower. Unfortunately she chose the other one, so Sudharma concluded that he was indeed not fated to get a son. Sudeha felt very unhappy at this and begged her husband to marry her niece, Ghushna in order to get a son. At his wife's insistence, Sudharma married Ghushna. She was a great devotee of Lord Shiva. In order to get a son she took a vow that she would make a hundred and one *lingas* out of clay every day and worship them. At the end of the daily *puja* she would immerse the *lingas* in the pond nearby. When she completed the worship of one *lakh* of *lingas*, she conceived and gave birth to a lovely baby boy. As expected, the first wife's nature changed as soon as the child was born and she began to be very jealous of Ghushna. One night, she killed the baby and threw the corpse into the pond where the *lingas* had been immersed.

Next morning, Ghushna got up as usual and started to prepare for her daily worship of Shiva. In the meantime her husband found out that the baby had disappeared. But Ghushna was not to be distracted by this and continued with her *puja* of the *linga.* Shiva was impressed by her devotion and restored the baby to her. As Shiva raised his trident in order to kill Sudeha, Ghushna, who had a most forgiving nature, begged him to spare the life of her aunt. Shiva was very pleased by her generous and forgiving nature and offered her a boon. She begged that Shiva would always be present in the *linga* near the pond which she worshipped daily. He granted this boon and this *linga* is known as Ghushnesha.

Devotees of Shiva consider it a rare good fortune to be able to make a pilgrimage to all these twelve *jyotirlingas.*

Lord Shiva is called Bhuteswara or the Lord of the elements. There are five temples to Shiva, in Tamil Nadu, South India, which correspond to these five elements. The five elements are *akasha* or ether, *vayu* or air, *tejas* or fire, *apas* or water and *prithvi* or earth. The *akasha-linga* is found in Chidambaram, the *vayu-linga* at Sri Kalahasti, the *tejo-linga* at Arunachalam in Tiruvannamalai, the *ap-linga* at Jambukeshwara in Tiruchirapalli and the *prithvi-linga* at Ekambaranath at Kanchipuram.

ॐ *Namashivaya*

"Prostrations to the one who is the eldest and the youngest. Prostrations to the primordial cause and the subsequent effect. Prostrations to the eternal youth who is also the infant. Prostrations to the one who is in the loins and in the seed. Prostrations to the one who is present in vice and virtue!"

Sri Rudri. Yajur Veda

There are three things which are rare indeed in this world. Birth in the human body, desire for liberation and the care of a perfect master.

Having by some means obtained a human birth and that too a male body, and mastery over the Vedas, the foolish person who does not strive for liberation verily commits suicide. He kills himself by clinging to things that are unreal.

Kathopanishad

ॐ

Sookshmathanaye Namaha!

PART – II

"The Perennial Philosophy is primarily concerned with the one divine Reality substantial to the manifold world of things, lives and minds. But the nature of this one Reality is such that it cannot be the directly and immediately apprehended except by those who have chosen to fulfill certain conditions, making themselves loving, pure in heart and pure in spirit.... But in every age there have been some men and women who chose to fulfill the conditions upon which alone, as a matter of brute empirical fact, such immediate knowledge can be had. And of these a few have left accounts of the reality they were thus enable to apprehend and have tried to relate in one comprehensive system of thought, the given facts of this experience with the given facts of their other experiences."

By Aldous Huxley

The devotees of Shiva who are described here belong to this class of beings.

ॐ

Jagatgurave Namaha!

CHAPTER XXV

DEVOTEES OF SHIVA

"O mouth of mine, note that you praise the Lord,
Who, donning the hide of the rutting elephant,
Dances in the cremation ground,
Where dwell the ghouls.
O mouth of mine, note that you praise Him!"

Saint Appar

No story of Shiva can be complete without mention of the great Shaivite devotees of Southern India who were known as Nayanmars. References to Shiva and his worship are extant even in the earliest Tamil literature, but the theology was systemised only in the late 13th century by Meykanda *Deva* in his *Shiva-jnana-bodham* which became the basic text of the Shaive Siddhanta philosophy which considers Shiva to be the supreme deity. The golden age of Shaivism dawned at the time of the sixty-three canonical saints, called the Nayanmars or Adiyars. They pointed out to people the perfect way of devotion to Shiva, the supreme Lord. The Periya Puranam of Sekkizhaar is a literary masterpiece dealing with the lives, deeds and sayings of these devotees of Lord Shiva. It was composed in the 11th century AD.

In the spiritual history of the world, it would be difficult to find such matchless devotion to God as evinced by these sixty-three saints. Since we cannot deal with all of them we will touch upon the lives of some of the greatest of them. Of these, four are without parallel. They are popularly known as Appar, Sambandar, Sundarar and Manikkavachakar. Three of them were really child saints but within the short period of time allocated to them, they performed miracles of piety. Sambandar died at the age of sixteen, Sundarar, when he was eighteen and Appar when he was past eighty. But these facts mean nothing. All of them were infinities scooped out of infinity and their names are hallowed for all eternity.

Though these four belonged to the Brahmin caste, many of the Nayanmars did not belong to the upper castes. They hailed from various castes and communities, rich and poor, high and low. One was a hunter who killed a boar and roasted the carcass and not only ate it, but also offered it as a fitting food for Shiva, the Lord of his heart. Another was a fisherman. A third was an untouchable who belonged to a community whose staple diet was the flesh of dead cows. None of them had the type of life one would expect a saint to have. Most of them had no learning or pedigree. All they had in common was an uncommon love of God. The life of any of these saints is an example to us how devotion to the Supreme alone can emancipate the human being from the coils of *karma*. By the purity of their love and the childlike innocence of their faith and their firm will to attain the object of their devotion, they were able to bind the boundless one, like the *gopis* of Vrindavana did to Lord Krishna. How we understand the stories of these saints would depend on the mentality of the reader. If perused with faith and devotion, these stories will help to elevate our own lives to a high degree.

In the history of the human race we find that along with the biological evolution of mankind, there occurs simultaneously a cultural and spiritual evolution. This takes place mainly by imbibing the ideas, codes and conduct of the saints. India has produced many such great souls who have helped to keep up the eternal verities of the Sanatana Dharma or the eternal religion of the Hindus. The Nayanmars belong to this category. They understood the true nature of the world and of God and had opted for God alone. Their devotion did not stem from ignorance and fear of the unknown but from the wisdom of those with inner sight who are established unshakeably in the Truth. Love of God completely removes attachment to the body. It also cuts at the root of our attachment to the world. These saints were ready to sacrifice everything including their own bodies and those of their dear ones, if they stood as an impediment to the worship of their beloved deity, Shiva. Some of the astonishing incidents described in the lives of these saints may be difficult for the modern mind to swallow. However, those whose hearts have not been clogged with materialism, will be able to understand that in the realm of God-love, there can be no second to the divine and miracles become commonplace, since God alone pulls the strings of our lives. All problems melt in the burning fire of His grace. These saints of Tamil Nadu never asked God for a favour, not even for liberation. All they prayed was to be admitted into the galaxy of devotees.

One of Sundarar's songs begins with these words, "I am the servant of the servants of the servants of the Lord of Thillai (Shiva)." The devotee is considered as even superior to the Lord. This interesting fact is brought out in many stories even in the Sreemad Bhagavad Mahapuranam. This is because the true devotee is one who has been able to subjugate the divine through the intense power of his devotion. It is easier for us to worship such a devotee and get his blessings so that we may also accomplish the same feat.

All the sixty-three saints of the Periya Puranam were ascetics but not of the usual order. What these saints renounced was not their kith and kin, or their villages and houses or their occupations. What they gave up was anger, theft, violence, pride, hurting others, attachment and desire. What they donned was not the external clothing of the ochre robe but the internal habit of non-violence, endurance, truth, and austerity. Externally they seemed to be no different to their neighbours but in their hearts they were ascetics. According to the popular notion of how saints should act, none of them appeared to have done anything spectacular that would have qualified them to gain *mukti* or liberation. But the fact is that all of them did gain it. The trap that every one of these saints laid for God, was the trap of love. Maybe this type of love is not developed in a day or even in a lifetime. It may need lifetimes before one can develop the type of love, which makes a prisoner of God in one's heart.

Manikkavachakar sang, "Behold God who falls into the net called Love."

Though this type of love or *bhakti* as it is called, might be difficult to achieve yet it is the one thing which all human beings can acquire without exception of sex, caste, creed, language, nationality, profession, poverty or wealth. No externalities can stand in the way of a human being acquiring this one qualification, by which one can imprison the divinity in one's own heart. It is a love without reservations — a total love, a love that does not try to possess, or be possessed. It is a love, which alone is worthy of merging in the very source of love, which is God. The separate entity called the individual disappears and what is left is God and God alone —"*Shivoham, Shivoham*" — I am Shiva, I am Shiva. The devotee melts into the arms of the divine beloved and nothing is left of the separate ego. The message of all these saints was simple — "Give up all attachments and love God alone, serve Him in all humanity and liberation is yours!"

Shiva himself is supposed to have said this about his devotees, "Shortcomings they have, none!"

Let us find out how this love or *bhakti* was evinced by the different saints. Did they follow the same standard or was there any difference in their devotion? Seven of them followed the accepted mode of conduct and sang their way to liberation. Nine persisted in their worship despite the difficulties of old age and poverty. Seventeen performed righteous acts of violence. They gave up their lives rather than their worship. One gouged out his own eye and placed it on the eye of an idol of Shiva, which was bleeding profusely. Another was prepared to sacrifice his only son to Shiva who came in the guise of a devotee. One used his elbow in place of a piece of sandalwood and rubbed it on a stone and used it in the worship of the Lord. Another flung a stone instead of a flower at a *linga* of Shiva daily, on his way to take his food. One rewarded a thief for stealing rice from the public granary in order to feed the devotees of the Lord. One kept prostrating at the feet of a washerman, whose body was covered with earth and reminded him of the body of Lord Shiva, covered with ashes. Some chanted the *rudri* — the garland of hymns to Shiva. Some chanted the five-syllabled *mantra* of Shiva constantly. Some took the vow of feeding the devotees of Lord Shiva through days of plenty and poverty before partaking of any food themselves. Thus we see that the criteria for *mukti* ranged from the sublime to the ridiculous and from the heroic to the mundane. The truth that emerges from this is that the Lord does not look into the act, but the love behind the act. Lord Krishna accepted the sweat-soaked bundle of rice flakes from his poverty-stricken friend, Kuchela and showered him with all the riches of Dwaraka. So also Lord Shiva did not notice how ridiculous some of the acts of his devotees were, but looked into their hearts and found the love overflowing therein.

ॐ *Namashivaya*

"Prostrations to the one who is present in death and liberation. Prostrations to the one who is present in the green fields and the barnyards. Prostrations to the one who is present in the Vedic mantras *and the* Upanishads. *Prostrations to the one, present in trees and creepers. Prostrations to the one who is both sound and echo!"*

Sri Rudri. Yajur Veda

"Prostrations to the one, present in marshes and ponds. Prostrations to the one, present in rivers and lakes. Prostrations to the one, present in wells and pits. Prostrations to the one, present in rains and drought. Prostrations to the one, present in thunder and lightning."

Sri Rudri. Yajur Veda

ॐ

Devaya Namaha!

CHAPTER XXVI

THE GREAT FOUR

"He grabbed me lest I go astray,
Wax before an unspent fire,
Mind melted, body trembled,
I bowed, I wept, I cried out loud,
I danced and praised Him."

Saint Manikkavachagar

The four great saints or Nayanmars whose lives are given below are known in Tamil literature as the "Fathers of the Faith." Each of them followed a different path in their approach to God. They are popularly known as Sundarar, Appar, Sambandar and Manikkavachagar. Sundarar followed the *sakhya-marga* or the path of friendship. Appar followed the *dasa-marga* or the path of the servant. Sambandar followed the *satputra-marga* or the role of a son and Manikkavachagar followed the *jnana-marga* or the path of knowledge.

THE FRIEND OF SHIVA

Sundaramurthi Nayanar lived in the 8th century. His life shows us how one can lead a householder's life and still be an ardent devotee of God. It also shows us that the Lord is deeply interested in all our problems. There is nothing in our lives, which God considers small or petty. We are the ones who fail to approach him for what we consider as petty, household problems. This is the great lesson that we learn from the life of Sundarar—that he did not hesitate to involve the Lord in every single incident of his life, even in his love affairs! He lived for only eighteen years but in that short span of life, he composed some of the most beautiful songs on Lord Shiva, known as Thevarams. Shiva loved his songs so much that he constantly tested him, and made him sing before he allowed him to pass the test.

In his previous life, Sundarar had been a servitor of Lord Shiva and had lived beside him in Mount Kailasa. It was his duty to offer the Lord the sacred ashes to anoint his body, as well as a garland of honey-laden flowers. One day it so happened that as he was plucking flowers in Parvati's garden, he fell in love with her two maids called Kamalini and Aninditi. Knowing his desire, Lord Shiva told him to incarnate himself in the world along with the girls and thus fulfil his wishes.

"You have set your mind on these damsels, therefore you will be born with them in the Southern region. After consorting with them in the pleasures of love, you may come back to me." These were the words of the Lord.

Another reason why Sundarar had to take a human birth was that he had not totally exhausted all the bonds of his *karma.* In the theology of the Sanatana Dharma, God's grace does not take the form of absolution of all sins, even for the greatest devotee. If that were the case there would be an end to the game of life. Life is a game in which the *jivatma* for some reason thinks itself to be separate from the *Paramatma* and has to find its way back to its original status. The *Paramatma* is our unseen companion, constantly encouraging us. The Lord stands beside the devotee and illumines him about the working of the Law of *karma* and strengthens his will to surrender totally to the will of God, thereby eradicating the desire for the fruits of *karma* and severing the link from the chain of births and deaths. The other reason for Sundarar's apparent downfall was that the Lord wished him to compose his divine music, which would be an inspiration for all those in the world. He was thus born on earth in a noble Brahmin family.

The king of the land saw the beautiful child and adopted him. At the age of fourteen he wanted to get him married. But to the great consternation of all concerned, an old Brahmin with ashes on his body and a garland of *rudraksha* beads round his neck, stormed into the wedding hall and declared that the boy was his bonded slave and had no right to marry without his permission. He took Sundarar to his own town and before an assembly of elders, he produced a document, which proved that the boy was indeed his slave. After thus establishing his rights over the boy, the Brahmin entered the temple of Shiva and vanished. Sundarar realised that this was none other than the Lord himself. Later the Lord appeared to him in his dream and told him to compose songs about him. From that day on, Sundarar wandered all over the place, from temple to temple singing the praises of the Lord. At the temple of Tiruvavur, a heavenly voice told him, "Sundarar I have made you my friend. From now on you will be a bridegroom for the rest of your days on earth."

Parvati's attendant, Kamalini with whom Sundarar had fallen in love, had been born as a beautiful woman called Paravayar. They met at the temple of Tiruvavur and fell in love with each other. Then Lord Shiva, who had once broken up Sundarar's marriage, now became his marriage broker and arranged for them to be wedded the very next day after the two lovers had met.

Once when their town was afflicted by famine, Sundarar begged the Lord to appease the hunger of the people and miraculously heaps of grain were found in the village. Paravayar was in the habit of distributing money to the poor on the festival of Holi. She requested her husband to give her the necessary funds. Without hesitation, Sundarar went to the temple of Shiva and asked him for gold! In the morning when he woke up he found that the bricks on which he had rested his head during the night, had turned into gold. So Paravayar was able to distribute as much gold as she desired.

At another time when he was travelling, Sundarar once again requested the Lord for more gold to feed the needy. The Lord gave him a heap of gold coins. Sundarar did not know how to transport it to Tiruvarur. So Shiva told him to throw the lot into the lake and collect it when he returned to Tiruvarur. Sundarar kept one piece back for identification. When he returned to his hometown he dived into the lake and found the coins but they were inferior in value to that which had been given to him. This was another trick of Shiva's to encourage Sundarar to sing. Again Sundarar composed another of his divine songs and the Lord changed the gold to its original value!

The other girl, Aninditi, whom Sundarar had loved in Kailasa, had been born as a great devotee of Lord Shiva. She was called Sangiliyar.

She refused to marry the man of her father's choice and took up her residence in an *ashrama*. She used to make garlands daily and take it to the Lord in the nearby temple. Once when she went to the temple, Sundarar saw her and due to his past association, he fell in love with her. With the familiarity of an intimate relationship, he asked Lord Shiva to solve his problem, since he had heard that Sangiliyar was a celibate. Shiva spoke to Sangiliyar in a dream and told her to marry Sundarar. She was willing but when she knew that Sundarar w*as* already married she made him promise not to desert her under any circumstance. Lord Shiva told her to make him take this oath under a nearby tree and not in the temple. Sundarar did as told and they got married. When spring came, Sundarar remembered his first wife and how she would be singing and dancing before the Lord in the temple of Tiruvarur. He was filled with a desire to see her again. For a long time he desisted, remembering his promise to Sangiliyar, but at last he could not help himself and left without a word to Sangiliyar. Just as he crossed the border of the town, he lost his eyesight and fell to the ground. Sundarar realised that the Lord was teaching him a lesson since he had broken his promise to his wife. He burst into song and with his devotional fervour unabated, he went from temple to temple, begging the Lord to restore his eyesight. He knew the Lord had tricked him into making the promise outside the temple near the tree and with the intimacy born out of close friendship, he pestered the Lord to forgive him and give him back his eyesight. At the temple of Kamakshi, the goddess of the beautiful eyes, in Kanchipuram, Parvati who knew his distress restored the sight of one eye. He was delighted and composed many songs to her. Before he reached Tiruvarur, he begged the Lord once more to restore his vision. Shiva asked him to go and bathe in the temple tank. When he came out, he was the colour of gold.

He was not satisfied with this and begged the Lord to give him both eyes so that he could feast them once more on the vision of the Lord in the temple. At last Shiva relented and gave him back his eyesight.

In the meantime Paravayar had heard of Sundarar's bigamous behaviour and refused to let him into her house. Once again Sundarar approached his one and only friend, Shiva, to help him in this new predicament. Shiva went as a Brahmin to Paravayar's house and pleaded

Sundarar's case. At first she refused since she did not recognise him but when Shiva showed her, his real form, she fell at his feet and happily agreed to take Sundarar back. Thus the two were reunited.

Many stories are there about how the Lord saved Sundarar from every predicament and gave him everything he asked for. But each time before granting his desire, Shiva would ask him to sing for him. It is said that on three occasions, Lord Shiva himself suggested the first line for his song. Once when Sundarar was struggling with the first line, Shiva prompted him, "O Thou who are difficult of being experienced in the mind and of being expressed in words!"

On the second occasion when Sundarar could not decide on a suitable word to begin his sonnet, Lord Shiva suggested with a smile, "What is the difficulty about this. You once called me Pitthan (madman) when I came to rescue you from the marriage hall, so why not start your stanza with that word!"

The third time the Lord told him to start with the famous words, "I'm the servant of the servants of the servants of the Lord dwelling at Thillai."

Sundarar thus joined the galaxy of the servitors of the Lord and became a *jeevan mukta*, or one who was liberated even while living in the human body.

The Lord treated Sundarar as his friend. This is known as the *sakhya-marga.* The greatness of this path is that the Lord puts up with all the familiarities taken by the devotee. As the great poet Thiruvalluvar writes, "If you ask what intimate friendship is, it is that which does not object to the liberties taken by a friend."

One day, when Sundarar was praying at the temple, the sight of the idol made him crazy with longing to return to Kailasa. He rolled on the ground with sorrow and begged the Lord to take him back to his abode. He sang one of his most plaintive melodies. He was only eighteen at that time. In this short span of time on this earth, he had composed some of the most heartrending songs on the Lord, which are sung even today in all Shiva temples. The Lord was also equally anxious to have him back in Kailasa and he ordered the divine white elephant to go and bring him. His physical body was discarded then and there and those who happened to look at the sky saw Sundarar mounted on the white elephant sailing across the sky to Kailasa. His two wives also shed their mortal coils and returned to their divine abode.

THE SON OF SHIVA

Another Nayanar who wrote a collection of songs on Lord Shiva called Thevaram, is Tiru Jnana Sambandar. He is called the son of God, an *Iswarakoti*, or *avatara.* These are the divine incarnations who can liberate themselves whenever they want. Sambandar's entry into this earth and his departure at a very young age of sixteen and all the miracles he performed in that short span of life, prove that he was indeed an *avatara* — God, descended to earth, in the form of a man. At that time Jainism was becoming popular in Tamil Nadu and Sambandar's parents prayed for a son who would be able to bring the land back to its original *Vedic* beliefs.

Once at the age of three, Sambandar was left on the banks of a lake while his father went for a dip. The child, who was filled with love and desire to see his true father, began to cry piteously as he looked up at the heavens. Lord Shiva sent Parvati to comfort him. She came and fed him from her own breasts. When his earthly father returned, he found the child drooling milk from his mouth and wondered who had fed him. The child of three stood with one foot raised like a statue of Shiva and pointing one finger to the heavens, sang his immortal song, "Behold Him with a ear-plug of a rolled palmyra leaf stuck in His ear!" Obviously he had the beatific vision of Lord Shiva at that time and began his ministry even at that tender age. At an age when most children cannot lisp more than a few words, Sambandar sang this song of eleven stanzas conforming to the rigid rules of Sanskrit grammar, set to an ancient Tamil melody. No doubt this was due to the milk imbibed from the breasts of Parvati, the divine mother of all arts.

Like Sundarar, he also went from temple to temple singing songs in praise of the Lord, which melted the hearts of all who heard him. The Lord is supposed to have presented him with a pair of gold cymbals to keep time.

At his sacred investiture ceremony at the age of seven, well before he had any formal education, he astonished the priests by standing up and reciting all the *Vedas*. He taught the priests that the *panchakshari mantra* of Lord Shiva, "*Namashivaya*" contained all the *Vedas* and that this alone was his source of knowledge.

Since he had so little time to accomplish all that he had come to do, he was carried on his father's shoulder from place to place, from the age of three onwards. At many of the temples he visited, he performed miracles and alleviated the troubles of the devotees. Once the wife of a devotee died of snakebite. It is said that Sambandar revived her with one of his songs. At this time the Jain influence was growing all over Tamil Nadu and in the city of Madurai, even the king had been converted. Only the queen and the chief minister were ardent Shiva *bhaktas*. When she heard of the child-saint, the queen sent the minister and begged him to come to the city. The Jain monks were perturbed at his coming and decided to set fire to his camp, using black magic but they were unable to do so and the fire, which had been sanctioned by the king, traced its path back to him. He was seized with a dreadful burning sensation all over his body. The queen urged him to call Sambandar. The Jain monks came along with the child-saint and challenged him to demonstrate his powers. The king promised to accept Sambandar's faith if he could cure him. The monks told him to cure the right side while they attempted to cure the left. The monks chanted *mantras* and passed peacock feathers over the king's left side but the burning continued unabated. Sambandar sang a song in praise of the sacred ashes of Lord Shiva and smeared the king's right side with ash and immediately the king was free of the disease. He begged him to do the same for his left side and this was done with the same result. The king and his consort fell at his feet. The Jains insisted on more tests. They ordered him to throw the leaves of his song into the fire. Both parties threw their respective palm leaves into the flames and the leaves of the Jains were burnt to cinders. Again they insisted that both sets of leaves should be thrown into the river and that which floated against the current should be considered superior. Sambandar was victorious in this test also and the whole land was converted back to Shaivism.

After undertaking a number of pilgrimages, Sambandar returned to his hometown at the age of sixteen. His father wanted to see him married.

Sambandar agreed and participated with secret amusement in the wedding ceremony. It is to be noted that Sambandar sang of the glory of the *panchakshari mantra* for the first time during his investiture ceremony and for the last time at his wedding ceremony, dressed gorgeously as a bridegroom. As he went round the ceremonial fire with his finger entwined in the little finger of his child bride, the fire grew into effulgence and engulfed him along with his bride. Those who had come to attend the wedding were also taken up into this effulgence and reached the abode of Lord Shiva. In his short span of life he did as much for Shaivism as Adi Shankara did for *Advaita.* Through his thousands of songs, he rekindled in the heart of his people, faith in their religion and their ancient modes of worship.

THE SERVANT OF SHIVA

Saint Appar's role was to be a forerunner to the son of God — Sambandar — just as Kumarila Bhatta was to Adi Shankaracharya and John the Baptist to Christ. His life revolves round the life of Sambandar. He lived at the same time as Sambandar even though the historic meeting between the two of them took place only when Appar was in his fifties and Sambandar but a boy of seven. At that time Jainism had taken a strong hold over the people of Tamil Nadu and Appar decided that he should find out more about the religion so that he could help Sambandar in his mission. He went to Pataliputra and entered the Jain monastery in order to study its precepts. He was branded as a defector from the true faith, but the fact was that Appar was a mystic who knew of the coming of Sambandar and the purpose for which he was coming. He decided that he would have to learn something of Jainism if he wanted to help Sambandar, whom he knew would live only for sixteen years.

For twenty years Appar lived as a Jain monk but when Sambandar was seven years old, Appar knew that the time had come for him to leave the monastery and go to his aid. He was wondering how he could leave the monastery without antagonising the Jains when Shiva came to his aid by giving him a severe colic, which could not be cured by the Jains. He went to his sister who cured him, by using the five-syllabled, *panchakshari mantra* of Shiva.

Appar himself sang thus, "O Lord, who roams about receiving alms in a dry skull, do graciously rid me of the colic which is inside my body."

At this time the king of the region had become a Jain and the Jain monks compelled him to kill, Appar since he had defected from their order. They imprisoned him in a burning kiln of limestone. When they opened the kiln after seven days they found Appar alive and in deep *samadhi*. They attributed it to the *mantras* he had learnt from them and gave him poison. Appar repeated the *panchakshari mantra* and drank the poison as if it was the elixir of life and survived.

Then they put him in the way of a rampaging elephant. Appar faced him with a beautiful verse on Shiva. The elephant bowed before him and turned its fury on the monks. Lastly they tied a granite stone round his neck and flung him into the sea. The stone started to float as Appar began to sing, "He is the Word, He is the saviour, He is the *Veda* incarnate, He is the effulgence...". He ended with the words, "The name of the Lord is nothing but *Namashivaya*."

The amorphous state of the Godhead as represented by the *linga* is *Nada* or sound which is the word — "*Namashivaya*." The stone carried him to the shore and as he walked into the town. His form was brilliant with ashes on his body and *rudraksha* beads round his neck.

However, even the orthodox Shaivites were angry with him for they thought that he was a traitor and boycotted him, so he decided that it was better to leave the town and go and meet Sambandar. At the historic meeting, both the great ones recognised each other. Without a moment's hesitation, they prostrated at the feet of each other since both were aware of the other's greatness. Appar saw in the child, the saviour of Shaivism. He stayed several days with Sambandar.

At their second meeting, a famine was raging in the land and both of them prayed to Shiva to end the suffering of the people. The Lord promised to give them one gold coin daily with which they could buy food for the people. Daily they would find a gold coin at the eastern and western entrances of the temple with which they bought food for the poor. After this, they travelled together for some time, visiting shrines and performing many miracles.

Their third and last meeting was when Sambandar was returning from Madurai after defeating the Jains. Appar saw the procession approaching and with the humility of a true saint, he quietly went and helped to carry the palanquin in which Sambandar was seated. When Sambandar saw him, he jumped out of the palanquin and embraced him with the greatest of love. They stayed together for some time and parted, never to meet again.

It was at the temple of Tiruppunthuruthi that Appar sang his famous song, "O head of mine bow down to the Head of the universe..." in which he commanded every limb of his body to worship Lord Shiva. Once while Appar was digging the temple gardens, Lord Shiva tested him. Gems and gold came up with the dirt. Appar took them with his spade and flung them, along with the dirt, into a lake filled with lotuses. Then heavenly damsels descended on him and tempted him with their alluring charms but he was totally unmoved by them and was intent on his repetition of the five-syllabled *mantra*.

He sang, "Thinker that I am, what should I think of, but of the holy feet of the Lord.... I see nothing but Thy anklet-girt feet.... Here and now O virtuous One, I am coming to Thy feet." So saying, Appar abandoned his body at the age of eighty-one. His motto was humble service and he always carried a hoe with which he used to work in all the temple gardens.

THE KNOWER OF SHIVA

Manikkavachagar was born to Brahmin parents. Even as child he was so bright that the king of the land made him, his Prime Minister. But very soon the youth realised the ephemerality of the world and decided to go and find his *guru*. At that time the cavalry was getting depleted and the king ordered his Prime Minister to go and get horses. Manikkavachagar was delighted since he took this as an opportunity to find his *guru*. When he reached a temple, he found a Brahmin seated beneath a tree holding the book, "*Shiva Jnana Bodham*" — The Knowledge of Shiva. As soon as he saw him, Manikkavachagar realised that this was indeed his *guru*. He ran forward and prostrated at his feet and begged him to accept him as his disciple. The Lord himself had come in the form of a Brahmin in order to initiate Manikkavachagar into the mysteries of the knowledge of Shiva. He immediately surrendered all his wealth to his *guru* and sang a most melodious song to him. This was the garland of jewels he offered to his *guru* and thus Lord Shiva called him Manikkavachagar since his words were like gems. Soon after, the Brahmin vanished and Manikkavachagar realised that this was none other than Lord Shiva. He was filled with sorrow at the disappearance of his *guru* and forgot the mission for which he had come. Moreover, all the money meant for the horses had been surrendered at the feet of the *guru* who had given it for the reconstruction of the temple. He sent word to the king that he would come within a month.

The month went by and the angry king sent another message. Manikkavachagar went and reported the matter to the Lord in the temple. Shiva came in a dream and told him to return to the king and he himself would bring the horses. Manikkavachagar returned and told the king that he had already arranged for the horses and they would be brought to the palace on an auspicious date. In the meantime the other ministers reported to the king all that had actually occurred in the temple and that Manikkavachagar had given the money meant for the horses, to his *guru*. The king was furious and ordered him to be tortured.

Manikkavachagar bore up with the agony patiently for he was sure that the Lord would keep his promise. Seeing his devotee being tormented, Lord Shiva changed all the jackals in the nearby forest into horses and sent his own messengers as riders. He himself took the form of a horse trader and they reached the city of Madurai on an auspicious day, as promised. When the king saw the horses, he felt very sorry for having inflicted this unnecessary punishment on his Prime Minister and apologised profusely.

As soon as he saw the horse trader, Manikkavachagar realised that he was none other than Lord Shiva and prostrated to him. The horses were led to the stables. However, with his usual puckish humour, Shiva decreed that during the night the horses regained their previous forms and fled howling, to the forest.

The king was furious with Manikkavachagar and ordered that he should be caught and tortured once again, since he felt that Manikkavachagar had made a fool of him once again. The saint prayed to the Lord to help him and immediately the river next to the town began to rise. There was panic in the city. The soldiers fled and Manikkavachagar went to the temple and prayed for help. In the meantime the king ordered everyone in the city to go and help in the making of an embankment to stop the floodwaters from rising further. There was an old woman in the town who was unable to carry anything and she prayed to the Lord to help her. Shiva came in the form of a labourer and started to throw mud at the breach with such force that it opened up again. The king who happened to be there at that time was furious when he saw this. Taking a stout stick he beat the man on his head. Everyone in the world, including the king felt this blow. It was only then that the king realised that this was all a play of the Lord. An invisible voice told him to go and beg Manikkavachagar's pardon for all the injustice done to him. The king ran to the saint and apologised profusely and begged him to accept the rulership of the country. Manikkavachagar refused and took leave of the king once and for all. He had had enough of politics and realised that he had come to this earth for a higher purpose. All he wanted was to meet his *guru* once again. He wended his way to all the temples of South India, in the hope of seeing the Lord once more in the form of his *guru*. In order to please him, Lord Shiva appeared to him in the form of his *guru*, at every shrine. At last he reached the glorious temple of Chidambaram where Shiva is in the form of Nataraja. This is the place where he composed his famous song called the Tiruvachagam.

At that time a Buddhist monk from Sri Lanka, accompanied by the Sri Lankan king and his dumb daughter came to Chidambaram. He came to enquire about the existence of a god other than the Buddha. The king of the land decided to arrange a debate between the Buddhist and a Shaivite. Manikkavachagar was chosen to represent Shaivism since he was the one who was most knowledgeable. At the end of the debate, the Buddhist monks were literally struck dumb.

The Sri Lankan king was amazed and said to Manikkavachagar, "You have made my eloquent teachers dumb. Now if you are able to make my dumb daughter speak, we will all renounce our faith and join yours." Manikkavachagar requested the Lord to help him and the dumb girl started to speak fluently and refute the arguments of the Buddhist monks in a faultless manner. Needless to say the king was converted.

One day Lord Shiva came to Manikkavachagar in the form of a Brahmin and asked him to sing the Tiruvachagam for him. The Lord proceeded to write down the song on palm leaves as Manikkavachagar sang. Manikkavachagar was so overwhelmed by the Lord's love and grace that tears started rolling down his eyes and he prostrated himself on the temple steps and could not rise up. When the temple priests came they found the palm leaves written by the Lord, on the steps of the temple. They also found Manikkavachagar in a state of ecstasy. Of the Brahmin there was no sign. The temple priests approached Manikkavachagar and asked him to explain the meaning of what was written on the leaves and also who had written them. With trembling hands, Manikkavachagar pointed to the idol within the temple and said, "He alone is the subject matter of these songs. He alone has written them!" He was so overcome with emotion as he uttered these words that he could not rise up and merged himself at the feet of Lord Nataraja.

ॐ Namashivaya

"O hands of mine! Join together And worship that transcendent Being, Who has a snake with the poisonous mouth as a waistband. Strewn at His feet are fragrant flowers, O hands of mine! Join together and worship Him."

Saint Appar

Words cannto express that state; the mind cannot grasp it,
The senses cannot perceive it
Except through firm belief in God and Self,
It cannot be understood.

ॐ

Anaghaya Namaha!

CHAPTER XXVII

THE VIOLENT VOTARIES

"His birth was in a family of hunters,
That robbed honeycombs and ate flesh.
He roamed about the forest in the mountains where roamed the tiger.
He bred red-eyed dogs and decoy animals.
He wielded the cruel bow, the spear, the sword,
And dwelt with butchered carcasses.
His form, a brawny forearm chewed by a tiger.
A rock-like chest hacked with mighty weapons, face marked by the teeth of bears.
Thigh slashed by the sharp-tusked boar.
Dense upstanding tuft, bloodshot, terrifying eyes,
Resounding harsh speech!"

Saint Nakeera

This was written about Kannappa Nayanar who was one of the earliest of the saints. He was a brutish creature, born of brutish parentage, living in a brutish terrain! He was born as the son of the chieftain of an aboriginal tribe. It is said that he was the incarnation of Arjuna, who had dared to fight with Lord Shiva who had gone to him in the guise of a hunter, because of which he was now born as a hunter.

Once on his maiden hunt, Kannappa chased and killed a boar. While his friends roasted it, he decided to visit the temple at the top of the hill. When he reached the temple and saw the *linga*, a remarkable change came over him. He ran towards the *linga* in ecstasy and began to hug and kiss it for he saw his beloved Lord, therein. Being a hunter, Kannappa was totally devoid of all knowledge of ritualistic worship but his friend told him that the method of worshipping Shiva was to pour water over the idol (*abhisheka*) and then offer flowers and food. Though he was loathe to leave his beloved alone, he sped off and took the best portions of the pork which had been roasted and after tasting each piece to see if it was nicely done, he laid the pieces lovingly on a bed of leaves. Then he ran to the river and took some water in his mouth since he had no vessel, and gathered some flowers and kept them in his hair since he had no basket and rushed back to the temple. He spat the water in his mouth over the idol as *abhisheka* and brushed aside the flowers in his hair with his sandals so that they fell over the *linga*. He then placed the pork on its bed of leaves in front of the *linga* and said, "Here is the meat, which I have roasted to a turn and tasted with my experienced tongue. Pray be gracious enough to eat it." He waited anxiously, never taking his eyes off the idol, like a mother watching her beloved child.When the sun set, his friends did their best to make him go back home but he refused to budge from the side of the idol. He stayed there for five days. In the morning he would dash off to get some meat for offering the Lord and then return for his worship, carrying the usual offerings in this unusual way.

While he went hunting the next day, the Brahmin priest, who used to come for the daily worship of the deity, arrived and was horrified to see the desecration of the temple. He noticed the imprint of sandals and the pug marks of dogs inside the sanctum sanctorum and the strange flowers on the idol and the stench of meat everywhere. He performed the necessary purificatory rites. He then brought water in a copper vessel for the Lord's bath with a cloth tied round his mouth lest his breath should pollute the water. He brought flowers in a rush basket and made a delightful concoction of milk and rice for the offering, untasted by anyone. After finishing the ritual he returned home.

Kannappa came back soon after and messed up everything which the priest had done and performed the rites in his own unorthodox fashion. This went on for five days much to the chagrin of the priest. On the fifth night the Lord appeared in a dream to the priest and told him to hide himself, if he wanted to see something special. The priest hid himself behind the *linga*. On the sixth day when Kannappa returned with his hoard of fresh meat he saw a dreadful sight. A stream of blood was gushing out of the right eye of the Lord in the *linga*. Kannappa ran forward and tried to stem the flow but it continued unabated. He dashed off and got some herbs and applied it to the bleeding eye but without any effect. At last he had a brilliant idea. He gouged out his own eye with the tip of his arrow and placed it lovingly over the bleeding eye and stanched the wound. But immediately the other eye also began to bleed. This time Kannappa knew exactly what to do but the problem was to find the exact spot of the eye on the idol, after gouging out his second eye. Then he thought of a splendid idea. He placed his left foot on the bleeding eye to mark the place and put his arrow to his remaining eye.

The Lord could bear this no longer. He jumped out of the *linga* and caught Kannappa's hand and said, "Stop! Kannappa!"

Three times he cried thus and Kannappa was thrice blessed. From that day onwards he was known as Kannappa. His sacrifice was equivalent to the one made by Vishnu, the lotus-eyed one who had given his own eye to the three-eyed Lord. Unparalleled was Kannappa's love and to this day, poets sing of his glory.

ॐ ॐ ॐ ॐ ॐ ॐ ॐ ॐ ॐ

Arivattayar Nayanar was a great devotee of Lord Shiva. Daily he offered cooked red rice, red spinach and some mango pickle to the Lord. To test him, Lord Shiva took away all his wealth but Arivattayar worked in someone else's field and with the wages that he received there, he continued to offer the same things to the Lord. He and his family ate inferior rice and offered the best quality to Shiva. But a time came when only red rice was available, so Arivattayar ate only the greens from his garden and not the rice, which was offered to Shiva. One day as he was carrying his usual offering to the temple, his legs faltered due to weakness and he fell on the ground, spilling the food.

He began to weep bitterly and said, "O Lord if it is true that you are omnipresent, you must be here on this spot, right now. Pray accept my offering which has fallen on the ground. If you do not eat it I will give up my life."

With these words he took up a sickle and started to hack his throat. Just then he heard the crunching sound of someone biting into the mango pickle. Simultaneously the holy hand stretched forth and caught the sickle and prevented him from killing himself!

ॐ ॐ ॐ ॐ ॐ ॐ ॐ ॐ ॐ

Murthi Nayanar used to adore the idol of Shiva by anointing it daily with sandal paste. A time came when a Jain king ruled the land. He began to persecute the followers of Shiva. Murthi Nayanar continued his worship undaunted. In order to convert him, the king declared that no sandalwood should be used in the land. Murthi prayed to Lord Shiva to give them a king who would be favourable to Shiva devotees. He was fast exhausting his stock of sandalwood and the day came when he did not have even a small piece for his daily worship. He searched the whole city without being able to get a single block of sandalwood. When the time came for his daily worship, he went to the temple and in desperation, began to rub his own elbow on the grinding stone, in lieu of sandalwood. It started bleeding profusely. Lord Shiva appeared and stopped him and told him that he had accepted his sacrifice and that he would be made king of the land. That night the cruel king died. In accordance with their ancient custom, the ministers sent the palace elephant to choose a worthy successor. The elephant went unerringly towards the temple and seeing Murthi Nayanar, it bowed to him and taking him on its back, it returned to the palace. The ministers begged Murthi to accept the kingship. He agreed on certain conditions. He said that he would not be anointed with perfumes but only with ashes, he would not wear any jewels but only *rudraksha* beads and his crown would be his matted locks. The ministers agreed. Murthi became king and once again Shaivsim flourished in the land.

ॐ ॐ ॐ ॐ ॐ ॐ ॐ ॐ ॐ

Chandeswar Nayanar was a child prodigy. One day he saw a cowherd beating a cow and he was so unhappy that he offered his own services to the householders who employed the cowherd. The cows prospered under the care of the child and yielded milk of their own accord. The boy used to make a mud *linga* on the river-banks and pour milk over it every day since there was so much of surplus. One day his father caught him in the act and angrily came and kicked the *linga*, which the child was worshipping. The boy looked up and saw that it was his own father who had obstructed his *puja.* He took up a stick, which turned into an axe in his hands and chopped off his father's feet. He continued with his worship, unmindful of his father lying on the ground. The Lord appeared and blessed him for his extreme devotion which could not tolerate an insult to the *linga* and who would not let any personal attachment stand in the way of his convictions.

ॐ ॐ ॐ ॐ ॐ ॐ ॐ ॐ ॐ

Sakkiyar was a Shaivite who became a Buddhist monk but he could never eradicate the ingrained love of Shiva from his heart. Even though he did not change his garb, he used to worship a *linga* on the way to his *biksha.* A Buddhist monk is supposed to beg for his food and this is called *biksha.* Every day he had to pass the *linga* on his way. He would throw a stone at it as an offering to Lord Shiva. A large heap of stones grew up in this barren place as a result of this strange floral offering. He continued this unique form of worship every day. The flinging of the stone itself became an act charged with love and the Lord accepted it as such. Once when he was just sitting down to eat, he remembered that he had not made his usual offering to the Lord and leaving his food he ran back to the *linga.* Just as he flung the stone, the Lord appeared and blessed him.

ॐ ॐ ॐ ॐ ॐ ॐ ॐ ॐ ॐ

Siruthonda Nayanar was a *bhakta* who never ate his meal without first feeding a devotee of Shiva. One day Shiva came to him in the guise of a *bhakta* just before his meal time. Siruthonda was delighted and begged him to come and be seated. Shiva said that he had taken a vow that once in six months he would eat the meat of a five-year-old child who had to be the only son of his parents. This happened to be the right time. Without a moment's hesitation, Siruthonda agreed. He realised that his son met with both these requirements. His wife agreed that it was their great good luck that they were given the opportunity to serve a devotee of Shiva in this unique fashion! The unsuspecting child was brought and kept lovingly on his mother's lap. The father chopped off his head and the meat was cooked and served to their guest. The Shiva devotee insisted that the host should eat with him so

Siruthonda sat to feast on the flesh of his only son. Then their demanding guest insisted that the son of his host should also eat with them. Siruthonda made some lame excuses but the guest insisted that the wife should go out and call the son. To the astonishment of the parents, the boy came running in as soon as he was called. When they returned to the kitchen with the son, they found the place empty. Neither the mendicant nor the meat was there and they realised that the Lord had tested them to the utmost.

ॐ Namashivaya

The Atman is self-existent, all pervading – pure.
It is beyond the concept and range of sin.
It has no form or body and hence cannot be hurt by weapons,
The Atman in its personal or individualized aspect is God,
the omniscient and all-inclusive One.
It is the inspirer of saints and seers.
It is omnipotent and is the final refuge and bestower of the fruits of actions.

The one who does not know the truth of the Atman and leads a life
Wedded to the senses falls into blinding darkness.
But the one who knows the truth of the Atman,
Yet leads a sensual life, falls into deeper darkness.

ॐ

Shaswathaya Namaha!

CHAPTER XXVIII

WOMEN DEVOTEES

"She who saying, 'I will not tread with my feet, the sacred mountain of the Lord',
Walked on her hands with both her feet pointing to the sky,
Who was privileged to be hailed, 'My mother', by the Lord of red golden body,
When Uma laughed at the sight,
She is the treasure of the family of Karaikkal,
Where pure honey seeps from the boughs of trees."

Saint Nambi-andar-nambi

Punithavathi was the daughter of a rich merchant. She was a devout wife. Once her husband sent two mangoes from the market with instructions to keep them for his lunch. In the meantime a visitor came for lunch and she served one of the mangoes to him. When her husband came home, she brought the other mango and gave it to him. It was so delicious that he asked her for another. She was in a dilemma and dared not tell him the truth lest he got angry with her for having given his mango to a guest. She went and begged the Lord to help her. He gave her a mango, which she happily cut and placed before her husband. But this mango was really out of the world, so the husband naturally asked her where she had got it. She had to tell the truth. The husband did not believe her and asked her to get another one from the same source. She went to the prayer room and begged Lord Shiva to save her from the ignominy of being called a liar. He gave her another mango. When the husband saw this miracle, he concluded that his wife must be some sort of a goddess and decided to leave her since it would be sacrilegious to have any sexual relationship with her. He went off on a mercantile expedition and never returned to her.

When he came back, he settled in a different part of the country and married another lady and had a daughter by her whom he decided to call Punithavathi after his first wife. Very soon the parents of the first Punithavathi heard of his whereabouts. They took their daughter to him and demanded that he take her back. As soon as he saw Punithavathi, he prostrated at her feet and begged her to forgive him. It was most unusual for a husband to prostrate at his wife's feet. He explained to the irate parents that in his eyes, Punithavathi was a goddess and he could not regard her as a wife any more. When she heard this, Punithavathi decided that all worldly ties were a bondage and the only one, to whom she was really bound, was Lord Shiva. She decided to go to the holy mountain of Kailasa in order to see her true Lord. When she reached the mountain she could not bear to tread the holy ground with her feet so she decided to climb it on her hands. She was just a bag of bones by this time and Parvati laughed when she saw this strange apparition coming up the mountain.

Lord Shiva chided Parvati and said, "Note, O Parvati! She who is coming up in this odd fashion, is the mother who cherishes us." As she approached them, Shiva addressed her as "O Mother!"

In response Punithavathi cried, "O Father" and fell at his feet.

He asked her to choose any boon and she chose to have undying love towards him. He told her to return to the world and see his *thandava* dance and sing about his glories. She did this till the end of her life when she was taken up to his abode. She has the unique privilege of being the only one of the devotees mentioned here who returned home after having gone to Kailasa.

ॐ ॐ ॐ ॐ ॐ ॐ ॐ ॐ ॐ

Sundarar's mother, Isai-gnaaniyaar, as well as Mangayarkkarasi, queen of Madurai who was responsible for getting Sambandar to Madurai and defeating the Jains in debate, are two other women saints who have been mentioned by Sekkizhaar in the Periya Puranam.

ॐ ॐ ॐ ॐ ॐ ॐ ॐ ॐ ॐ

Thilagavathi the sister of Appar was a saint on her own. Without her help, the world would never have known about Appar. She was his only relative and she was the one who brought him up and saved him from an untimely death.

She had been betrothed to a warrior but before the wedding could take place, both her parents died. Soon after, the man, whom she was engaged to, also died in the war. She decided to end her life along with him but at the pleas of her younger brother, Appar, who begged her to stay alive for his sake, she desisted and brought him up. When her brother decided to join the Jains she was quite devastated. She dedicated herself to Lord Shiva and spent her days in his divine service. She begged the Lord to save her young brother. It is said that Shiva agreed and gave Appar a severe colic pain, as we have seen, which the Jain monks could not cure. He was forced to take refuge with his sister who cured him purely by the repetition of the five-syllabled *mantra* of Lord Shiva and by the application of the sacred ash over his body. Then she told him to enter the temple of Shiva and beg his pardon. We have seen from the story of Appar what happened to him after that. Thus, his sister who was already a mother and father to him now became his *guru.* She not only cured his physical disease but also gave him spiritual redemption. She was indeed a gem amongst women.

ॐ ॐ ॐ ॐ ॐ ॐ ॐ ॐ ॐ

Our next woman saint was the wife of a Brahmin called Neelanakkar. We do not know her name. She used to accompany her husband daily to the Shiva temple and offer worship along with him. One day while her husband was muttering the five-syllabled *mantra* with great concentration, the lady noticed that a spider had fallen on the top of the *linga.* Impelled by her motherly instincts, without thinking of what she was doing, she blew off the spider. When the Brahmin saw this he was shocked. One should never blow on an idol, in case it gets defiled with our spit. He shouted at her for her foolishness and declared that he would not have her in his house again! The poor woman was forced to stay the night in the temple. That night the husband had a dream, in which Shiva appeared and showed him his body, which had been totally affected by the poison. The only place that was free from the effects of the poison was the place where the spider had fallen and which had been removed by his wife's breath! Needless to say, the stupid husband rushed to the temple and begged his wife to return with him. Her spontaneous action had been inspired purely by maternal love and the Lord took it as such. We have seen that Shiva had a friend, a son and a servant but this was the first time that we hear of him, who was never born of a woman's womb, to have acquired a mother!

Of course, all the doings of these ladies pale into insignificance when we think of the great sacrifice made by the wife of Siruthondar Nayanar. As we have seen in his story, she was prepared to take her only son on her lap so as to make it easy for her husband to chop off his head! She also cooked and served the meat to the so-called Shiva *bhakta* without batting an eyelid! Such a sacrifice can hardly be emulated and she certainly deserves a prominent place in our account of women saints.

ॐ ॐ ॐ ॐ ॐ ॐ ॐ ॐ ॐ

We might wonder how it is that Shiva sanctioned such apparently heartless actions by his devotees. A culture and religion perish due to the apathy and indifference of its followers rather than by their excesses. Shaivites have always been known for the violent way in which they expressed their intense love for Shiva and he seems to appreciate it. The devotees of Vishnu however are known for their peace-loving and calm natures akin to the nature of Lord Vishnu himself. Hinduism, with its great ability to accept all natures, has no difficulty in allowing people of different types to follow the path that is best suited to their temperaments. There is no fixed rule or laws of conduct that is mandatory on all human beings without exception. God has no favourites! What he values above all is the *bhavana* or the feeling with which the devotion is given.

There are many, many more saints who have been mentioned in the Periya Puranam and whose names are sung even today in Tamil Nadu. For lack of space we have touched on the lives of just a few.

We will conclude with the words of Thomas Merton, "A mystic is one who surrenders to a power of love that is greater than human. He advances towards God in a darkness that goes beyond the light of human reason and conceptual knowledge. When we speak of mysticism, we speak of an area in which man is no longer completely in command of his own life, his own mind, and of his own will. Yet at the same time his surrender is to a God who is more intimate to him that his very self."

The devotee reaches a peak of realisation in which she does not even want to be in control of her life. She has no separate life or mind or will. She has surrendered herself body, mind and soul to the core of her being which is God and remains content that his grace and his intelligence will carry her on the waves of his divine compassion to the farther shore of existence. In this path of total submission, there is no fall and no mistake for the Master of her Being who is also the beloved of her heart, accomplishes all.

ॐ *Namashivaya*

"I have neither hatred nor attachment, nor greed or infatuation. I have neither pride nor a competitive spirit, I am not after duty, wealth, passion or liberation. I am the essence of consciousness and bliss — Shivoham! Shivoham!"

Nirvanashtakam by Adi Shankaracharya

"Prostrations to you who are formless and manifested in diverse forms. Prostrations to you who manifest as the noble and the lowly. Prostrations to you who are in those who ride the chariots and in those who do not. Prostrations to you who are both the chariots and their owners."

Sri Rudri. Yajur Vedawsg

Day by day, a man comes closer to death,
His youth wears away.
Transient as the ripples on a stream, is the goddess of fortune.
Fickle as lightning is life itself.
O Shiva! O giver of Shelter!
Protect me who have taken refuge at Thy feet.

Adi Shankaraacharya

ॐ

Anantaya Namaha!

EPILOGUE

"Prostrations to the source of bliss, earthly and heavenly.
Prostrations to the auspicious one, more auspicious than anything else.
Prostrations to the one present in holy rivers and in idols installed on their banks."

Sri Rudri. Yajur Veda

The *Vedas* are the great storehouses of philosophy and they are the oldest spiritual treatises known to humankind. They are the corner-stones of the Hindu philosophy and are four in number: *Rig-Veda*, *Yajur-Veda*, *Sama-Veda* and *Atharvana Veda.* Of these the first three are considered more important. In this threefold classification we find that the *Yajur-Veda* comes in the middle. The *Rudri*, which is a hymn dedicated to Lord Shiva, comes in the centre of the seven cantos of this *Veda.* The *panchakshari* or the five-syllabled *mantra* of Shiva comes in the centre of the *Rudri.* The word Shiva comes in the centre of the *panchakshari* as can be noticed, when it is written in Sanskrit. The *Rudri* is thus considered to be the eye of the *Veda-Purusha*, who is Lord Shiva. The five-syllabled *mantra* then becomes the pupil of this eye. The *Rudri* is chanted at all fire sacrifices or *yajnas.* There are eleven forms of Shiva as Rudra and at these *yajnas*, eleven priests chant the *Rudri* eleven times invoking Lord Shiva in eleven pots of sanctified water. Shiva is also Bhuteswara or the Lord of the elements. So the five letters of the *mantra* stand for the five elements. Hence we end our chapters with this unique *mantra* by chanting which all people will be released from the cycle of births and deaths.

We will end this book on the Play of Lord Shiva by initiating all readers into the mystery of the sacred *panchakshari*, the five-syllabled *mantra* of Lord Shiva — *Na-Ma-Shi-va-ya.* It is always preceded by the *pranava mantra*, which is *Aum.* So the whole *mantra* reads as...**Aum Namashivaya**. Those who chant this *mantra* regularly, with faith and devotion to Shiva will undoubtedly be blessed by him and attain all happiness, prosperity and liberation.

It is usual to end all *pujas* or ritualistic worship of Shiva with an *arati* or the waving of lights lit with camphor. A little verse is chanted while the lights are being waved in front of the *linga* of Shiva. This book itself is a *puja* to my three-eyed Lord, Vanamali. So we will end it with the usual *arati* to Lord Shiva.

Karpoora gauram, karunavataaram,
Samsarasaaram, bhujagendrahaaram
Sada vasantam, hridayaravinde,
Bhavam Bhavani sahitham namaami.

"I bow to Shiva along with Parvati,
Who resides ever in the lotus of my heart,
Who is the colour of camphor, who is filled with kindness,
Who is the support of the world and who wears a snake as a garland."

ॐ *Namashivaya!*

Hari Aum Tat Sat

GLOSSARY OF SANSKRIT TERMS

abhisheka	ritualistic bathing of an idol or a king
achala	immovable
adharma	unrighteousness
advaita	non-duality
advaitic	pertaining to *advaita*
aham brahmasmi	I am Brahman; *Vedic mantra*
ahamkara	ego
ahimsa	non-violence
ajna chakra	spiritual centre between the brows
akasha	ether
amrita	nectar of immortality
anahata chakra	heart *chakra*
ananda	bliss
apana	the downward breath
apas	water
apsara	celestial dancer
arati	waving of lights before a deity
ardhra	a star
ashrama	hermitage
asura	demon
asuric	demonic
asvini	name of month. September/October
aswamedha yaga	horse-sacrifice
atharvana veda	the fourth *Veda*
atma	soul
atmic	pertaining to the soul
aum	*mantra* denoting the Supreme
avatara	incarnation

avidya	ignorance
avyaktha	unmanifest
bel	a type of leaf used in Shiva's worship
bhadra	name of month. August/September
bhagavan	God
bhakta	devotee
bhakti	devotion
bhang	marijuana
bhasma	ashes
bhavana	attitude
bhiksha	food got by begging
bhikshu	one who begs for food
bhogi	one who lives to eat
bhutas	five elements; spirits
bindu	a dot
brahmachari	a celibate
chaitra	name of a month. February/March
chakora	a bird
chakra	an energy centre in the spine
chandrakala	crescent moon
chaturyuga	the four epochs
chidakasha	the divine ether
dakshina	fee given for any spiritual benefit
damaru	Shiva's drum
darbha	a type of grass
darshan	the vision
dasa	servant
dasa-marga	the way of the servant
deva	one of the lesser gods
devataru	type of tree
devipurana	a scripture about the divine mother
dharma	eternal law of righteousness
dundhubhi	a percussion instrument

ganapatis	leaders of the *ganas*
ganas	the assorted followers of Shiva
gopi	milkmaid
guna	one of the three modes of nature
guru	spiritual preceptor
halahala	a type of virulent poison
indriyas	sense organs
Iswara	God
jiva	individual soul
jivatma	embodied soul
jnana	spiritual knowledge
jnana-marga	the way of knowledge
jyotirlinga	one of the twelve *lingas* of Shiva
kala	art; phase
kamandalu	a water-pot carried by sannyasis
karma	action
karma-mala	impurity from action
keora	a type of cactus flower
kinnaras	celestial beings
kundala	a man's earring
kundalini	the spiritual energy coiled at the base of the spine
kusa	type of grass
lakh	hundred thousand
lasya	the movements of a woman
lila	play
linga	rounded stone signifying Shiva; sign; token; phallus
maha-pralaya	the night of Brahma where all worlds up to the world of Brahma dissolve

mahayogi	great *yogi*
mahout	elephant keeper
malaya	southern breeze
mantra	sacred word
manipura chakra	third *chakra* at the navel
manvantara	the lifetime of Manu
marga	path; way
margashirsha	name of a month; December/January
maya	cosmic illusion
maya-mala	impurity caused by *maya*
modaka	round sweet loved by Ganesha
mooladara chakra	first *chakra* at base of spine
mudra	mystic symbol made with the fingers
mukti	liberation
mythya	illusory
nada	cosmic sound
nadi	spiritual energy rising from spine
naga	serpent
naimittika-pralaya	same as *Maha-pralaya*
namashivaya	five-syllabled, sacred *mantra* of Shiva
navadurgas	the nine Durgas
nitya	constant
nitya-brahmachari	eternal celibate
nitya-pralaya	dissolution of personality experienced during sleep
nritta, nrittya	dance
omkara	sound of *Aum*
panchakshari	five-syllabled *mantra* of Shiva
paramatma	the Supreme soul
pasa	rope
pasu	creature
pasupata	missile of Shiva
pati	master

peethas	spiritual seats of the goddess
pishachas	ghouls
prakrittika-pralaya	total dissolution of everything including Prakriti into its ultimate cause - Brahman
pralaya	dissolution; deluge
prana	vital breath
pranava mantra	*Aum*
prasad	left-overs from offering to God
pratah sandhya	morning twilight
pretas	ghosts
prithvi	earth
puja	ritualistic worship
purana	scripture
puranic	pertaining to *Puranas*
rajas	one of the modes or *gunas* of nature
rajasic	passionate, lusty
rakshasa	demon
Rig-veda	one of the four *Vedas*
rishis	saints
rudraksha	the seed of a tree loved by Shiva
rudram/Rudri	a hymn to Shiva in *Yajur-Veda*
rudravina	a type of lute designed by Ravana
sadhana	spiritual practice
sadhu	a holy man
sahasrara	the seventh *chakra* on top of the head
sakhya-marga	the way of friendship
saligrama	a round stone typifying Vishnu
salokya	staying in god's world
Sama-veda	one of the four *Vedas*
samadhi	super-conscious state
samhara	annihilation
samipya	staying near to god
samsara	transmigratory existence
sandhya	twilight

saras	type of grass
sarupya	having the form of God
satchidananda	existence-consciousness-bliss; definition of Brahman
satputra-marga	the way of the son
sattva	quality of harmony; goodness; one of the *gunas*
sattvic	pertaining to *sattva*
sayujya	entering into the godhead
shakti	force or energy of the goddess
shastras	scriptures
shrishti	creation
shyama sandhya	evening twilight
siddha	one having supernormal powers
siddhi	supernormal power
sthithaprajna	person of firm intellect
sthiti	conservation
sudarshana chakra	the discus; weapon of Vishnu
sushumna nadi	energy coil rising from the bottom of the spine
swadhistana	second *chakra*
tamas	inertia, lethargy; third *guna*
tamasic	pertaining to *tamas*
tanmatras	subtle energy underlying the elements
tantras	esoteric scriptures
tantrik	pertaining to *tantras*
tapasya	askesis, austerity
tarakamudra	position of the fingers when the tip of the forefinger touches the tip of the thumb
tat twam asi	*Vedic mantra*; that thou art
tatanka	earring worn by a woman
tattvas	elements; twenty-four in number
tejas	glory
thandava Nritta	cosmic dance of Shiva

udana	a part of the vital breath
upanayanam	ceremony of the investiture of the sacred thread
upanishad	last portion of the *Vedas* dealing with the philosophy of *advaita*
urdhva-thandava	Shiva's cosmic dance in which one foot is raised vertically beside the ear
vairagya	detachment
vajra	thunderbolt
vayu	wind
veda-Purusha	The Lord of the *Vedas*
vedas	earliest spiritual scripture of the Hindu religion; four in number
vidya	knowledge
vishuddhi chakra	*chakra* at the base of the throat
yaga	fire sacrifice
yajna	ritual by fire; same as *yaga*
yajna-shala	place where the *yaga* is performed
Yajur-veda	one of the four *Vedas*
yaksha	demi-gods; guardians of the wealth of the nether-world
yantra	a mystic, geometrical figure
yoga	any activity which leads to union with the supreme
yoga-maya	Lord's power of illusion
yogi	one who practises *yoga*; one who is in union with God
*yogi*ni	a female *yogi*
yoni	a seat; base; vulva; usually has reference to the base of the *linga*
yuga	epoch

ॐ *Namashivaya*

ॐ

Bhoothapathaye Namaha!

METHOD OF WORSHIPPING LORD SHIVA

"Now fragrant flowers, incense, lamps, materials for the bath of the Lord,
With these i hand go to a suitable place and place a seat for the Lrod.
Install the image therein and meditate on His form and the light that is God.
Invoke Him to descend and occupy the image
Worship Him with great devotion
With flower offerings, songs and obeisance
Perform with ardour all the religious acts.
Those who do these acts daily
Will abide by the side of the Lord"

Shiva-jnana Siddhiyar

GLOSSARY OF MANTRAS

ॐ *Viveshvaraya Namaha!*	Salutations to the Lord of the Universe
ॐ *Ganeshaya Namaha!*	Salutations to Sri Ganesha
ॐ *Mrityunjayaya Namaha!*	Salutations to the conqueror of Death
ॐ *Gagatpitre Namaha!*	Salutations to the father of the World
ॐ *Shivaya Namaha!*	Salutations to Lord Shiva
ॐ *Giripriyaya Namaha!*	Salutations to the lover of mountains!
ॐ *Panchavaktraya Namaha!*	Salutations to the five-faced one!
ॐ *Sri Gurave Namaha!*	Salutations to the Guru!
ॐ *Mahadevaya Namaha!*	Salutations to the great God
ॐ *Maheswaraya Namaha!*	Salutations to the great Lord
ॐ *Shambave Namaha!*	Salutations to the one who grants prosperity
ॐ *Ambikanathaya Namaha!*	Salutations to the Lord of Ambika
ॐ *Pinakine Namaha!*	Salutations to the wielder of the bow-Pinaka
ॐ *Sasishekaraya Namaha!*	Salutations to the one who wears the moon on his head
ॐ *Rudraya Namaha!*	Salutations to the wild avenger
ॐ *Viroopakshaya Namaha!*	Salutations to the odd-eyed one
ॐ *Kapardine Namaha!*	Salutations to the one who ties his hair in the form of a conch
ॐ *Kamaraye Namaha!*	Salutations to the enemy of Kama
ॐ *Shankaraya Namaha!*	Salutations to the one who confers happiness
ॐ *Srikandaya Namaha!*	Salutations to the one with a beautiful neck
ॐ *Shivaapriyaya Namaha!*	Salutations to the beloved of Shivaa (Parvati)

ॐ *Laladakshaya Namaha!*	Salutations to the one with an eye on his forehead
ॐ *Sharvaya Namaha!*	Salutations to the cosmic archer
ॐ *Tripurantakaya Namaha!*	Salutations to the destroyer of the three cities
ॐ *Shoolapanaye Namaha!*	Salutations to the one who carries a trident
ॐ *Neelakandaya Namaha!*	Salutations to the one with a blue neck
ॐ *Gangadaraya Namaha!*	Salutations to the one who carries the Ganga
ॐ *Somaya Namaha!*	Salutations to the guardian of the sacred herb — Soma
ॐ *Sadashivaya Namaha!*	Salutations to the ever auspicious one
ॐ *Kripanidaye Namaha!*	Salutations to the one who is a storehouse of compassion
ॐ *Bhaktavalsalaya Namaha*!	Salutations to the one who is kind to devotees
ॐ *Haraya Namaha!*	Salutations to the one who takes away (sins, minds)
ॐ *Sookshmathanaye Namaha!*	Salutations to the One with a subtle body!
ॐ *Jagadgurave Namaha!*	Salutations to the preceptor of the world
ॐ *Devaya Namaha!*	Salutations to God
ॐ *Anaghaya Namaha!*	Salutations to the one without a blemish
ॐ *Shaswathaya Namaha!*	Salutations to the one who is eternal
ॐ *Anantaya Namaha!*	Salutations to the one without an end
ॐ *Bhoothapathaye Namaha!*	Salutations to the Lord of all creatures
ॐ *Namashivaya!*	Salutations to Lord Shiva. The five-syllabled mantra of Shiva

ॐ *Namashivaya*

GLOSSARY OF CLASSICAL CHARACTERS

1.	Achala	name of Parvati; the immovable one
2.	Adishesha	serpent couch of Lord Narayana
3.	Aditi	mother of the gods
4.	Agastya	sage
5.	Agni	god of fire
6.	Ananga	name of Kama
7.	Anasuya	wife of Atri
8.	Andhaka	blind son of demon Hiranyaksha
9.	Angiras	one of the seven celestial sages
10.	Annapurna	manifestation of Parvati; giver of food
11.	Aparna	name of Parvati; one who subsisted on dry leaves
12.	Arundhati	wife of sage Vasishta
13.	Asikni	wife of Daksha
14.	Atri	sage
15.	Bana	demon
16.	Bhadra	one of the nine Durgas
17.	Bhadrakali	destructive aspect of the goddess
18.	Bhavani	name of Parvati, eternal transformation
19.	Brahma	one of the trinity; the Creator
20.	Brighu	one of the seven celestial sages
21.	Brihaspati	preceptor of the gods
22.	Buddhi	wife of Ganesha
23.	Chamunda	one of the nine Durgas
24.	Chandra	moon
25.	Dadichi	sage
26.	Daksha	father of Sati
27.	Dakshayani	name of Sati; daughter of Daksha

28. Dambha	demon
29. Dasaratha	father of Rama
30. Dattatreya	son of Atri; manifestation of Vishnu
31. Devasenapati	name of Kartikeya; general of the army of the gods
32. Devayani	Kartikeya's wife; daughter of Indra
33. Dhanya	daughter of the manes
34. Diti	mother of the demons
35. Durga	one of the names of the goddess, Parvati
36. Durvasa	son of Atri; manifestation of Shiva
37. Ettumba	demon
38. Ganapathy	name of Ganesha; leader of the *ganas*
39. Ganesha	son of Shiva; elephant god
40. Ganga	the river; wife of Shiva
41. Garuda	Vishnu's eagle vehicle
42. Gouri	name of Parvati; the radiant one
43. Guha	name of Kartikeya; the secret one
44. Himavan	king of the Himalayas
45. Hiranyakashipu	demon; brother of Hiranyaksha
46. Hiranyaksha	demon
47. Indra	king of the gods
48. Isani	one of the nine Durgas
49. Jalandara	demon
50. Janaka	father of Sita
51. Jaya	Parvati's maid
52. Kaali	goddess of destruction
53. Kala Bhairava	fierce manifestation of Shiva
54. Kalanemi	demon
55. Kalavati	daughter of the manes
56. Kama	god of love
57. Kamalaksha	son of Taraka
58. Kardama	one of the patriarchs
59. Kartikeya	Shiva's son; son of the Krittikas
60. Kartyayani	one of the nine Durgas
61. Kasyapa	name of sage

62. Kratu	one of the seven celestial sages
63. Krishna	incarnation of Vishnu
64. Krittikas	the constellation Pleides; foster-mothers to Kartikeya
65. Kshema	Ganesha's son by his wife Buddhi
66. Kubera	Lord of wealth
67. Kumara	name of Kartikeya; young boy
68. Kumuda	son of the serpents
69. Labha	Ganesha's son by Siddhi
70. Lakshmana	brother of Rama
71. Lakshmi	wife of Vishnu; goddess of wealth
72. Mahakali	one of the nine Durgas
73. Manibhadra	one of Shiva's *ganas*
74. Manmatha	god of love, Kama
75. Marichi	one of the seven celestial sages
76. Mayan	architect of the demons
77. Medathiti	sage
78. Mena	wife of Himavan; mother of Parvati
79. Mundamardini	one of the nine Durgas
80. Muruga	name of Kartikeya
81. Nandi	bull vehicle of Shiva
82. Nandiswara	bull vehicle of Shiva
83. Narada	the celestial singer known for meddling
84. Narayana	one who sleeps on the cosmic waters
85. Nishumba	demon
86. Parvati	wife of Shiva; daughter of the mountains
87. Pavakatmaja	name of Kartikeya; son of fire
88. Pradyumna	son of Krishna
89. Prahlada	son of Hiranyakashipu
90. Pralamba	demon
91. Pulaha	one of the seven celestial sages
92. Radha	Krishna's childhood sweetheart
93. Rama	*avatara* of Vishnu
94. Rati	Kama's wife
95. Ravana	King of *rakshasas*

96.	Rohini	wife of Chandra
97.	Sanaka	one of the four boy sages
98.	Sanandana	one of the four boy sages
99.	Sanatana	one of the four boy sages
100.	Sanat-kumara	one of the four boy sages
101.	Sandhya	Brahma's first creation; twilight
102.	Sarabhu	name of Kartikeya; born among reeds
103.	Saraswati	wife of Brahma; goddess of learning
104.	Sati	Shiva's first wife
105.	Shakti	the active power of the Lord
106.	Shankachuda	demon
107.	Shanmukha	name of Kartikeya; having six faces
108.	Shatarupa	the first woman
109.	Shivaa	name of Shiva's consort
110.	Shukra	preceptor of the demons
111.	Shumba	demon
112.	Siddhi	wife of Ganesha
113.	Sita	wife of Rama
114.	Soma	moon; sacred herb used in *yajnas*
115.	Sradha	wife of the manes
116.	Sri Hari	incarnation of Vishnu
117.	Subramanya	name of Kartikeya
118.	Sudama	friend of Krishna
119.	Svetavahara	incarnation of Vishnu as the white boar
120.	Swaymabhu Manu	the first man
121.	Taraka	demon
122.	Tarakaksha	son of Taraka
123.	Tulasi	wife of Shankachuda, the sacred basil plant
124.	Twarita	one of the nine Durgas
125.	Uma	name of Parvati; do not go
126.	Vaishnavi	one of the nine Durgas
127.	Vajranga	demon
128.	Valli	Kartikeya's wife

129.	Varangi	Vajranga's wife
130.	Vasanta	spring
131.	Vasishta	preceptor of the royal house of the solar dynasty
132.	Vayu	wind god
133.	Veerabhadra	manifestation of Shiva
134.	Velayudha	name of Kartikeya
135.	Vidyunmali	son of Taraka
136.	Vigneshwara	name of Ganesha; remover of obstacles
137.	Vijaya	Parvati's maid
138.	Vinayaka	name of Ganesha
139.	Virini	wife of Daksha
140.	Vishnu	one of the trinity; the harmoniser
141.	Vishwarupa	one of the patriarchs
142.	Visvakarma	architect of the gods
143.	Visvamitra	sage
144.	Vrinda	wife of Jalandara
145.	Vrishabhana	Radha's father
146.	Vyasa	author of the Mahabharata and all the *Puranas*

ॐ *Namashivaya!*

VEDIC INVOCATION FOR WORLD PEACE

Aum sarvesham swasthir bhavathu,
Sarvesham shantir bhavathu,
Sarvesham poornam bhavathu,
Sarvesham mangalam bhavathu.
Sarve bhavanthu sukhinaha,
Sarve santhu niramayaha
Sarve bhadrani pashyantu,
Makaschid dukhabav bhaveth

Let everyone be healthy,
Let everyone enjoy peace,
Let everyone live in fulfillment
Let everyone be filled with auspiciousness
Let all be happy
Let all the free from pain
Let all see only auspiciousness
Let not anyone be unhappy

Aum asato ma sad gamaya
Tamaso ma jyotir gamaya
Mrityor ma amritam gamaya.

From the unreal lead me to the Real,
From darkness lead me to light,
From death lead me to immortality.

Aum Poornamadam poornamidam,
Poornath poornamudachyathe,
Poornasya, Poornamadaya,
Poornamevavashishyathe.
Aum Shanti, Shanti, Shanti!

That is full and this is also full,
From the full comes the full
From the full if you take away the full,
Fullness alone will remain.
Aum Peace! Peace! Peace!

GLOSSARY OF NAMES OF SHIVA

1.	Adi-purusha	the first Lord
2.	Ardhanareeswara	half-male, half-female form of Shiva
3.	Ashutosha	one who is easily propitiated
4.	Bhairava	one who brandishes a blood-soaked sword
5.	Bhava	eternal Being; source; origin
6.	Bhola	the simple one
7.	Bhutesvara	Lord of the elements
8.	Chandrachuda	one who wears the crescent moon in his hair
9.	Chandrashekara	one who wears the crescent moon in his hair
10.	Dakshinamurti	the cosmic teacher; one who faces South
11.	Gangadhara	one who upholds the Ganga
12.	Girisha	Lord of mountains
13.	Guhesha	Lord of caves
14.	Hara	one who removes the sorrows and sins of the world
15.	Ishana	supreme Lord of the universe
16.	Kalakanta	the devourer of time
17.	Kapalin	one who carries a skull
18.	Kirata	the hunter
19.	Krittivasa	one who wears animal hides
20.	Mahadeva	the great God
21.	Mahayogi	the great *yogi*
22.	Maheswara	the great Lord

23. Nageswara — Lord of serpents
24. Nataraja — the cosmic dancer
25. Natesha — king of dance
26. Neelakanda — the blue-throated one
27. Pasupati — Lord of all creatures; divine herdsman
28. Rudra — the fierce one
29. Sadashiva — name for Shiva as given in the *Shiva Purana*; refers to Brahman
30. Shambunatha — one who grants prosperity and success
31. Shankara — one who is benevolent and confers happiness
32. Sharva — the cosmic archer
33. Shiva — the auspicious one
34. Somasundara — one who is as beautiful as the moon
35. Somnatha — the Lord of the sacred herb
36. Sundaramurti — the handsome one
37. Tripurantaka — slayer of the demons of the three cities
38. Tryambaka — the three-eyed one
39. Vaidya — the keeper of the *Vedas*; the physician
40. Vaidyanatha — the Lord of physicians
41. Veda-Purusha — the Supreme personality of the *Vedas*
42. Vireshvara — Lord of martial arts
43. Virupaksha — the odd-eyed one
44. Vishveshvara — Lord of the cosmos

ॐ *Namashivaya!*